D1556514

A Missionary Nation

A Missionary Nation

Race, Religion, and Spain's Age of
Liberal Imperialism, 1841–1881

SCOTT EASTMAN

University of Nebraska Press
LINCOLN

Library of Congress Cataloging-in-Publication Data
Names: Eastman, Scott, 1971– author.
Title: A missionary nation: race, religion, and Spain's age of
liberal imperialism, 1841–1881 / Scott Eastman.
Description: Lincoln: University of Nebraska Press, [2021] |
Includes bibliographical references and index.
Identifiers: LCCN 2020052171
ISBN 9781496204165 (hardback)
ISBN 9781496228307 (epub)
ISBN 9781496228314 (pdf)
Subjects: LCSH: Spain—Foreign relations—19th century. |
Spain—History—19th century. | Spain—Ethnic relations—
History—19th century. | Nationalism—Spain—History—19th
century. | Church and state—Spain—History—19th century. |
Catholic Church—Spain—History—19th century.
Classification: LCC DP203 .E368 2021
DDC 325/.32094609034—dc23
LC record available at https://lccn.loc.gov/2020052171

Set in Questa by Laura Buis.

To Kara

Contents

List of Illustrations . . ix

Acknowledgments . . xi

Introduction . . 1

1. "The War of Africa Has Been the Dream of My Entire Political Life" . . 23

2. They "Were Calling Us Their Liberators": The Taking of Tetuán . . 42

3. The Visual Culture of Mid-Nineteenth-Century Spanish Imperialism . . 68

4. Order, Progress, and Civilization: The Annexation of the Dominican Republic . . 92

5. Anatomy of an Uprising: Race War and Dominican Independence . . 113

6. Death to Spain! Mexican Views of Spanish Intervention . . 134

7. The Traveling Society of La Exploradora: Imperial Enterprises in the Río Muni . . 156

Epilogue . . 177

Notes . . 183

Bibliography . . 215

Index . . 225

Illustrations

MAPS

1. The western Mediterranean .. xvii

2. Hispaniola .. xviii

FIGURES

1. "The Jews of Tetuán" .. 44

2. "Puerta de la Victoria, en Tetuán" .. 47

3. "Spanish soldiers come to the aid of the hungry residents of Tetuán" .. 48

4. "Entrance into Madrid of the troops from the army of Africa," 1860 .. 49

5. "Misa de campana en la Plaza de España, de Tetuán" .. 50

6. "Plaza del Teatro, en Tetuán" .. 55

7. "Blueprint for the Catholic church, consulate and hostel, 1861" .. 56

8. "Principal facade of the Catholic church, consulate and hostel" .. 57

9. "Chronicles of the War of Africa: A street in Tetuán" .. 58

10. "Reception of the Moroccan ambassador Prince Moulay El-Abbas, 1860" .. 65

11. José Villegas y Cordero, *Moroccans Inspecting Weapons*, 1871 .. 70

12. "An encampment during the campaign of Africa, 1860" . . 78

13. "Chronicles of the War of Africa: The Moorish slave prisoner" . . 79

14. "Panoramic view of Tetuán" . . 82

15. "View of the citadel and cemetery of Tetuán" . . 83

16. "The Moorish woman Hatima of Tetuán" . . 84

17. "Chronicles of the War of Africa: Jewish types of Tetuán" . . 86

18. "Precedents to the War of Africa" . . 88

19. Lieutenant General Don José de la Gándara . . 93

20. "Barbarous attack committed in Mexico against two Spaniards" . . 151

21. "Island of Fernando Po—The king of the Bubis of Basupu and his family" . . 164

Acknowledgments

I was inspired to begin this project on a visit to Omaha's Joslyn Art Museum. My students, in an undergraduate class on imperialism, race, and the formation of national identities, had come across a small collection of Orientalist works of art from the nineteenth century, and we decided to make a trip to see them in person. Walking across the street and down a block from Creighton University, we discovered that one of the paintings had been composed by the Spaniard José Villegas y Cordero, who would later become the director of Madrid's renowned Prado Museum. I started to build in a trip to the Joslyn each time I taught the course, precisely when we were set to discuss bourgeois culture and the role that the arts played in the spread of imperial ideologies. I enjoyed the break from the classroom, and I learned more about artistic production and Orientalism in nineteenth-century Europe. Subsequently I was invited to deliver a lecture at the museum on the paintings within the context of empire building, and I've included some of the material in chapter 3 of this book.

Both of my mentors in graduate school, José Álvarez Junco and the late Carolyn Boyd, worked on issues related to identity and empire in their long and brilliant careers, sparking my lasting interest in the subject matter. While Álvarez Junco examined the rise of nationalism spurred by conflicts such as the Spanish-Moroccan War of 1859–60, Boyd explored the military and the praetorian politics of turn-of-the-century Spain, especially the brutal campaigns in Morocco in the early 1920s.[1] As I completed my first book manuscript on national identities and religion in the Hispanic Atlantic world, I increasingly found myself drawn to the rise and fall of Spanish imperial dreams in the mid-nineteenth century.

I'm very thankful to have received funding for research trips to multiple cities in Spain, Mexico, and the Dominican Republic. I worked in fourteen different archives, including the military repositories in Mexico and Spain as well as Seville's Archivo de Indias. I had the pleasure of working in Alcalá de Henares for the first time, and I found incredible documents at Mexico's Archivo Histórico Genaro Estrada de la Secretaría de Relaciones Exteriores as well as Spain's Foreign Relations Archive, parts of which are now relocated to the Archivo Histórico Nacional. The University of Minnesota's Program for Cultural Cooperation awarded me an early grant, and I later received Hispanex funding from Spain's Ministry of Education, Culture, and Sport in 2014. Creighton University's Dean's Office funded travel to Mexico City, Madrid, and Seville during my sabbatical, and the Department of Academic Affairs and a CURAS Fellowship permitted me to return to Spain for multiple summer trips. Gail Jensen in the Graduate School has always been tremendously supportive, and she helped with funding as well. Last, I enjoyed a teaching position in Creighton's Encuentro Dominicano program in 2016, which gave me the opportunity to work in Santiago's small historical archive.

A wonderful colleague, Chris Schmidt-Nowara, undoubtedly shaped the outlines of the manuscript. He encouraged me and wrote on my behalf when I first applied for grants. Arguably the foremost scholar in the field of nineteenth-century Spanish imperial studies in the United States, Chris passed away tragically and unexpectedly in 2015, and all of us who knew him lost a friend and a role model. He always had time to talk and email, and when I traveled to Spain to start this new project, he alerted me to a seminar on the subject of empire building during the age of Napoleon III. So, during my first summer of work in Madrid, I was able to sit in on a talk by Juan Antonio Inarejos Muñoz as he celebrated the publication of his book *Intervenciones coloniales y nacionalismo español*, and he graciously gave me a copy. The dialogue and even the disagreements between the author and the scholars in the room motivated me to dig deeper into my topic and historical period.

These kinds of presentations are invaluable. Invited to speak at the Seminario Ortega y Gasset by Javier Muñoz Soro and Pilar Mera Costas a few years later, after having completed the initial stage of my research, I also faced a barrage of tough questions from experts in the field. I had a great time and especially appreciated the incisive commentary by María Luisa Sánchez-Mejía. At a symposium hosted by the University of Chicago in 2016, I got to know Josep Fradera and gave a talk on his magisterial *La nación imperial*, which has influenced my work and caused me to rethink key aspects of Spanish colonialism in the nineteenth century. Over the past decade I presented my findings at a number of conferences hosted by organizations such as the Association of Spanish and Portuguese Historical Studies, the International Network of Nineteenth-Century Hispanists, and the American Historical Association (AHA). At the AHA meeting in New York, I benefited from an excellent panel discussion with Gregg French, Andrés Sánchez Padilla, and Bonnie Miller on the "new" imperialism of the nineteenth century.

I have a long list of people to thank. Emily Berquist Soule, Clint Young, Sasha Pack, and Adrian Shubert have provided important insights along the way. John Calvert translated material from Arabic, which proved extremely useful. I very much appreciate that Anne Eller graciously shared her dissertation with me before its publication with Duke University Press. Susan Gilson Miller introduced me to Eric Calderwood, who read the first chapters of the book and generously offered critiques. He and Jamie Jones are some of the most hospitable people I've met; they were amazing guides in Tangier and helped facilitate a short trip to Tetuán. Josh Goode served as one of the peer reviewers and gave me pages and pages of thoughtful feedback. I'm grateful to both Josh and an anonymous reader who spent countless hours putting together comprehensive evaluations that have helped to make the book much better than it would have been otherwise. I have to acknowledge Alisa Plant, my initial acquisitions editor, and Bridget Barry, Haley Mendlik, and Kenneth Wee at the University of Nebraska Press, who each helped shepherd the book through various stages prior to publication.

My writing has been aided and abetted by friends such as Chris McClellan at the Blue Line and Barbara Wenger in Madrid. Of course, my family has supported me the most on this journey, and I couldn't have researched and written the manuscript without them. This book is dedicated to my wife, Kara, who, while running for the United State Congress, helped with the editing process, for which I will be eternally in her debt. But any errors in the text are completely my own. Finally, I've been inspired by my daughter Sabina's incredible art and political activism, which I know will continue in the years to come, revolving around issues of gun violence and antiracism. I hope she likes this book.

A note on transliteration: I have followed the practice of scholars such as Susan Gilson Miller, who retains the spelling of place names commonly found in English such as Tangier, although I include accents for the city of Cádiz, among others. For most Arabic names, Miller defers to the guidelines of the *International Journal of Middle Eastern Studies*.[2] Thus, like her, I will use "'Abd al-Qadir" instead of "Abdel-Kader," which was commonly found in Spanish-language sources from the nineteenth century.

A Missionary Nation

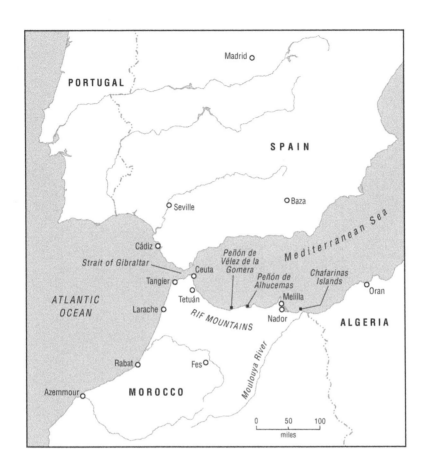

MAP 1. The western Mediterranean. Created by Erin Greb.

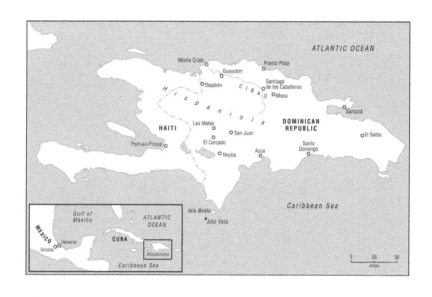

MAP 2. Hispaniola. Created by Erin Greb.

Introduction

An anonymous pamphlet published at the height of the Spanish-Moroccan War in 1859 predicted Spain was destined to re-create a once mighty empire: "To civilize northern Africa . . . is our dream, our duty, our glorious future." Why not follow the example of the eighteenth-century statesman Floridablanca, the author asked. He argued that if the Ottoman state had crumbled under the weight of revolutionary turmoil, the monarchy of Charles III could have seized the Mediterranean coast of Africa. Why not bombard a coastal port like Algiers in a show of force, just as the British had done in 1816? The author, purporting to be a diplomat, opined that the subsequent "French conquest of Algeria [was] a historical warning, a lesson" that must be heeded. If it were to be ignored, the French would grab what undoubtedly belonged to Spain. And just like the United States and even Russia, actively engaged in imperial expansion and conquest, the Spanish had the right to permanently occupy and maintain a presence within their spheres of influence, especially across the Strait of Gibraltar. Race, religion, and national honor provided the most convenient justifications. Spain would emerge triumphant in the name of civilization and Christianity, because the Moroccans, and "the African race" in general, were tied to the past, "their institutions, religion, and customs chained to barbarism."[1]

Writers and intellectuals such as Pedro Antonio de Alarcón, later renowned for books such as *The Three-Cornered Hat*, had enlisted in the army and experienced the combat in North Africa firsthand. Alarcón tied nostalgia for fifteenth-century imperial grandeur to a profound religious sensibility, plainly stating that the war represented "a kind of pilgrimage to undertake or martyrdom to suffer in the name of God."[2] According to Susan Martin-Márquez, Alarcón avidly believed that modernity was "only accessible to those who . . . accepted Christ."[3] He described the journey in his *Diary of a Witness to the War of Africa* and worked alongside the Italian photographer Enrique Facio Fialo to document what the soldiers saw and encountered in a foreign land.[4] Artists such as Marià Fortuny and José Villegas y Cordero also visited Morocco in the wake of the Spanish invasion of 1859.[5] The products of their labor, including images and stories of the conflict—many of which came directly from the battlefront—made a deep impression on a Spanish public eager for daily news from the front. From the 1850s on, a romanticized culture of imperialism spread through the public sphere.

Most scholarship on empire has followed the trajectory of the British and French and, to a lesser extent, Dutch and German experiences. A case in point is Edward Berenson's *Heroes of Empire*, a text that presents fascinating microstudies but entirely neglects Spanish expeditions and men such as Alarcón, who worked tirelessly to revive the spirit of imperial glory. If "genuine national heroes in the second half of the nineteenth century . . . had to be peaceful conquerors—or appear as such," as Berenson claims, then many figures in Spain certainly fit the pantheon of charismatic individuals who galvanized public opinion through their commitment to Christian values, humanitarianism, and empire building.[6] Ordinary citizens who may not have expressed great interest in the daily exercise of power, politics, and policy did follow the exploits of those who captured the collective imagination, especially in the course of overseas adventures.

This book will, in part, rectify shortcomings in the literature by examining the cultural and political fabric of nineteenth-century Spanish imperialism in four episodes—beginning in

Morocco (chapters 1–3), proceeding to the reincorporation of the Dominican Republic in 1861 (chapters 4–5) and the attempted conquest of Mexico in 1862 (chapter 6), and concluding with expeditions to the Gulf of Guinea over several decades (chapter 7). These targeted campaigns against lesser global powers, what Stephen Jacobson has called "micromilitarism," will be analyzed in addition to interventions in Vietnam and Peru.[7] As midcentury Mexican liberals continued to be preoccupied with the possibility of a Spanish invasion like the abortive mission of 1829, Spaniards, conversely, were animated by the prospect of a renewed cycle of imperialism. For example, in November 1861, just months after Spanish soldiers had marched into the North African city of Tetuán and diplomats had cemented the annexation of the Dominican Republic, one journalist excitedly reported that ministers were on the cusp of signing a treaty giving Spain commercial and territorial rights in Annam. This would, naturally, provide just compensation for the lives lost and the "sacrifices made for our patria and in the interest of humanity and civilization."[8] Less than a week later the same newspaper reprinted an editorial from England predicting in no uncertain terms that Spain would soon be reconquering Mexico. On the next page an article lauded the peace reigning in Hispaniola, as Dominicans had realized their hopes of attaining order and security.[9] Though facile examinations might point to the limited successes of such ventures as the French pushed Spain aside in Vietnam and Mexico and factionalism devolved into war in the Dominican Republic, a Spanish overseas presence proved durable and lasted well into the twentieth century, especially in northern Morocco and Guinea.

Spanish culture, actualized through various forms of media as well as clerical and political rhetoric, built on the norms, assumptions, and stereotypes of nineteenth-century bourgeois societies. These movements lent support to empire building. A shift toward a popular and mobilizing culture of imperialism occurred in the first several decades of the nineteenth century. This came at about the same time as it did in other

European nations, or perhaps even earlier. For example, amid the Napoleonic wars in 1811, the Cortes discussed jettisoning extra European possessions, such as three of Spain's North African military presidios.[10] Between the 1820s and early 1840s, by contrast, a new current of imperial thinking spread. In reference to French campaigns in Algeria, Spanish periodicals began to laud "the civilizing principle" of "social progress," thereby decrying Islamism, fanaticism, and barbarism.[11] By this time liberal nationalists ardently wanted to hang on to all of their imperial territories, whether in the Caribbean, Asia, or Africa. This book, therefore, begins in 1841, when popular opposition voiced in the press thwarted a bill that had been introduced in the Cortes to sell Fernando Po (Bioko) to Britain.[12] Some journalists described the West African island as an integral part of national territory, especially important in the face of continued English incursions.[13] They embraced the fact that on the island of Corisco, just two hundred miles to the south, the island's inhabitants apparently were "naturalized at their own request" during the expedition of Juan José de Lerena in 1843.[14] In 1846 Dominican officials made inquiries into annexation by Spain, and the Chafarinas Islands off the Moroccan coast were seized in 1848. A modern and muscular Spanish liberal imperialism had begun to take shape that, much to the chagrin of many committed nationalists, reached its apex in the 1860s and 1870s. Only in the early twentieth century would it be resurrected under the auspices of so-called Africanistas and a powerful new conservative form of nationalism. The taking of Tetuán in 1860 figures as the apogee of this age in Spain; after the fall of the Liberal Union government in 1863, active interventions and funds to pursue colonialism were pulled back. Following the Conference of Madrid in 1880, Spanish influence, even in Morocco, waned.[15] According to J. A. Hobson, writing about the new imperialism of the 1880s, "Spain may be said to have definitively retired from imperial competition."[16]

This transnational history will reexamine the rise of nineteenth-century Spanish imperialism by focusing on the politics and culture that produced it as well as the cohesive social movements that offered sustained anticolonial resistance. In addition each chapter will assess the roles played by key protagonists, from unlikely surrogates for the cause of expansion such as Secretary of State Saturnino Calderón Collantes to Emilio Castelar y Ripoll, the influential president of Spain's First Republic in 1873.[17] Castelar, author of more than ninety works, will provide a voice throughout the text, from private letters to editorials and public speeches, but his unbridled advocacy was not unique. Chapter 1 will highlight the destructiveness of figures such as Brigadier Manuel Buceta del Villar, who single-mindedly fought for the projection of Spanish power. He headed Spain's military outpost in Melilla during the start of the Spanish-Moroccan War and subsequently became notorious for atrocities committed in the Dominican Republic during hostilities in the Cibao region, the subject of chapter 5. Chapter 2 focuses on the 1860 charge to take Tetuán, Morocco, led by General Juan Prim y Prats, while chapter 6 explores his deployment to Veracruz, Mexico, the following year. At the same time republican leaders, including the rebellious Dominican general Gregorio de Lora and the Mexican diplomat Juan Antonio de la Fuente, fiercely resisted the reimposition of Spanish rule.

Using a variety of tactics, the diplomats Juan Blanco del Valle, Mariano Álvarez, and Gabriel Tassara pressed Spain to reclaim the status of a great power and would use almost any means necessary to achieve their goal. Conspiratorial consuls and military leaders, examined in depth in chapters 4 through 6, planned years in advance to seize both the Dominican Republic and Mexico. Whether through dissimulation, espionage, or alliance building, they actively pursued a foreign policy bent on territorial enlargement. Spanish field commanders, such as Buceta and José de la Gándara y Navarro, tried to maintain control of presidios in the Caribbean and in West Africa, the focus of chapter 7. All shared a commitment to Spanish nationalism, the values of Roman Catholicism, and the unquestioned ideals of racial supremacy.

The chapters that follow, therefore, dig into the decades of transition between what Eric Hobsbawm has called the "classical period of liberal nationalism" and the rise of a more conservative discourse tinged with racism starting in the 1870s, marked by the emergence of an exclusionary National-Catholicism in Spain.[18] In between, thinkers like Donoso Cortés inveighed against liberalism and urged a return to religion as the indestructible foundation of human societies.[19] In 1882 the eminent Spanish historian Marcelino Menéndez y Pelayo succinctly defined the underpinnings of a new nationalist ideology premised upon religious bonds: "Only common religion can provide a people with its own specific life, with the consciousness of a strong unanimity; only religion can legitimate and found the laws." Because "Christianity gave its unity to Spain," he concluded, "we have been a Nation, even a great Nation, and not a multitude of individuals."[20] National-Catholicism plainly drew on traditional interpretations of the faith as the central marker of identity. While many scholars present these eras in dichotomous terms, contrasting the nationalist rhetoric of the latter half of the century with the fraught liberal version dating back to 1812, this book traces more continuities than stark differences, as the Catholic faith informed both liberal and conservative nationalisms in Spain and Latin America over the course of the nineteenth century.[21] In turn, religion infused Spain's civilizing mission from Asia and Africa to the Caribbean.

Race and Empire

What did race and empire mean to contemporary men and women who lived in both metropolitan and imperial spaces in the mid-nineteenth century, and how were these ideas forged? As Anne McClintock asserts, racial discourse has been historically unstable, overlapping with other lexicons of gender, sexuality, culture, and religion.[22] Influential writers correlated masculinity with physical strength, contrasting white civilization and manly virtues with degeneracy and effeminacy.[23] In the Spanish-speaking world notions of racial difference and their corresponding attributes could be used to distinguish Black Dominicans, mestizo Mexicans, and Sephardic Jews from European Spaniards. But were distinctive characteristics understood as fixed and ingrained products of biology, or had they been determined by climate?[24] Did culture play a role?[25] Although Joshua Goode has explored the development of racialized thinking in turn-of-the-century Spain, less has been written about the 1850s and 1860s, a defining era that saw the publication of some of the most important racial theorists of the age, such as the Frenchman Arthur de Gobineau.[26] While scholars note that the works of Victor Courtet de L'Isle and Gobineau initially had been "received with deep silence," Spanish intellectuals had waded into debates over their veracity by the end of the 1850s.[27]

The question of race posed complications for even the most outspoken democrats of the nineteenth century and exposed the contradictions and limits of their radical thought. Castelar was no exception. While formally espousing the equality of all races, he correlated absolutism and backwardness with Eastern societies.[28] Others continually associated barbarism and tyranny with Blackness—as archetypal African traits. Contrary to those who preached a doctrine of innate racial difference, however, a number of important scholars dismissed the vitriolic scientific racism of Frenchmen like Courtet and Gobineau. Castelar said, "Mr. Courtet holds that racial difference explains all of history. He says that the enslavement of inferior races, of poor and ignorant races, is based upon human nature. There always will be a race privileged by nature. From here he makes the absurd claim that societies cannot be happy where all men are of the same race, and that it is necessary that two distinct races exist, one that is free, rich, and happy, and the other poor, enslaved and despondent. These absurdities do not need to be refuted."[29] Likewise Alexis de Tocqueville privately admonished his friend Gobineau, criticizing his extreme ideas on inherent inequality. Yet, as Goode has shown, racial thinking based upon an inclusive premise that disavowed scientific racism was often in practice no different than an ideology grounded in exclusionary claims.[30] In other words, Europeans advancing a civilizing mission as well as practitioners of scientific racism operated the same way, especially in the colonial world. Mid-nineteenth-century Spanish imperialism and the edifice of a Catholic civilizing rhetoric, as witnessed and propagated by Castelar, is a case in point. Though often downplayed at the time, the idea of biological racial inferiority in many ways served to justify expansion overseas.

Nineteenth-century politicians and statesmen spilled a great deal of ink explaining how culture, ethnicity, and race differentiated Europeans from Africans and Asians. Prior to the invasion of Morocco, for example, one diplomat insisted that Maghrebis tended to "conserve their primitive language and their traditional independence." Drawing on a current of essentialist thinking, he wrote that they therefore embodied "a state of misery and desolation in which the country will remain."[31] A popular song that celebrated the Catalan volunteers in the Spanish-Moroccan War condemned all Moroccans as a "race of slaves."[32] Castelar publicly castigated the despotism of the "Orient" and contrasted Islam's aristocratic, hereditary priesthood with the democratic meritocracy of Christendom.[33] Christianity was, he said emphatically, "the exaltation of humanity."[34] The explorer Manuel Iradier y Bulfy, describing the people of the Río Muni region of West Africa, definitively stated, "The only thing I dare to affirm is that the blood of the black vengas [Benga people] is not the same as we, the men of the Caucasian race, have."[35] In private diplomatic correspondence Spain's consul to Haiti in 1862 claimed that the entirety of the Black race showed "great defects and inherent vices"; they only would respond to the language of force and violence.[36] The broad brushstrokes of Orientalism and mid-century racism, which began to dovetail with conclusions of phrenologists, certainly affected ideology and praxis prior to the Restoration (1874–1923). One particularly telling letter reprinted in a newspaper, written by a seventy-four-year-old father of a soldier, paid tribute to the men fighting in North Africa against the vile "African Caribs."[37] No sarcasm had been intended. Europeans used epithets for Moroccans, Berbers, Dominicans, and Indigenous peoples of the New World interchangeably, erasing ethnic, cultural, and linguistic differences.[38] Ultimately, many Spanish imperialists employed a similar language of declension and fundamental difference to justify their actions in Africa and in the Caribbean.[39]

Clearly, racial thinking also remained tied to polemics over slavery in both the French and Spanish colonial worlds, notably in Cuba and Puerto Rico. Seymour Drescher writes that prominent nineteenth-century European liberals, including Tocqueville, maintained the idea that "[w]hites and blacks could nowhere exist without either subordination or racial conflict."[40] In his analysis of emancipation within French dominions Tocqueville suggested European domination could continue under a regime of legalized equality that precluded former slaves from purchasing property. Thus his commitment to both empire building in Algeria as well as the abolition of slavery can be seen as an extension of his quintessentially nineteenth-century liberal views, rife with paradox and prejudice. Likewise, Spaniards vacillated on the subject, seeing economic benefits while also understanding the trend toward manumission. The government officially declared slavery a "necessary evil" at the time, although the proclamation emphasized its importance as well.[41] Spain declared all slaves on Fernando Po free in 1859 and did not reestablish slavery in the Dominican Republic after reincorporation into the monarchy in 1861, despite its proximity to Cuba, where the institution persisted until 1886.[42] Due to the perceived threat represented by the large free Black population of Haiti, diplomats like Álvarez entertained the idea of whitening the Hispanic Caribbean by "neutralizing the influence of other races" through white immigrants, especially Canary Islanders emigrating to the island of Hispaniola.[43] Others looked to Spanish emigration to Mexico to prevent further racial degeneration on the mainland.[44] But even the radical revolution of 1868 did not provide the impetus to abolish slavery once and for all, with Cuba viewed through the lens of Spanish nationalism rather than through the prism of race and slavery. *La Época*, a moderate periodical that had been tied to the Liberal Union government in the early 1860s, ran the sensationalistic headline "Cuba is lost!" in December 1868. The paper expressed horror and frustration over the insurrection yet did not mention slavery at all.[45]

The concepts of race and civilization came to be fundamentally intertwined during the second age of European imperialism in the nineteenth century. Kwame Anthony Appiah finds that an emergent discourse extolling modern Western civilization dates back to the 1890s.[46] Accordingly, the West had triumphed over its imagined antithesis. Edward Said detailed the artistic, intellectual, and scientific origins of European Orientalism through its flowering in the twentieth century. He insisted that it was used by Europeans to define themselves, an inversion of supposed Western values and technological prowess.[47] Bernard Bailyn has tied the development of the idea of Western civilization to the history of the Atlantic World during the interwar period and the rise of the United States as a global power following World War II.[48] However, self-identification with the West, connected to the idea that the occident reigned supreme over a fallen and decadent East, appears in the rhetoric of Spaniards in the 1860s. One journalist manifestly stated, "We owe much to the East: great institutions have come from these countries where the sun rises; and the truth is that we westerners [occidentales] do nothing more than imitate them even as we appear more distant from their uses and customs."[49] This apparently self-evident notion of a declining "East," sandwiched between a discussion of Morocco, Berbers, and a reference to José Cadalso's *Cartas marruecas*, perfectly captures the sense of historicism and teleology that underlay nineteenth-century European Orientalism and empire building.

In dialogue with Said, historians of late have debated vigorously the interrelated issues of culture, race, and imperialism. Bernard Porter has challenged the idea that the British Empire played a significant role in shaping metropolitan culture and everyday life, insisting that the entire venture was to a degree the product of a confluence of unusual circumstances.[50] Porter's contention that the empire required very little commitment prior to the end of the nineteenth century does not correlate with an assessment of Spain's imperial fortunes. Their overseas expeditions necessitated significant expenditures and received the blessing of competing political factions of Progressives (*progresistas*), Moderates (*moderados*), and Conservatives. On the other hand, the idea of a civilizing mission certainly resonated across Europe and in many ways underpinned Spain's war efforts in Morocco, the Caribbean, and the Pacific. The Archbishop of Madrid insisted that the campaign in Africa represented a struggle against the enemies of the *patria*, God, and religion. This sentiment was echoed by the anticlerical intellectual Castelar, who clamored for troops to fight in North Africa armed with the sacred fire of patriotism, their imminent victory blessed by heaven.[51] Castelar, who would later become a leading republican political figure, unapologetically wrote that Spain was destined to civilize the primitive races of Africa and to baptize them into Christian civilization.[52]

While scholars have dated the use of the term "civilizing mission" to the early 1840s, the concept has Catholic roots in the Hispanic world.[53] Clerics fulfilled the duty of proselytization in part by spreading the ideals of Christian civilization, and the language of a civilizing mission morphed from its origins in the church to a more secular call to arms. In 1836, at the end of a polemical debate over disentailment in Spain, the press highlighted the historical role of the clergy as teachers and intellectuals with a clearly delineated "misión civilizadora."[54] As contemporary clerics no longer served these same functions and had been replaced in many respects, journalists argued that much of their wealth and many of their holdings could and should be nationalized for the good of society as a whole. Shortly thereafter advocates used the term in the context of European imperialism. For instance, a Spanish periodical from 1844 lauded France for completing its "civilizing mission" in

Morocco and standing firm in its demands for reparations for treaty violations and aggressive acts.[55] Alice Conklin has explored the "idea of a secular *mission civilisatrice*" and the blindness of nineteenth-century French republicans toward West African cultures.[56] Yet Spaniards did not in any way preach secularism, rather emphasizing that their efforts must "shine the light of Christianity" upon colonized peoples.[57] They unambiguously situated imperialism under the umbrella of the civilizing mission, with an emphasis on religiosity, and Progressives such as Castelar often were the most vocal.[58] This paternalistic brand of Catholicism, however, tended to intensify anti-Spanish sentiment, as the following chapters will demonstrate.

Chronologically, government-sponsored empire building, dubbed the new imperialism, has been dated to 1870 and the rush to cobble together territories sparked by German unification and the aftermath of the Franco-Prussian War. Hobson noted that "the year 1870 has been taken as indicative of the beginning of a conscious policy of Imperialism," though he saw that the movement truly gained steam in the 1880s, during the Scramble for Africa. He also linked this history to "an expansion of autocracy" and the repression of civil liberties in occupied lands.[59] Yet at this point the regime in Spain remained nominally liberal, with Castelar elected as a deputy once more in 1881. And the government in Madrid, like the July Monarchy in France, had resolved to rebuild its imperial presence well before 1870, responding to internal dynamics and nationalism as well as international pressures and competition.

All of this runs contrary to conventional wisdom regarding the driving forces of nineteenth-century colonialism—economic and social domination. If, as Josep Fradera astutely observes, nineteenth-century colonialism served to transform African and Asian societies into economic engines that functioned in accordance with European needs and demands, then Liberal Union adventurism did not adhere to the same rationale.[60] While economic factors certainly pushed Spain to join France and Britain in besieging Mexico in 1861, they do not provide a complete explanatory paradigm for the invasion of northern Morocco or the war in the Dominican Republic during Leopoldo O'Donnell's administration.[61] One colonial administrator went as far as to say that "the possession of the island of Fernando Po for the Spanish had been a question of national luxury [lujo]," an ostentatious and extremely expensive venture untethered from cost-benefit analysis.[62] To avoid budgetary shortfalls, a governor of Fernando Po, Antonio Vivar, had high hopes for developing commodities like palm oil. Likewise, the expansionist-minded Spanish consul to Haiti expressed great interest in Dominican mahogany and gold deposits.[63] Such plans did not match the scale of engagement in West Africa and the Caribbean, however, which cost in the neighborhood of $10 million (close to $300 million today, but far more as measured by percentage of GDP).[64] One discerning journalist advocated making economic inroads into Morocco rather than conquering territory, yet he conceded that the war's popularity was tied almost entirely to the idea of raising Spain's profile above that of the rest of the nations of Europe.[65] New research into culture and empire building shows that historians must reframe their questions and challenge preconceived truisms. H. Glenn Penny provocatively claims that German imperial aims "were much richer and more multifarious than a simple colonialist drive. These included humanism, liberalism, pluralism, monogenism, and a persistent desire to know more about the world."[66] This assessment helps illuminate the variety of motives driving Spanish imperialists from the 1840s through the 1870s.

As demonstrated in a diverse array of sources, from letters and diplomatic correspondence to newspapers, plays, and military records, Spaniards tended to portray their imperial wars as racial and religious struggles, and the cultural conflicts that resulted were mediated through the lens of Spain's history and Catholic faith. A gendered rhetoric of imperial benevolence often came couched in paternalistic overtones, depicting the colonized and colonizer in binary terms. But a belief in humankind's inexorable progress, an idea that dates back to the

Enlightenment and philosophes such as the Marquis de Condorcet, informed many of the protagonists as well. In *Sketch for a Historical Picture of the Progress of the Human Mind*, Condorcet wrote, "These vast lands [Africa and Asia] are inhabited partly by large tribes who need only assistance from us to become civilized, who wait only to find brothers amongst the European nations to become their friends and pupils; partly by races oppressed by sacred despots or dull-witted conquerors, and who for so many centuries have cried out to be liberated."[67] Castelar similarly idealized the benevolence and charity of Europeans who offered liberation to those suffering under tyranny and despotism. He did not imagine civilization would be enclosed and fenced off in Europe and America. Rather, the modern world would extend outward "to make natural rights and justice universal." He juxtaposed Christian civics and liberty with their antithesis—African cities across the Mediterranean, populated by "races enslaved by their own ignorance."[68] The weight of history in the Orient had led to a degeneration of man, while "progress, then, had been consecrated by Christianity."[69] Castelar channeled Georg Wilhelm Friedrich Hegel, emphasizing a Christian teleology and the rise of the West, as well as Immanuel Kant, who noted that preenlightened people had been mired in self-incurred tutelage.[70] By way of a remedy Castelar encouraged commerce, exploration of the interior of Africa, and industry, a progressive process that would overcome the blind forces of nature. And this imperial vision absolutely correlated with his firm belief in democracy and natural rights.

The Progress of Modern Spanish History

For men like Emilio Castelar (1832–99), liberty and democracy heralded union and the elision of arbitrary borders, principles they did not view as antithetical to colonization. Castelar romantically opined that the doctrines of the French Revolution, notably fraternity, would bring together people on both sides of the Atlantic Ocean who would embrace the values of Hispanic civilization.[71] The Spanish Monarchy's kaleidoscopic "Age of

Revolution" and its echoes in the Americas provided inspiration and the impetus for a later generation of Progressives and democrats to develop new social and political identities. Key actors such as Castelar and his political mentor Nicolás María Rivero, among many others in both peninsular Spain and in the Spanish Caribbean, transformed politics in the 1840s and 1850s. They published widely, founded periodicals like *La Discusión*, and contributed to a growing political opposition.[72] By appropriating the discourses of earlier revolutions—in 1812, 1820, 1836, and 1848—republicans in the mid-nineteenth century presented themselves as the true heirs to a unique tradition of radical Hispanic liberalism. Concomitantly they pushed for a liberal imperialism that was grounded in Enlightenment ideals of progress and civilization.

In December 1847, immediately prior to the outbreak of revolutionary movements across Europe, the moderate newspaper *El Eco del Comercio* (The echo of commerce) put forward a strong, clear defense of Spain's outposts on the northern coast of Africa. Addressed to its patriotic readers, the brief article insisted that Spain's interests must be protected at all costs; abandoning its imperial possessions would constitute "traitorous" acts of foolishness. The piece focused on the old, established Spanish presidios in Africa as well as on the "precious" Chafarinas, three islands off the coast of Morocco in the gulf of Melilla that form a natural barrier and protective enclave on the border of French Algeria.[73] Castelar, musing about the importance of recent French imperial triumphs, understood that the successes of the war in Algeria had begun "to excite national sentiment" in Spain.[74] Just a few years prior national honor had been offended by the assassination of Spanish consular agent Víctor Darmon in Morocco, and public opinion supported a strong response. Although that specific incident did not escalate into a conflict, when France initiated negotiations with the Moroccan sultan, the Moderate-led Narváez government preemptively sent several ships to formally take control of the Chafarinas and declare them to be Spanish possessions

in early January 1848.[75] As other European states found themselves convulsed by revolutionary agitation, Spain looked to
cement territorial expansion in the Mediterranean.

But radicals also pushed for major changes in Spain. On
March 4, 1848, Rivero, a deputy in the Cortes, gave a speech that
effectively undermined the legitimacy of the state and the ruling Bourbon monarchy. He proclaimed, "Revolutions are not
a whim of the people; they are always a necessity."[76] He urged
reforms in electoral laws to open up the franchise, changes in
taxation, and the creation of a national militia to supplant the
conservative Constitution of 1845. As a move away from the
liberalism of Spain's first Constitution of 1812, promulgated in
Cádiz during the French occupation, the Constitution of 1845
established a joint form of sovereignty, with power shared by
the Crown and the elected legislature. Only one percent of the
total population could cast a vote in elections.[77] Sovereignty was
not vested solely in the people, which had been the rallying cry
of the first liberal generation. While one Spanish conservative
lamented the "universal shipwreck" of the year 1848 and held
out hope for monarchies "standing strong against the impet-
uous whirlwinds" whipped up by radicals like Rivero, abortive
uprisings took place at the end of the month in Madrid, Barcelona, and Valencia.[78] There were dozens of casualties, and
the government in Madrid suspended normal constitutional
protections and even rescinded freedom of the press for more
than a month. In Paris, Spanish refugees demonstrated their
support on the same day and proudly unfurled the banner of
Rafael Riego, which had flown during the Trienio Liberal of
1820–23.[79] There were more disturbances in Madrid and Seville
in May, resulting in the forced exile of seven hundred accused
conspirators. This pattern continued as unrest rocked a number of other key municipalities from Galicia to the Spanish outpost of Ceuta in northern Africa. Protestors included military
figures and civilians reacting to the news of revolutionary agitation across Europe that spring. Events culminated not in a
break with the remnants of an Old Regime state but with the

formation of the Democratic Party in Spain, founded in 1849 by Fernando Garrido, Rivero, and others to spearhead the cause of universal suffrage and republicanism.[80] While there would be no wave of revolutionary fervor cresting over Spain and Latin America in 1848, Progressives would come to power in 1854 in an echo of the radical impulses that had swept through European capitals six years earlier.

In ex post facto liberal narratives of the period, the cycle of revolution and reaction in the Hispanic world had roots in 1789. Garrido declared that "Paris had given . . . the great example of the new evolution into which humanity had entered." He saw it as the "combustion that would purify the world."[81] Writing with a similar historicist sensibility, Gaspar Melchor de Jovellanos had noted as early as 1794 that "the human spirit is progressive." During the height of the French Revolution he urged moderation, insisting that "it is necessary to pursue progress gradually." At the same time, however, he praised the liberal model that initially came out of France: "Certainly it would be great" to aspire to "a constitution like the one that Louis XVI swore to in 1791."[82] Yet Spain would have to wait until the extraordinary events of the War of Independence provided space for liberals to muscle their way into power. Castelar, in an extended history lesson published a decade after the revolutions of 1848–49, eulogized the "audacious legislators of 1812" as the font of the progressive movement in the nineteenth century.[83] What had they done to draw such praise from Castelar? They had dismantled the Inquisition, broken the "chains" of absolutism, ended seignorialism, and provided natural rights to the Spanish people in the form of a constitution. Castelar called it the "immortal code of 1812." Yet he went further in claiming it as an authentic artifact of democracy—a constitution for all Spaniards. Accordingly, the doceañistas, embryonic democrats, "established the sovereignty of the nation, its autonomy, its independence . . . equality before the law, free speech, the abolition of privilege, universal suffrage . . . the independence of the municipality; in one word, the seed of all the rights and ideas that today are the symbols of democracy."[84] Was he right to connect early nineteenth-century liberals, the men to whom the appellation *liberal* was first applied, with midcentury democrats? Certainly, the architects of the Constitution of 1812 had sowed the seeds of democracy and self-consciously created a uniform, modern nation-state for Spaniards on both sides of the Atlantic, including the Indigenous peoples of the New World. Yet their radicalism had its limits, just as was the case in the United States. Deputies to the Cortes did not abolish the slave trade nor did they eliminate the institution of slavery, and they excluded those of African descent, women, and non-Catholics from citizenship. Elections were indirect and took place in three stages, erecting a barrier between the people and their representatives. On the other hand, conservatives quickly read the document as a fundamental challenge to the old order and worked tirelessly to prevent its resurrection. Ferdinand VII had it revoked immediately upon returning from captivity in France in April 1814. The three-year stretch of liberal rule during which the Constitution was reinstated in the early 1820s represented such a threat to the Holy Alliance that the French dispatched a hundred thousand troops to Spain to put down the vestiges of the *doceañista* revolution in April 1823. The symbols of that liberal triennium, from the tricolor flag to Riego's hymn, which was named the national anthem in 1822, remained potent reminders of the promise of liberal politics.[85]

Castelar's reflections provide a window into questions of empire and identity in the mid-nineteenth century. In *The Formula of Progress*, he presented the Hegelian idea of evolution toward a more perfect state. He argued that the "space that separates 1789 from 1848, the age of the middle class, the time that now begins, is the age of justice . . . the age of democracy." Accordingly, he stated his firm conviction that "the law of progress was liberty."[86] The march forward necessitated the embrace of equal rights and universal suffrage, both of which, Castelar mused, were aspects of Spain's nineteenth-century history dating back to the Constitution of Cádiz in 1812.

The next revolutionary turn, following this logic, took shape in the tumultuous 1830s during the First Carlist War in Spain. The backdrop to the struggle against traditionalists in the north, with their slogans hearkening back to the Catholicism of an earlier age, was a sustained campaign of disentailment of church lands and dissolution of religious orders, including the Jesuits. Belatedly, the Inquisition was shut down in 1834. With Carlists railing against perceived heretics and atheists and speaking out against constitutionalism in general, the government accepted the Constitution of 1812 as a provisional legal code and called the Cortes to convene. From as far away as eastern Cuba, key officials promulgated the Cádiz Constitution and implemented its representative protocols.[87] But the resulting Constitution of 1837 enfranchised a mere 5 percent of male voters and ushered in a period of moderate liberal rule.[88] Castelar decried the "bitter deception" of a charter that had backed away from the ideal of popular sovereignty and corrupted freedom of the press. He fumed that "liberty was mutilated by those who would call themselves sons and heirs to the glorious legislators of Cádiz."[89] Yet he would find inspiration in the events of February 1848 in Paris, just as Mexican radical Valentín Gómez Farías did from his diplomatic post across the channel in London. Gómez Farías wrote to his son that he hoped "the revolutionary movement [would] spread to Spain and other [monarchical] nations."[90] However, a growing fear of communism, expressed by conservatives as well as democrats such as Garrido, soon muted the voices that had initially applauded revolution in both Spain and Mexico.

In the wake of liberal uprisings quelled across Spain in 1848, Castelar had to reimagine the ways in which progressivism would take hold in the Iberian Peninsula. To realize the twin goals of democracy and republicanism, Castelar postulated the idea that a charismatic, "enigmatic" man of the people had to seize the mantle of revolution. He plainly stated that Baldomero Espartero, a hero of the Carlist War and the "incarnation of the Progressives," was destined to fulfill the role of Spanish revolutionary. With a quintessentially Spanish character tinged with

Arabism, according to Castelar, Espartero symbolized the revolutionary aspirations of liberal Spain. He was not a man of ideas; instead, his fatalistic instincts would allow him to lead the process of reform and change.

For democrats like Castelar the revolution took place in 1854, as Progressives under General Espartero formed a government and attempted to shift power away from their Moderate rivals. This revived the spirit of 1812, and by 1856 a democratic constitution had been proposed. In Mexico liberals enacted a new constitution in 1857, and rebels in the Dominican Republic put forward a radical new charter in 1858. Castelar argued that "the result of the revolution of 1854 was in large measure beneficial to Spain: the public spirit rose up . . . the treasury was strengthened . . . the press, endowed with greater liberty, could play its central role. . . . Then it was possible to speak of an Iberian union, this great mission of the current generation; then the coasts of Africa became a promised land; then one spoke of Spanish politics in America."[91]

The contradictions between Castelar's democratic principles and his vision of imperialism would become increasingly apparent when Spain invaded North Africa in 1859, annexed the Dominican Republic in 1861, and supported French intervention in democratic Mexico by 1861. The two years between the fall of Tetuán in February 1860 and the withdrawal of Spanish auxiliary forces from Mexico in April 1862 marked a period of great optimism for imperialists of all stripes in metropolitan Spain. Front-page editorials in the opposition periodical to which Castelar contributed, Madrid's *La Discusión*, illuminated a vision of liberal empire, one that was shared by both Progressives and Moderates in O'Donnell's government. General Espartero felt that the conflict in Morocco evoked medieval chansons and conjured up the age-old struggle between Muslims and Christians.[92] But with more than religious hegemony at stake, the war exposed tensions between universal ideals and hardening attitudes toward race. The Cortes had excluded its overseas representatives beginning in 1837, maintained slavery in Cuba and Puerto Rico, and embarked on a renewed campaign of territorial aggrandizement in the 1860s.[93] Castelar, like his liberal compatriots, articulated a dismissive kind of racial superiority when he compared a "people without the understanding of their rights, without being conscious of their obligations," to "a black African slave, who, when he breaks his chains, rides roughshod over everything, destroying everything."[94] The actions and beliefs of a generation of radical thinkers undermined the promise of liberalism even as they delivered constitutional regimes as well as a brief respite from the monarchy throughout the course of the nineteenth century in Spain.

If revolutions are to be understood as efforts to transform the values, myths, and institutions of a given polity, then intellectuals and politicians such as Castelar, Garrido, and Rivero certainly qualify as revolutionary agitators.[95] Marked by the historical reference points of liberal Spain, a new discourse emerged. Castelar called for sweeping change and a rupture with the past, even with the Bourbon dynasty itself. Yet he would soon become a central apologist for the liberal imperialism and racism that characterized the postrevolutionary age.

ONE

"The War of Africa Has Been the Dream of My Entire Political Life"

The year before Spain invaded Morocco with forty-five thousand men, an incident occurred that threatened to undermine the already tense relations between Spanish authorities and the Moroccan sultan. According to the consul general in Tangier Juan Blanco del Valle (1822–77), a Muslim woman and her two daughters had been preparing to flee the country because, having been educated as Christians, they wanted to "embrace Catholicism." Caught in the company of a "renegade" Spanish soldier, the three were imprisoned. Blanco del Valle wrote an impassioned letter describing the scene to the secretary of state in Madrid, claiming that the women "began to shout that they were Spaniards [españolas], as evidenced by their clothing, and that they wanted to be presented before me." When the family was transported to the residence of the consul, disturbances took place, as one of the three was to be executed. Just as the exemplary punishment was about to take place, Blanco del Valle, "in harmony with the humanitarian sentiments of the government," intervened on her behalf.[1] Ultimately the consul could not find any justification in the treaty between the countries to provide the women with asylum, as they were subjects of the Moroccan emperor. But he agreed to return them to the sultan only with a formal promise that they would not be punished and would be able to reclaim their liberty immediately. He ended the note by confidently stating that he had upheld the national honor and dignity of Spain, and he subsequently received accolades from his superiors. This episode, and many others similar in tone and content, linked the protection of the faith and of the faithful to national pride—a key element of mid-nineteenth-century Spanish nationalism.[2] Gendered and racial markers intertwined as Spaniards took up the mantle of the civilizing mission. In turn, this rhetoric became a linchpin of Spain's growing involvement in North Africa and the Caribbean in the 1850s and 1860s.

This chapter explores blustering diplomats and military officials in Tangier, Ceuta, and Melilla who paved the way for a declaration of war in October 1859 and inaugurated an age of expansion for a nostalgic public back home. It also ties together a culture of storytelling and articles in the periodical press that served as outlets for imperial dreams. A narrative of nineteenth-century Spanish imperialism wove together a complex cast of characters, the core of which included an intrepid soldier or diplomat vanquishing an aging tyrant, the defender of an antiquated political and social system epitomized by the subjugation of women. Spaniards believed their efforts to shelter non-European females within the orbit of the Catholic church served as proof of their progressive values. Whether fact, as in the case of Blanco del Valle in the prelude to the Spanish-Moroccan War, or fiction, exemplified by popular plays from the era, heroic Spaniards were presented as noble and disinterested protectors of Christian mores in the colonial world. For instance, the 1859 zarzuela *The Martyrs of Cochin China* underscored the religious justifications for Spain's participation alongside the French in the invasion and occupation of Tourane, Annam (Da Nang, Vietnam). Catholicism took center stage, as the murder of a missionary in 1857 had precipitated Spanish intervention in the Far East. The play used the backdrop of actual events to make an emotional appeal for an imperial venture ostensibly designed to protect Annamese Catholics.

The Martyrs of Cochin China begins as two protagonists, both "indigenous Christians," are to marry, their vows presided over by a Spanish missionary in defiance of the local sovereign's

attempts to extirpate Roman Catholicism. The governor of Saigon, Thi-ur, the embodiment of a stereotypical Oriental despot, is furious that they have professed publicly the religion of
the "European barbarians."[3] When the bride-to-be refuses to
join Thi-ur's harem and abandon her spouse, the entire Christian community is put on trial, accused of betraying Annamese
laws and their sovereign.[4] Before being sentenced to death they
are asked to renounce Christianity and defile a cross by tram-
pling it on the ground. The plot twists and turns as the bride,
María, realizes that she is the daughter of one of Thi-ur's ten
wives. As the Christians are about to be executed, cannon fire
is heard in the background, and the Spanish and French flags
are seen on the horizon. The soldiers come and save the day,
and the Spanish captain says, "Before the divine Cross / I swear
to die, / to avenge the affronts / to my country."[5] Such popular
dramas offered a version of the civilizing mission as a duty to
atone for the crimes of patriarchal tyrants such as the fictional
Thi-ur and provide for their ouster. Offenses committed against
women and against the Catholic faith served as pretense for a
revived, sentimental brand of imperialism.[6]

Despite the staging of empire to popular acclaim, the dominions of the Spanish Monarchy stood in stark contrast to the
global reach of rival empires in the 1860s.[7] Spanish imperialists looked at French successes in Algeria as a model, especially
for their having put down the resistance of 'Abd al-Qadir, but
they also celebrated France for having rebuffed British entreat-
ies to negotiate a settlement to end the conflict in the 1840s.[8]
Spaniards appreciated French bravado in the face of intense
British pressure to scale back imperial ambitions, and a jin-
goistic press urged Spain to "imitate France."[9] After a series of
perceived slights, including hostile acts committed against its
outposts in North Africa, Spain went to war in October 1859.
Shortly thereafter the Spanish Monarchy reincorporated Santo
Domingo and sent troops to Mexico with the French.[10] British
diplomacy, however, ultimately prevented further incursions
southward and ended the conflict in Morocco. By April (Mex-

ico), May (Morocco), and June (Annam) 1862, Spanish imperial advances had been thwarted.[11] In each case, officials, notably Secretary of State Saturnino Calderón Collantes (1799–1864), justified withdrawal with the spurious claim that Spain had not been pushing for territorial aggrandizement. Spaniards, speaking with near uniformity, insisted otherwise, because imperial adventures had galvanized popular culture and invigorated the public sphere.[12]

As France and Britain continued to expand into Africa and India, Spain held only a tenuous grip on the north of Morocco. Few long-term economic gains were seen. Yet Queen Isabel II was lavished with praise for having initiated a new Reconquest in the tradition of Isabel la Católica. The Spanish government invested the war in Morocco with great symbolic significance. In the Philippines Jesuits established the St. Ignatius church in 1863 and named the parish "Tetuán" to honor the bravery of the soldiers who had fought in the conflict. Having melted down artillery captured on the North African battlefield, artisans crafted statues of lions, emblematic of Spanish fortitude, to guard the entrance to the Spanish Cortes in Madrid.[13] How can we understand such contradictions? Is it possible to reconcile the limited successes of Spain's imperial enterprises with the hold that an empire had on the popular imagination? And despite deep support across regions and classes, why did a nascent civilizing mission in Africa, followed by campaigns in the Caribbean and the Pacific, not unify Spain politically?

C. A. M. Hennessy observes that "the period of greatest internal stability in the fifty years after 1833 was the five years of [Leopoldo] O'Donnell's Liberal Union between 1858 and 1863 when . . . the Army was engaged . . . in Morocco, Mexico, in the Pacific war, San Domingo, and Cochin China." Thus he asserts that "O'Donnell had little to fear from the opposition of either Progressives or Democrats."[14] Other historians emphasize political turmoil, even within the ranks of enlisted men, that epitomized the era. Albert Garcia-Balañà describes a scene of soldiers parading through the streets of Barcelona in triumph upon returning home from Morocco in 1860. They caricatured the Spanish general Ramón Narváez and the moderate faction of liberals, equating them with an Oriental despot, the likes of whom they had just defeated.[15] José María Jover stresses the domestic ramifications of military interventions, arguing that overseas expeditions allowed political elites to maintain order and mitigate social tensions in the metropole, while others note the economic importance of commercial treaties pushed by Spain.[16] The short-term success of such wars, however, did not seem to temper rising social and political discontent, and O'Donnell himself resigned from power in February 1863. The "Glorious Revolution" brought more radical figures into power in 1868, followed closely by the declaration of Spain's First Republic in February 1873.

Toward War in Africa

Piracy and smuggling certainly contributed to deteriorating relations between Morocco and Spain, as a number of hostile acts had been reported in the late 1850s.[17] French forces seized key strategic areas just inside Morocco's border with Algeria, and Spanish strongholds faced continuing incursions launched by the restive towns surrounding them.[18] Even Sultan 'Abd al-Rahman (r. 1822–59) failed to quell unrest on the western coast of Morocco in Azemmour.[19] In 1858 a series of disturbances in the northern reaches of Moroccan territory, many occurring outside the jurisdiction of the both the Moroccan state and Spanish frontier posts, foreshadowed the war that began in October 1859. Violence in the east around Melilla proved just as important as unrest around Ceuta, pushing policymakers toward conflict with the Makhzan. A British memorandum predicted that "the Sultan may therefore finally have to choose between a war with Spain, and a rebellion among his own subjects."[20] The British ambassador John Drummond Hay reasoned that all depended upon "the words 'Valley of Melilla.'"[21] Symbolized by the occupation of Tetuán, the Spanish-Moroccan War of 1859–60 saw a burgeoning jingoism spread across Spain, in part a response to British machinations designed to prevent the rise of a second Spanish Empire.[22]

In the spring and summer of 1858 the British engaged in a series of diplomatic maneuvers to cement their position in the increasingly unstable environs of North Africa. First, they provided a steamship for three sons of the sultan who were headed to Alexandria on their pilgrimage to Mecca. The sultan returned the favor with the gift of a tiger, a "unique and strange way" of showing appreciation, according to a Spanish diplomat.[23] More significant, the British were open to selling arms to the Moroccans. The sultan, with the memory of the 1844 bombardment of Tangier still fresh in his mind, sent a delegation to London to purchase 120 cannons, weapons that would be used to fortify their ports and defend against future French attacks.[24] But they also could be used in the event of conflict with Spain. In July the Spanish periodical *La América* ran a headline article listing the reasons why Spain should absorb the Rif, including historical analysis back to the fifteenth century. The author, Manuel Ortiz de Pinedo, confidently predicted that a military operation with ten thousand troops would be celebrated in the European press.[25]

The Rif comprises a region of northern Morocco spanning over three hundred kilometers of mountainous terrain on the coast of the Mediterranean. According to nineteenth-century European observers as well as contemporary scholars, the communities there, many of whom are Berber, "don't recognize the authority of the Sultan."[26] This area, in addition to Atlantic ports such as Larache, had been contested for centuries, dating back to the seizure of Ceuta by Portugal in 1415, subsequently sanctioned by Pope Eugene IV. The Ottomans had established control over Algiers by 1555, but their loss at the Battle of Lepanto, coupled with the defeat of King Sebastian of Portugal in 1578, demonstrated that the Spanish Monarchy had become the most important Mediterranean power. Spain had a permanent presence in Melilla beginning in 1497 and in the rocky enclave of Peñón de Vélez de la Gomera in 1564. They also took Larache in

1610 and Peñón de Alhucemas in 1673, challenging the English as the latter occupied Tangier between 1662 and 1684. Along with piracy, competition over the lucrative ports on the north coast of Morocco continued into the nineteenth century.

Spanish language sources referred to communities such as Kalaya (Qal'iya), populated predominantly by Berber peoples, as *kabilas*.[27] In what is the town of Nador today there were five significant settlements—the Mazuza, Benibuyfuror (Bni Bouifrour) Benibuyllafar (Bouyafar), Benisidel (Beni Sidal Jbel) and Benisicar (Beni Chiker)—numbering between one thousand and three thousand inhabitants. These extended clan networks, according to one observer, spoke a corrupted form of Arabic but understood and spoke Spanish, albeit imperfectly.[28] A Spanish diplomat described a "state of complete insurrection and anarchy" in the region, disparaging the Mazuza in particular as the most "bellicose and piratical of all of them."[29] They were so divided amongst themselves, he noted, that elections for new village heads had resulted in disturbances and deaths.[30] The British saw that divisions between communities might be exploited: "Orders might be immediately given to the Sheikh Maimon of Benissnassel [*sic*] to act against the Akkalayans; and Mr. Hay informs me that the Chiefs of the Beni Said tribe have expressed their readiness to assist the Sultan's troops in chastising the refractory Akkalayans." Siding with the sultan and the Beni Said, who were acting in "good faith," British diplomats decried the others as "half-independent and uncivilized Tribes of the Reef." At times, the British seemed to welcome the idea that "the Sultan would no longer delay to use force, to cause his authority to be respected in the Reef."[31]

In September 1858 near the presidio of Melilla, close to the border of French Algeria and the city of Oran, Spanish troops attacked the Riffian community and seized their lone cannon. In the wake of the provocation, the Mazuza and Benisidel took seven Spanish soldiers—including Francisco Álvarez, who would later write about his experience—as hostages to ransom for their cannon. In his memoir, Álvarez spoke of the terror inspired by the mere mention of the name Manuel Buceta del Villar (1808–82) among his captors.[32] Known for being a fearless and aggressive leader who clamped down on Riffian piracy with fierce determination, Buceta had been named as military governor in 1854. Buceta had been injured in the struggle to suppress local rebellions and illicit commercial activity between 1854 and 1856, but his forces had captured a significant number of pirate vessels in the process.[33] He had to navigate the complexities of competing political systems and local factions to free the seven men. With unrest plaguing Spanish strongholds in North Africa, however, diplomatic officials in Tangier and Madrid crafted a policy of territorial expansion to counter the threat of continued violence and lawlessness.[34]

By October rumors swirled of an alleged assassination of a Spanish consular agent by the "moros" of Tetuán, located over two hundred miles to the west, news that was denied vigorously by diplomats.[35] Such a slight, they realized, might have been used as a pretext for war.[36] In private correspondence, exactly one year before the Spanish-Moroccan War, Drummond Hay presciently called attention to the possibility of a large-scale Spanish invasion of the Rif:

> With regard to the supposed scheme of invading Reef by an army of from 15,000 to 20,000 men, and the intention attributed to the Spanish Government of making themselves complete masters of the Reef country, I beg to say from my knowledge of the warlike character of the people of Reef, the mountainous and almost inaccessible territory they inhabit, . . . and from the experience we have had of the results that have been obtained by the French Army in Algeria, that it would require a sacrifice of many millions of Dollars and of many thousands of men, and a war of many years before the Spanish Government could attain the object they are alleged to have in view. . . . [T]he only result that could be obtained after the shedding of much blood and the loss of millions of Dollars, would be perhaps, the reestablishment of the old

lines under the guns of the Spanish fortress of Melilla, an arrangement which might perhaps be attained by peaceful negotiation.

He concluded, "If the Reefians and Moorish troops were defeated and the Sultan's government were overthrown, . . . and a general revolution took place throughout Marocco, . . . the Spanish Government might then discover, perhaps, when *too late*, that it had entered precipitately into a rash and unprofitable war which would lead to complications, over which it could have little or no control."[37] His astute analysis suggested that Spain would face myriad challenges in prosecuting an imperial war and in consolidating new territories. What many would later describe as small gains from the Spanish-Moroccan War, concluded with the 1860 Treaty of Wad-Ras, was foreseen by Drummond Hay well before the start of the conflict.[38]

On October 22, 1858, Spanish authorities sent warships to the Moroccan coast in an act of what might be termed gunboat diplomacy in support of Buceta. Due to the sultan's "indifference" to Spanish claims, the crown justified the operation in terms of an "obligation to protect the lives and interests of its subjects."[39] Spain had been seeking an indemnity for damages and harm caused by hostile actions at sea in 1851, 1853, and 1854 in the vicinity of Melilla and demanded the release of the prisoners. Diplomatic correspondence flatly stated that the naval vessels would stay on the Moroccan coast, weather permitting, until the conclusion of the affair. With the British as intermediaries, a small sum of "two thousand dollars" was suggested to bring an end to the escalating conflict. In turn, the Spanish would have to return the boats and merchandise that they had seized in retaliation. Drummond Hay said, "It is to be hoped that the Spanish Government will not object to what appears to me to be the reasonable request and proposition of the Moorish Government; and that all existing differences may be now arranged in an amicable and satisfactory manner."[40] By the end of the year one of the issues had been resolved, with the British facilitating. Morocco paid an indemnity to the Spanish, and Spain reciprocated by returning vessels to the Riffians.[41] The French, according to Spanish sources, appeared amenable to additional concessions, such as fortifying Spain's territories on the Algerian border with peninsular settlers sent to foster the ideals of European civilization.[42] The following month, it seemed to the Spanish consul Blanco del Valle that the sultan had approved the expansion of Spanish territory in Melilla and had secured the return of the imprisoned soldiers, representing great victories for the diplomat.[43]

The seven Spaniards, however, remained in captivity, and tensions soon flared again. Diplomats in Morocco received reports "that the Spanish Chargé d' Affaires had made a communication to the Maroccan Government, threatening that, if the Spanish prisoners were not liberated in fifteen days, the Ports of Marocco would be bombarded by a Spanish Squadron." The British discounted the news as a bluff, noting in private correspondence that "there is not the slightest probability of the threat of Don Juan Blanco being carried into execution."[44] Negotiations took place on two fronts, as the frustrated Buceta corresponded with the leader of the Benisidel while diplomats worked directly with the sultan and Moroccan dignitaries. To punish the Riffians, the combative Buceta ordered a blockade from the Chafarinas to Peñón de Vélez de la Gomera to disrupt local commerce.[45] The Riffians continued to demand the return of all impressed ships and their lone cannon in exchange for the release of Álvarez and his compatriots.[46] Spaniards portrayed the hostage Álvarez in sympathetic terms as a selfless and honorable warrior who, supposedly, maintained that his life mattered little in comparison to the honor of his *patria*. He was quoted as telling his captors, "I die nobly for my country. . . . for a sentiment that you do not understand, cowardly assassins."[47] Behind the scenes in Madrid, however, authorities privately spelled out their Machiavellian plan: "For now, we do not want to provoke a conflict with the Moroccan Government. . . . In actuality, we want to promote our influence in this country,

The War of Africa

obtain the indemnifications that we have justly asked for and wash our hands of the protectorate that Great Britain hopes to establish in this Empire." The Foreign Ministry then asked Blanco del Valle to interrogate Álvarez, upon arrival in Tangier, about the state of the *kabilas* and their military strength, information that could be "very beneficial."[48] Despite the ulterior motives of the Spanish and a number of missteps by the Moroccan sultan, Álvarez was liberated with the six others, leaving Melilla on a steamship on March 25, 1859.[49]

But as Spanish officials celebrated this diplomatic resolution, they also made some fateful calculations.[50] While Consul General Blanco del Valle welcomed a temporary end to tensions with the sultan, he urged officials in Spain to push for territorial expansion around all of their outposts in Morocco.[51] Official correspondence described this policy as a state "secret" that would be achieved through veiled diplomatic channels.[52] Accordingly, he wrote, "Neither France nor England would oppose [an augmentation of Spanish territory]; the former, because they would contribute, if it was necessary, to the dismemberment of this Empire, as they want it to disappear entirely; . . . the latter, to the contrary, because through their maritime commerce and their stronghold in Gibraltar they profit more from the Berbers than any other nation would."[53] He also realized that the sultan made all key decisions based upon the counsel of the English, and that diplomats in the region acted like satellites revolving around a planet. Within this metaphor, Drummond Hay exerted a kind of centripetal force around which everything turned. To foster his own designs, then, Blanco del Valle knew that London had to be tricked into serving the Spanish cause. The English had to believe that the Spanish desired a pretext to invade Morocco, which would cause a disastrous full-scale war, and would act to avoid it at almost any cost. They could not know the mundane truth—the diplomat simply wanted greater concessions around Ceuta and Melilla.[54]

The self-assured Blanco del Valle believed his scheme could work and that the British would agree to the expansion of Spanish frontiers. The British would recognize that their economic predominance would be maintained even as Spain gained a small amount of additional territory in the region. Blanco del Valle might have considered British warnings to the contrary, as Drummond Hay had cautioned: "The Spanish Government ought, however, to consider the peculiar position of the Sultan as Sovereign of the semi-independent and barbarous tribes of Reef, and bear in mind the fact that it would be impolitic to demand of the Sultan engagements for the future, which may be of too stringent a character, and which if His Majesty could not fulfill them, might bring about between the two governments a more serious difference than the present."[55] Many of the peoples that had threatened Ceuta and Melilla operated independently of the sultan's authority, and by treaty Spain was authorized to counter any acts of aggression with impunity.[56] Running contrary to some of the more hawkish and traditional military figures in Spanish Morocco, like Buceta, Blanco del Valle continued to craft a dangerous strategy of dissimulation. While internal papers indicate that he did not seek a military confrontation, he certainly made bellicose pronouncements meant to intimidate and force the Moroccan Empire and their British proxies to offer additional compensation for the acts of the largely autonomous Riffian pirates.[57]

In the spring tensions continued unabated. Buceta expressed concern that he would not be able to abide by "the same peaceful conduct" he had been upholding, and his forces seized a number of ships in the area. The Moroccan government protested, and Blanco del Valle insisted that Buceta use greater circumspection in his role as commander.[58] Benisicar and Benisidel men who had returned after taking six of the Spanish prisoners to Fez resumed hostilities, disobeying the orders of the Moroccan Emperor.[59] If they attacked, Buceta bluntly stated, he would have to respond with force. Within months between six and eight thousand men from Benisidel went on the offensive. Over the course of several days they humiliated the Spanish contingent, with dozens killed and hundreds wounded on each side.[60] The *Times* reported that two hundred Spaniards were slaughtered.[61] Brigadier Buceta soon faced court proceedings for his failures; he was convicted and sentenced to jail for two years.[62] This episode in the east had noticeable effects on Moroccan calculations.

Throughout the year 1859 the sultan seemed to be planning for an imminent Spanish intervention, providing the communities on the Atlantic coast around Larache with "gunpowder and munitions" and even sending "proclamations from the Emperor that called his subjects to arms," according to a Spanish diplomat.[63] The preparations conveniently helped on the domestic front, as he still faced a simmering revolt in Azemmour. The Spanish said Prince Mulay al'Abbas had arrived in the region around Tangier with two thousand cavalrymen and three thousand infantrymen, preparing to join up with his brother, who commanded between thirty thousand and sixty thousand men. Reports also circulated that an English warship carrying artillery for the Moroccans was on its way.[64]

Seemingly in response, authorities in Madrid presented the Cortes with a plan to call up twenty-five thousand additional men to arms. Critics in progressive circles immediately questioned its necessity and spoke to the sacrifice of those who would have to leave their work, their land, and their families behind. A military reserve already existed, the periodical *La Discusión* noted, and the police had public order under control. Why would the government institute this kind of program if ministers were not actively planning for or trying to prevent a major conflict, as Austria was at the time? Extra munitions and materials would need to be produced as well. In the end, the article stated, the public would tolerate such a "grand enterprise" only if it were an expedition to Africa, a "civilizing and humanitarian mission . . . to avenge the affronts to our nation's flag by the savage tribes that populate the Rif." They would happily support such a campaign, but most Spaniards did not imagine that an overseas war was on the horizon. The editorial condemned the ruling cabal as a "military oligarchy" for issuing the plan, contrasting the leaders with liberal men guided by principle and the general will of the people.[65]

Spain's domestic and foreign policies had unanticipated consequences. By the summer of 1859 a series of events had taken place in the west that served to heighten tensions once more between the Spanish and Moroccan regimes. On August 21 the Anjera breached the Spanish presidio at Ceuta, knocking down sentry posts and pillars that demarcated the borders and destroying Spanish coats-of-arms in the process. The "Moors of Anghera," seeing the Spanish refortify their positions, continued to attack on August 23 with more than a thousand men, according to Castelar's recounting of events.[66] The intensification of violence had a great impact on Spanish public opinion, and the groundswell of support for a war did not go unnoticed in the halls of government. The consul general in Tangier, Blanco del Valle, negotiated reparations with the heir apparent to the throne, because Sultan 'Abd al-Rahman had died on August 29. As the consul, in his own view, had already enjoyed great successes expanding Spanish influence in the region, he continued to demand that Spanish territory be augmented, this time in Ceuta. Discussing matters in September and October, the Spanish pressed the issue. They declared that "savage tribes" in the area had committed intolerable acts of violence against their property that had in turn violated their honor.[67]

Initially the new sultan, Muhammad IV (r. 1859–73), appeared amenable to the key points put forward by the Spaniards, but a few weeks later negotiations broke down. The sultan wrote to the consul general, "We admit that this ignorant population has committed a serious offense in crossing the well-known limits of the Spanish fortress at Ceuta and threatening the garrison there; but you know well that if the aggression continued against our will, and if they were not punished, it was because of the fact that it took place upon the death of our beloved Mulay 'Abd al-Rahman, and the new sultan, Sidi Muhammad, had not been announced."[68] The letter also disputed Spain's right to put to death those accused of the attacks, insisting that the sultan truly desired peaceful relations with Spain. The British supported Spain's effort to receive reparations, but they hesitated to endorse imperial ambitions. According to internal correspondence, if "the violent acts of the Moorish tribes serve as a pretext for conquest, particularly on the coast, the government of Her Majesty is obliged to safeguard the security of Gibraltar." Furthermore, the occupation of Tangier was considered "incompatible" with British interests.[69] Although Blanco del Valle clearly looked to enlarge Spain's possessions in North Africa, Spain's secretary of state Calderón Collantes had been publicly repeating the mantra that Spain did not harbor expansionist designs.[70] Therefore, when diplomatic documents were publicized in the press, first in Gibraltar and subsequently in Spain, it appeared to many that a weak O'Donnell government, abetted by Calderón Collantes, had been bowing to British pressure and would not respond militarily. The public was outraged and increasingly pushed for war.

Castelar described the sentiments of his fellow Spaniards as a war fever, especially after the exposure of British efforts to dissuade the Spanish from choosing a military option in pursuit of territorial aggrandizement.[71] In the end public opinion propelled O'Donnell to send a telegraph to major military installations with news that "relations with Morocco had broken down" and to declare war on October 22, 1859.[72] The next day, newspaper headlines served as battle cries of a final crusade that would complete the Reconquest in the name of Saint James: "We contemplate seven centuries of horrors. To Africa! Grandchildren of Isabel, finish the grandchildren of Boabdil. Long live Spain!"[73] Judging from the number of donations, the war drew upon tremendous popular support, even from as far away as Cuba.[74] Bishops across Spain, including the Archbishop of Seville, and financial institutions, such as the Bank of Seville, gave money. The Armory of Seville gifted six cannons to the Fifth Artillery Regiment for extra firepower.[75] Private citizens—men and women—as well as town councils and regional governments, from Lérida and Zaragoza to Burgos and

Córdoba, provided unsolicited funds. Plays, concerts, and even bullfights were organized to benefit the war effort.

In addition to the standing army more than six thousand men volunteered to serve in northern Morocco, and religious ceremonies often marked their departure.[76] In the Church of Saint Mary in Guernica local notables and clergy gathered in November to "implore Heaven to favor Spanish arms in the holy and glorious struggle against the Moroccan empire."[77] Troops embarked on vessels for the short journey across the strait (and returned) amid celebration and music. *Vivas* rang out in honor of god, the queen, and the Spanish people, while soldiers sang opera and zarzuela as they sailed.[78] For the first time in Spain periodicals covered an imperial conflict with up-to-date news on a daily basis, in part due to a newly installed telegraph cable that connected Ceuta to the peninsula. O'Donnell expressed great satisfaction with the new technology, exclaiming that now "Africa is united with Europe."[79]

As Christopher Schmidt-Nowara has argued, many Spaniards presented the conflict in terms of a battle between civilization and savagery, part of the eternal struggle between Christianity and Islam.[80] During a session of the Cortes, Nicolás María Rivero was effusive in praising the value of the war: "We are the only Latin nation that has been able to carry its religion and its laws, its language, its customs . . . to ferocious enemy races. The War of Africa has been the dream of my entire political life."[81] Castelar, who narrated the Spanish experience in Morocco in the periodical *Chronicle of the War of Africa*, referred to Africa as a "hieroglyph of History," a place where ideas were born and died without leaving behind any relics. All of the great monuments of ancient history in Africa were like "letters from a grand epitaph that had been erased by time" and were now lying in ruins. While once Spain and Africa had been connected, united by "mysterious" bonds, Africa had become an impenetrable wall in modern times, closed off to progress.[82] For Castelar, an oppositional racial component underpinned history, although he believed that in the near future peace would reign.

The War of Africa

He opined, "We will achieve this harmony in Africa: God will protect our cause—that of civilization and justice."[83]

Like Blanco del Valle, many Spaniards publicized their humanitarian efforts both before and during the Spanish-Moroccan War. Not limited to the Iberian context, the rhetoric of humanitarianism had become important in late nineteenth-century French colonial efforts as well, exemplified by Pierre Savorgnan de Brazza, the so-called "pacific conqueror."[84] Castelar often included stories that highlighted Spanish compassion on the battlefield. For instance, he wrote early in the campaign that the army had allowed a "moro," two children, and a Black man to return to the "enemy camp" after they had been discovered chasing livestock and unexpectedly encountered Spanish troops on the march.[85] Other stories showed a similar narrative arc, describing a family with two children being released and an older man allowed to go free with his cow.[86] Obviously such tales appearing in the popular press helped to put a human face on the otherwise bloody campaigns of the military and lauded Spanish efforts to treat civilians caught up in the war with kindness. Later Castelar praised the discharge of two prisoners, arguing that such actions "will diffuse among [the Moors] the idea of our generosity and our good behavior in regard to those who fall into our hands, and can make them understand that obstinate resistance that provokes the ire of the army is not only fruitless but is also prejudicial to their cause."[87]

Military regulations codified such benevolent intentions. A general order from December 1859 expressly forbade the burning of huts and shacks, as that kind of behavior was reminiscent of the "savages of Africa" rather than the "disciplined" Spanish army. Nonetheless, within two months, a regiment from Granada had burned 180 houses, supposedly abandoned, in the area of Anjera where unrest had sown the initial seeds of conflict. Local residents witnessed the rampage, crying out, "Get out, Christian dogs! [¡Fuera, perros cristianos!]"[88]

Many newspaper accounts emphasized that the true enemies of Spain were the Arabs. The *Chronicle* often vilified Arab-speaking "Moors" and their culture as bellicose and barbaric. One article repeated the trope of Arabs as militaristic tribesmen who learned to ride horses as infants and soon thereafter were given rifles. In combat, therefore, "The Arab is . . . robust, active, valiant and long-suffering. Their first thrust is terrible. . . . they wave their weapons, launching savage cries and, in the style of Homeric heroes, try to frighten their adversaries from afar. Once this passes, the Arab, upon encountering resistance, is easily dismayed and flees, saying: *God wants it this way, it is written thus.*"[89] Castelar described Morocco as an unknown and remote corner of the world with its inhabitants living in a semisavage state of existence: "The deplorable backwardness of the Moroccan Empire is well known; the absolute ignorance that reigns in regard to the arts and sciences, the stupor and intellectual darkness that the people find themselves plunged into by the stupidity of the government and an indolent character, is also well known." Accordingly, few knew how to read, and even fewer could write. Castelar opined that "it is possible that the vast majority go through life without taking the time to think." He breezily dismissed Islamic spirituality, saying that "a few prayers learned rapidly . . . and a few confused ideas about divinity and the other world suffice for their religious necessities."[90] For the Riffians, he continued, the struggle against Spain represented "a holy war."[91] In summing up his Orientalist vision, Castelar argued that "the Moorish race has lost the memory of their ancient glories."[92]

In many ways public opinion in the peninsula was tied to the idea of a second Reconquest, with Isabel II following in the footsteps of her namesake.[93] Northern Morocco had replaced Andalucía as the frontier for Spain's push southward. Playwrights quickly appropriated the discourse of conquest, presenting Tetuán, the "precious pearl of the sultans," as the denouement of fifteenth-century Spanish expansion in Iberia and the Americas. One popular drama, opening in 1860 to great fanfare at the Teatro de Príncipe, portrayed the generals in Morocco as heirs to the legacy of Hernán Cortés.[94] Castelar, in the vein of other

European imperialists, urged Spaniards to remember the necessity of "the honorable civilizing mission [la honrosa misión de ser civilizadora], of bringing to Africa, together with religion that ennobles you so much, the advances of modern civilization."[95] Spaniards, he grandiloquently pronounced, came to Africa "as soldiers of civilization, establishing tolerance, cementing all liberties. . . . [And] Spain has opened commerce to the world."[96] A liberal imperialism, premised upon a Catholic civilizing mission, clearly undergirded Spain's invasion of Morocco.[97]

TWO

They "Were Calling Us Their Liberators"

The Taking of Tetuán

The Spanish-Moroccan War of 1859–60 climaxed with a brief battle and a protracted process of negotiation and occupation before troops withdrew in 1862. The phrase "a great war and a measly peace [paz chica]" circulated widely, and many Spanish nationalists clamored for a larger campaign of territorial acquisition.[1] The press made the key protagonists into larger-than-life heroes who epitomized the mores of European Christian civilization by pushing for the spread of the faith and even the construction of a major church. For instance, in a formal ceremony the queen feted one of General Rafael Echagüe's regiments prior to departure. The cadets kissed her hand, and upon leaving, kneeled before a priest in a show of religious solidarity "against the enemies of Christianity."[2] Subsequently injured in battle in November 1859, a humble Echagüe chose to recognize the enthusiasm, valor, and honor of his troops rather than accept accolades himself.[3] The qualities of chivalry and a tempered strength exemplified nineteenth-century masculinity and played a major role in the construction of European empires. According to Edward Berenson, "after 1850, the British and French sense of their own superiority turned in part on being more 'civilized' than others, on their ability to resolve conflicts through negotiation and the example of a better life."[4] An analysis of the seizure of Tetuán and the two-year occupation of the city shows that Spanish imperial leaders similarly prized martial values and the norms of liberal imperialism alongside the restraint and caution that characterized the bourgeois masculinity of the age.

The commercial hub of Tetuán is located on the western edge of the Rif Mountains just a few miles from the Mediterranean Sea. Spaniards such as Gaspar Núñez de Arce felt drawn to and repulsed by the city, "lost on a green plain like a lily in the countryside." In the middle of a fertile valley and meadows punctuated by the occasional small white house, with doves flying overhead, he mused, "Tetuán stood out, dominated by a citadel, an ancient fortress situated on a hill; Tetuán, so dirty, so repugnant inside; so white, so beautiful, contemplated from outside."[5] Orientalist depictions presented the municipality's history of ethnic diversity, stemming from Jewish and Muslim diasporas out of Spain, in similarly dualistic terms. Jews, legally referred to as *dhimmi*, paid a poll tax and in return received the ostensible protection of the sultan.[6] Spanish occupation inverted these established relationships, as the Muslims now found themselves in a subsidiary position previously held by Jewish residents, exacerbating religious antagonisms.[7] Accounts published in Spain contrasted the narrow but straight streets of the Jewish neighborhood with the rest of the city's labyrinthine layout. But the Spanish occupiers also brought with them powerful anti-Semitic stereotypes that prejudiced their view of the Jewish community. One newspaper article published in 1860 proffered the idea that "the race is beautiful, but degenerate and extremely degraded," proceeding to deride Jews as stingy and sycophantic.[8] The author claimed that Spanish soldiers began to have more sympathy for the Arab population than for the Jews, who represented a much larger proportion of the residents. Of the occupied city's eleven thousand inhabitants, there were five or six thousand Jews, just over a thousand "Moors," and several thousand Spaniards.[9] Over the course of a more than two-year occupation colonial officials attempted to address Tetuán's ethnic and religious diversity by establishing a multifocal form of governance.

E. Facio fotª

FIG. 1. "The Jews of Tetuán," photograph by E. Facio.
Reprinted courtesy of the Archivo General de Palacio.

In order to expand Spanish possessions around Ceuta, Leopoldo O'Donnell, Juan Prim y Prats, Juan de Zavala, and Antonio Ros de Olano led Spanish forces to Tetuán, not much more than twenty miles to the south. The march along the coast from Ceuta proved extraordinarily difficult, and many men succumbed to an outbreak of cholera. In December they faced fifteen thousand soldiers from three enemy "tribes," reputedly flying the same banner as the Almohads did during the Battle of Las Navas de Tolosa in 1212. In spite of hardships Spanish journalists hailed the discipline and valor of the troops. Men and women such as Ignacia Martínez, an auxiliary to a battalion from Baza, received

The Taking of Tetuán

inordinate praise in the press. Martínez reportedly would pick up a gun and start shooting when a male comrade was injured in combat. Normally serving aguardiente and animating the men, she fought so valiantly that some proposed she receive a military pension for her service.[10]

By early February 1860 more than twenty thousand Moroccan troops had amassed outside Tetuán, including five thousand on horseback. On February 4 General Prim strategically attacked and pushed them back in a short battle. Mulay al'Abbas and his brother, Sidi-Ahmed [Ahmet], serving as commanders of the armies of the sultan, soon asked to establish the conditions for a peace settlement. A copla celebrated what the Spanish viewed as a major conquest: "The Saracens came / beaten and outgunned, / God helped the good, / even though there were more bad ones."[11] The few remaining Moroccan and Riffian soldiers began looting the city on the morning of February 6; Núñez de Arce spoke of Jewish women grabbing at the clothing of the Spanish troops, desperate to show them the serious destruction caused by the "mountain Moors."[12] Shortly thereafter Tetuán was taken definitively and occupied by a foreign army.[13]

Emilio Castelar, in many ways demonstrating both romanticism and naivety, argued for a simple campaign of pacification appealing to the hearts and minds of the local residents. He quickly noted that "it would be easy to open the door to civilization." The narrative of civilization conquering barbarism was enticing. The instincts that made the Moroccans into strong warriors likewise would facilitate the civilizing mission, he wrote, as "the same ferocity and lack of culture will make relations and communication easier, and therefore our domination. A semi-savage people will soon surrender to our yoke if we appeal to their sentiments and to their heart." As they were tied to their culture and religion, he intimated, "we should respect their institutions and their religion. . . . A few months of fraternal treatment of the enemies of our faith will be enough to make them change their minds about Christians."[14] Spanish liberal imperialists advocated a decidedly nineteenth-century ideal of humanitarianism. Castelar predicted that dialogue and exchange would triumph over violence: "Fortunately for humanity, the time has passed in which it was possible to exterminate a race in order to sow a new idea: today the work of civilization does not take such a brutal path: conviction and reason have substituted for brute force."[15] Nicolás María Rivero even proposed that the Spanish and African races were congruous.[16] Consequently, many liberal thinkers believed that commerce was key to Spain's success in Morocco and that Tetuán would become "the premier marketplace in Morocco."[17] Almost all of the residents engaged in business, including the principal merchants, were Jewish, according to Castelar, and he insisted that their religion be respected as well. Otherwise, he felt that they would abandon the city, taking their riches with them.

Publicizing the news from February 6, journalists described the festivities in Tetuán, with the "Marcha real" playing and the remaining Jewish and Muslim inhabitants receiving the Spaniards "with open arms."[18] In the central plaza, Spaniards reported that notable Jewish residents "were calling us their liberators . . . saying: Welcome! Long live the Queen!"[19] General O'Donnell used the same language in his dispatch from Tetuán on February 8.[20] Prim, in an address to his soldiers, stated that the local people "should find a protector, not an enemy, in each of us."[21] The artist José Vallejo sketched the "Puerta de la Victoria," a gate through the walls of Tetuán, with soldiers that appear to have just scrawled "Viva España" on a stone in the foreground (figure 2). The seven gates to Tetuán were renamed, paying tribute to Queen Isabel as well as famous figures from Spanish history, with Reconquest heroes foremost among them.[22] Likewise, the occupying forces immediately renamed streets after the royal family and different regiments.

Newspapers quickly pointed out the excellent treatment meted out to the city's population, including its Muslim inhabitants. One such item described as typical "a soldier who parted with his bread or a biscuit with a Moor or with a hungry Jew."[23] An artist drew an image of soldiers coming to the aid of Tetuán's

E. Facio foto

FIG. 2. "Puerta de la Victoria, en Tetuán," photograph by E. Facio.
Reprinted courtesy of the Archivo General de Palacio.

poor as corroboration of articles in the press (figure 3). O'Donnell reiterated this consensus in a communiqué, in which he
told of an emerging *convivencia*: "Today one sees Moors and
Jews mixing as it they had never been divided, and as if they
had passed all of their lives together."[24] With the excesses of
French imperial campaigns in mind, O'Donnell claimed that
the Spaniards would not treat residents like the French did in
Algiers and Tlemcen.[25] A subsequent account revealed to the
Spanish public the generosity of soldiers as they helped a poor,
old Muslim woman who had fled the city to return home, providing her with some food, then taking her on their shoulders
and carrying her to Tetuán.[26]

FIG. 3. "Episodes from the War of Africa: Spanish soldiers come to the aid of the hungry residents of Tetuán." Reprinted courtesy of the Biblioteca Nacional, Madrid, Spain.

The taking of Tetuán, completed by the morning of February 7, 1860, and the making of Spaniards went hand in hand in discursive terms. O'Donnell, the Count of Lucena, became the Duke of Tetuán. The *Chronicle* was effusive: "We have renewed our traditions: we are Spaniards, and now this name is spoken with respect in all the courts of Europe."[27] Even a satirical paper from Havana immediately released a special issue to solemnly announce the conclusion to "the glorious campaign . . . against the savage hordes of Morocco."[28] In cities across Spain, "[m]en, women, children, with tears in their eyes, were running wild in the streets and plazas . . . filling the air with enthusiastic cries of long live the Army and the Nation, and repeating the phrase: Glory to Spain!" There was a palpable enthusiasm with which Madrileños received the news of taking Tetuán: "The welcome that greeted [the victory] in all of Spain, and above all in Madrid . . . declares . . . how well the government responded to the need to cleanse our stained honor and raise the name Spaniard from the prostration in which it lay."[29] University students marched alongside people from all classes, waving Spanish flags as music played and *vivas* were chanted. Banquets and

FIG. 4. "Episodes from the War of Africa: 11 May 1860. Entrance into Madrid of the troops from the army of Africa." Reprinted courtesy of the Biblioteca Nacional, Madrid, Spain.

fireworks marked the festivities, and Te Deums were sung.[30] A lead editorial emphatically announced, "It is not the time to think, but to feel."[31] An emotional, romantic nationalism had taken root. One woman flew two flags from her balcony. One read, "Long live the Spanish army and death to Muhammad!" The other displayed a simple rhyming verse: "Muley-Habbas flees / and runs with such passion, / that he's broken two ribs / in leaving Tetuán."[32] A periodical stated that revelers went as far as shooting a mannequin of Abbas.[33] Within a week of the victory trophies taken from the battlefront, including tents, flags, and cannons, were presented to Queen Isabel in Madrid.[34] Verses to a popular song, composed in the name of "Spain's sacred, Christian cause," incited the audience to begin "extermination, extermination of their Masses."[35] More moderate voices in the *Chronicle* reminded readers that a Christian religious tradition continued to serve as the bulwark of a revived national spirit: "Finally, national sentiment was brought back to life, and with it, the God of our history."[36]

Muslim taboos did not seem to be of much importance to the Spanish. After seeing the city's main mosque, one newspaper

FIG. 5. "Misa de campana en la Plaza de España, de Tetuán," photograph
by E. Facio. Reprinted courtesy of the Archivo General de Palacio.

editor glibly dismissed "a sentinel [placed in the door of this
Muslim temple] to deny entry to Christians and Jews."[37] Reporting from Tetuán a few days after Spain's troops had entered the
city triumphantly, Castelar's newspaper highlighted efforts to
convert a mosque into a Catholic church, punctuated by a mass
and solemn recitations of Te Deum.[38] The military doctor Nicasio Landa, in his memoir, described clouds of incense slowly
rising above thousands of soldiers giving thanks for their victories and recognizing their fallen comrades as the new church
was consecrated. Although undated, one of Enrique Facio's photographs may depict that day's mass, showing well over a thousand troops in formation, some with heads bowed, in the main
square (figure 5). Exactly three months after the first Spanish
forces had arrived in Tetuán, authorities issued an urgent order
to the Muslim mayor. The decree insisted that, instead of having
local engineers occupied with "insignificant things," they immediately embark upon construction of a "spacious and respect-
able" Catholic church in the center of the city.[39] With religion
and clerics at the vanguard of the occupation, the Spanish sym-

The Taking of Tetuán

bolically invested in a form of religious reconquest that, in their view, complemented the economic aspects of empire building.

Public discourse tended to disparage the non-European culture of the city. Echoing the infamous claim of Lord Macaulay, Castelar argued that European knowledge far surpassed that of the colonized Moroccans: "Between some fifty volumes that can be found here scarcely one contains history or literature of true merit or importance."[40] At the same time he criticized the practice of forbidding Christians to read such texts—he was not allowed to buy a book on the history of Tetuán, even though he offered a more than fair price. But the ideal of the civilizing mission at times superseded the Orientalist lens through which Spaniards viewed the North Africans. For instance, by March, with a peace agreement in place, the peninsular press reported celebrations in Tetuán as news of the treaty spread: "Moors and Jews began to run through the streets shouting 'Long live Spain, we are all brothers.'"[41]

Spanish observers noted that Tetuán had the "trimmings" of a European city, although the buildings had no symmetry and the streets flooded when it rained. The supposedly distrustful character of the Arab was revealed through an examination of their housing, they stressed, as most dwellings had an "impoverished appearance."[42] Class divides in Tetuán often seemed invisible or indecipherable to occupying soldiers who had trouble distinguishing between homes of the poor and those of wealthy families. Lavish inner sanctums often belied simple exteriors. With a sexualized discourse, Castelar expressed the surprise felt by troops "at penetrating through a humble doorway and finding a twisting corridor with a beautiful patio of well-made arches, and with large rooms adorned with splendid carpets."[43] With a mixture of admiration and disgust, he gazed upon Tetuán as if he were seeing a city in Andalucía under Muslim rule: "With just a little work Tetuán would be converted into a city as beautiful as Granada."[44] And toward the end of February Spaniards marveled at the changes that the occupation had produced, from the political to the economic. Writers discussed the prospect of imminent rail service, the beginnings of a new municipal administration, and measures to improve safety and hygiene. Others proposed pleasure trips, with a special train from Madrid taking curious visitors to the port of Alicante and a steamship that would then bring them to Tetuán.[45] A theater had been established and, Castelar asserted, "so that nothing that constitutes modern life is lacking," the newspaper *El Eco de Tetuán* (The echo of Tetuán) would be published.[46] From this perspective, public health, administration, technology (both in terms of print and transportation), and culture constituted modernity. But Catholicism played a defining role as well. Spaniards boasted of a new Golden Age inaugurated by the Battle of Tetuán, connecting the victory to Habsburg triumphs such as Lepanto. A dispatch from troops from the Castilian town of Alba de Tormes summed up Spanish sentiment: "The period of decadence during which the Spanish lion appeared to be sleeping has been a brief parenthesis between our past and present glories."[47]

A Catholic Mission in Morocco

Journalists did not shy away from the political implications of a constitutional European state governing Muslim territory in North Africa. As the most well-known conquest of the brief war, Tetuán became the object of media speculation. Reports indicated the army had divided the city into four military districts occupied by the four brigades led by General Santiago de los Ríos. Muslim residents who fled were given ten days to return before they would lose the right to reclaim their possessions.[48] On February 19 General Prim met with emissaries of Abbas and greeted them with "sweets, coffee, and good cigars." Officials held a "*soirée*" hosted by Ríos, during which the Moroccan delegation, in the eyes of the occupiers, remained dignified and proud, never appearing to be humiliated.[49] In a dialogue with Ríos the newly selected Muslim mayor, *hājj* Ahmad Ab'ayir, explained that he would be faithful and obedient, but he recognized that his difficult position as an intermediary was compromised and fraught.[50]

On April 26, 1860, Sidi Muhammad and representatives of the Spanish government signed a peace agreement, the Treaty of Wad-Ras. The articles provided for an amplification of territory around Ceuta, the concession of Ifni—an abandoned port used to send expeditions to the Canary Islands in the early sixteenth century—and a compensation payment of 400 million *reales*. Article 11 stipulated that, in the event that Spanish troops evacuated Tetuán once the indemnity had been paid, the Moroccans would allow a space next to the Spanish consulate for the construction of a Catholic church and cemeteries for Spanish soldiers. These facilities had to be respected, according to the language of the treaty. Diplomats crafted a separate agreement to enlarge Spanish territory around Melilla.[51]

Spanish officials named two mayors—a Muslim and a Jew to serve the city's different faith communities—and created an *ayuntamiento* (town council).[52] The fifty-year-old "Moorish mayor," Ab'ayir, "obtained veritable celebrity in Spain." The *Chronicle* described him as "an accommodating person held in high esteem in the country. . . . He is a man of clear talent and has traveled a great deal in Europe."[53] A dedicated *esparterista* (a follower of General Baldomero Espartero), according to Núñez de Arce, Ab'ayir had been in Madrid in the early 1840s and spoke Spanish.[54] He even received a letter from a newspaper reader in a small Andalusian town addressed to the "señor *alcalde constitucional de Tetuán*" and reprinted in *La América*. The writer suggested that Ab'ayir take good care of the Spaniards in his city, because "*the Moors . . . are brutes that do not observe the sacraments*." He also recommended that the mayor become a Christian, and he ended his riposte with the phrase, "*Finally, death to Muhammad!*"[55] Extreme rhetoric of this sort mirrored that of the popular culture of the theater and of the public sphere in general, simultaneously exalting Christianity and denigrating Islam.

Government records detailing the occupation of Moroccan territory placed great emphasis on education and religion. For instance, a Spanish priest received significant funding to return to Tetuán with paper, catechisms, and other items for a school that had more than ninety children.[56] In the summer and fall of 1860, correspondence clearly shows that construction of a church, guest quarters, and a consulate remained priorities, with O'Donnell and even Queen Isabel highlighting the urgency of the matter.[57] The Spanish wanted to break ground as soon as possible, even though the treaty mandated that a church be built regardless of whether the city was occupied. Estimates projected that the buildings would cost close to a million *reales*, and prominent local residents as well as the town's newly appointed mayor, Ab'ayir, signaled their support of the proposal in November.[58] Legality and legitimacy remained paramount concerns during the process, especially because a local business owner, Abdel Krim Lucas, had sold land to the Spanish authorities for the groundbreaking. An interpreter had to take an oath in front of a military official to translate the contracts faithfully and truthfully. An imam, an administrator, a businessman, and a scholar, all residents of Tetuán, testified to knowing Lucas, who had his principal business in the renamed Plaza de España (Plaza Feddan) and others in the renamed Plaza de Pamplona. Within two months architects had created a blueprint, and officials signed papers on December 31, 1861. The church and consulate were to be built on a site measuring 8,139 square meters (*varas*), situated next to the four gardens in front of the theater on the streets now called León and Callejón de Oviedo. As late as March 1862, a little more than a month before Spanish troops were evacuated, a fourteen-page document was drawn up to legally divert water from the main hospital to the construction site at the newly minted Plaza del Teatro (figure 6). The project undoubtedly served as both a symbol and a concrete priority for the Isabeline regime.[59]

In the spring of 1862, with the occupation winding down, Spanish authorities began the withdrawal of their forces. But they wanted to ensure that work continued on the church; while handing over the city to the Moroccan military, they gave control of the construction project over to a Moroccan head archi-

E. Facio for°

FIG. 6. "Plaza del Teatro, en Tetuán," photograph by E. Facio.
Reprinted courtesy of the Archivo General de Palacio.

tect. At the end of April a priest delivered the last mass for the
Spanish in occupied Tetuán, retiring the tabernacle, the iron
cross, and other holy relics. They also exhumed the cadavers of
two priests to return to the peninsula and brought important
keys to a Moroccan military official.[60] The Spanish arranged a
final meeting with Abbas, and with the aid of an interpreter,
officially returned the city to the Moroccan prince. 'Abd al-Qadir
Ash'ash, named the new mayor, was called "a good man," a
"friend," and "a lover of justice" by Consul Isidoro Millas in private diplomatic correspondence. As the Spanish troops packed
up, Moroccan flags flew across the city. The consul wrote that

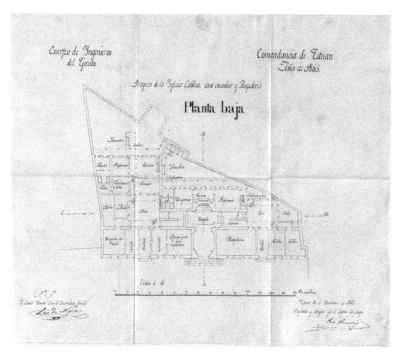

FIG. 7. "Blueprint for the Catholic church, consulate and hostel, 1861."
Reprinted courtesy of the Archivo Histórico Nacional, Madrid, Spain.

he had expected to see celebrations, but the people remained calm, and the Spanish merchants that remained circulated "freely through the city without being bothered at all," keeping their shops open even in the majority Muslim neighborhood.[61]

By this time the Spanish had spent almost 300,000 *reales* on construction and materials for the new church and consulate, with financial support coming from as far away as the General Commission of Holy Places in Jerusalem.[62] As seen in the blueprints, the ambitious design included a detailed floor plan, complete with ornate statues, stained glass, and ironwork to adorn the façade (figures 7 and 8). But with a revised cost estimate of 1,537,214 *reales* and 56 *céntimos*, the General Commission pulled its funding from the project, claiming they could not legally donate to a consulate, which constituted a secular venture. However, the Consul of Tetuán had secured a loan

The Taking of Tetuán

FIG. 8. "Principal facade of the Catholic church, consulate and hostel."
Reprinted courtesy of the Archivo Histórico Nacional, Madrid, Spain.

of 1,109,862 *reales* that covered most of the expenses. He ultimately recommended that the government cover the cost of the consulate and bring the matter to the Cortes.[63] The Church of the Immaculate Conception, completed in 1866, was built as a monument to a moment of imperial triumph. According to a contemporary Spanish diplomat, it was supposed "to perpetuate the glories of our African campaign and the occupation of this city."[64]

The Cultural Encounters of Prisoners, Spies, and Soldiers

Writers such as Pedro Antonio de Alarcón and artists, including Vallejo, traveled to Morocco with the troops, conveying descriptions and sketches of the campaigns (in addition to peace negotiations, landscapes, etc.) to a public eager for the latest information. Orientalist tropes infused the imagery, creating scenes of cultural dissonance that displayed the scars of modern warfare (figure 9). For example, Spanish soldiers described

FIG. 9. "Chronicles of the War of Africa: A street in Tetuán," José Vallejo.
Reprinted courtesy of the Biblioteca Nacional, Madrid, Spain.

with fascination coming upon Jewish residents of Tetuán, who appeared to them to be members of the "European race," unlike the Muslims of North Africa. Many spoke a variant of Castilian, and soldiers realized that they were the descendants of Jews expelled from Spain in an earlier age epitomized by "intolerance."[65] Other episodes illustrated the growing mistrust that pervaded occupied areas, as Spaniards were unable to navigate effectively the cultural milieu of northern Morocco. In one case a Spanish soldier, Ramón Rios, "spontaneously presented himself in [the Tetuán] Consulate." A dispute with the commander of his battalion had apparently sparked his decision to abandon his post and desert. Rios claimed to have been threatened with death by an armed man and said that he was taken into the mountains and forced to "embrace Muhammadanism."[66] After finally escaping and making his way back into Spanish territory, he appeared to have chosen Spanish military justice over the prospect of integration into the local society.

Conceptions of identity were crucibles of the conflict, and interconnected networks of consuls, spies, and collaborators worked to govern and legitimize colonial rule, suppress dis-

The Taking of Tetuán

sent, and even capture fugitive Spanish conscripts. Prisoners, spies, diplomats, and soldiers negotiated the interstices of a new Spanish imperial project throughout the 1860s, and their actions provide a window into nineteenth-century cultures and identities. Writing in 1861 to Secretary of State Saturnino Calderón Collantes, two collaborators implored their benefactors for aid, as they had fallen on hard times in the aftermath of the occupation of Tetuán. Both had been held prisoner— one by Prince Abbas during hostilities—and they spoke of losing all of their worldly possessions prior to being incarcerated. Ahmed el Morabet said both had been in the service of Spain for eighteen years and, most recently, they had been shuttling back and forth between Tangier and Tetuán during the negotiations over the frontiers of Ceuta and Melilla. The wife of Brigadier Buceta helped Morabet avoid being killed by Riffians and others who wanted to decapitate him; then he was imprisoned for more than seven months. Referring to himself as "a loyal servant of the Spanish government," he wrote, "And if you do not help us, we have no one else to turn to but God, because the Muslims consider us Spanish."[67] From the safe haven of the Spanish consulate in Tangier, Caid Ahmed Ez-Zaruali worried that, if abandoned, the two would be seen as spies and face harsh retribution. Other examples similarly demonstrate the fear inspired by perceived religious difference. In early 1862 reports that two hundred "Moors" had gathered on the streets one night caused great alarm in occupied Tetuán, and the Spanish immediately called up two battalions of soldiers to serve as reinforcements in case of a military engagement. Authorities soon realized that the crowd, far from expressing hostility, had congregated to celebrate Ramadan.[68]

The northern reaches of the Moroccan Empire and of the sovereignty of the sultan served as a metaphor of the imperial encounter, as a permeable frontier between north and south, between "civilization" and "barbarism."[69] Although the crown employed interpreters and soldiers and recruited guards and spies from the local population as they attempted to pacify the regions under their control, Spanish officials constantly expressed concern over the conflicting loyalties of their collaborators. In *Regulations of the Moorish Marksmen of the Rif*, for example, the protocols stated that Riffians maintained deeply held religious convictions and had to be considered "irreconcilable enemies of those who do not follow their faith." They resisted the rigid discipline of the modern military and, according to the manual, did not consider it "a grave offense to turn their backs on the Christian cause."[70] Spanish military reports, drawing lessons from the French war in Algeria, put this bluntly: "One of the captured chiefs, a prisoner [held by French general Thomas-Robert Bugeaud], explained to them the causes of the insurrection [in the 1840s]. 'The Arabs detest you because you don't practice their same religion, because you're foreigners who come to take over their country.'"[71] Yet Riffian soldiers served with distinction in the Spanish army, some even earning the cross of María Isabel Luisa, which came with a pension.[72]

Consular authorities also employed local men to capture Spanish deserters, and qualified individuals were brought on as spies.[73] Riffian leaders reported the capture of renegade Spanish soldiers and quickly informed military officials in the presidios through handwritten correspondence in Arabic, accompanied by translations into Castilian.[74] The son of the British consul in Tetuán, Eduardo Butler, who was said to know the language and customs of the regions extremely well, was asked to provide information to the Spanish in their struggle against the Moroccan sultan. He rejected the offer, claiming, "Neither my name nor my honor will permit me to spy on the side of the Spanish army."[75] Instead, he joined the Spanish forces as a soldier and soon died of illness. Muhammad el Tensamani, who traveled from Málaga to Melilla in early 1862, accepted the charge of assessing the state of public opinion among the peoples of the Rif. The Spanish recruited Tensamani because they believed that as a trader, he enjoyed the confidence of the local peoples. Tensamani requested authorization not to declare his mission upon arriving in Melilla, "out of fear that his coreligionists would inform on him."[76] In addition to a passport he was given a safe conduct pass that he could show to Spanish authorities in case of emergency. The military governor of Melilla permitted Tensamani's entry only after being presented with this secret document and threatened to shoot him if he made himself conspicuous during his travels.

While tensions certainly existed, examples abound of cooperation, negotiation, and cultural hybridity amid the war. The prisoner Álvarez, held against his will outside of Melilla for several months, relayed one of the most telling cases. A man from La Mancha named Victoriano Olivares, a Spanish grenadier corporal, had deserted and become a "renegade" in 1832. Known as the "moro manchego," the Moor from La Mancha, he had married into the local community.[77] Spanish soldiers just as often disappeared into the local population as Riffian leaders worked with Spain's military and diplomatic apparatus. For example, an influential governor in the Rif petitioned the Spanish authorities on the Chafarinas Islands for help with an irrigation project on the Moulouya River in 1861.[78] And Jews crossed cultural and religious boundaries as well. The Spanish consulates in Morocco were known for providing protection to local Jewish residents.[79] In 1862 two female novices of Jewish ancestry, in the charge of a missionary friar, presented themselves to the Spanish consul in Tetuán. They requested passports to travel to Spain so that they could be baptized and pursue their religious training.[80] As these examples demonstrate, the different faith communities and ethnic groups in northern Morocco overlapped in significant ways. Although Spain ceded Tetuán back to the Moroccan sultan in May 1862, the Spanish consul general nostalgically wrote in August that Tetuán still appeared "Spanish" in spite of the presence of a sizeable number of "Moors" in the city.[81]

Diplomatic Conclusions

Not only did common soldiers and merchants serve in intermediary roles within an emergent imperial system, but Prince

Mulay al'Abbas, brother of the new Moroccan sultan Sidi Muhammad, played the role of go-between as well. As commander of the troops that had entered into battle with the Spanish in the winter of 1859, he represented a formidable foe with tens of thousands of cavalry and possibly as many as forty thousand infantrymen.[82] But resistance crumbled as the Spanish pushed toward the interior, and diplomacy soon overshadowed the force of arms. On February 23, 1860, Abbas and O'Donnell sat down in what was described as a dignified meeting. O'Donnell wanted to make indefinite "possession" of Tetuán the centerpiece of the negotiations. He affirmed that the area under control of his troops "is now our territory, it is an integral part of our land and of our nationality." He noted the strategic importance of staving off the French from the east and putting an end to piracy, and, of primary importance, linking Ceuta and Melilla. Abbas, clearly in a difficult position, was described in Spanish diplomatic correspondence as "a deferential man, not a man of war, as the Moors here say." [83] Unfortunately for the Spanish general and head of state, Sidi Muhammad did not attend the meeting. O'Donnell, in a subsequent defense of his actions before the Cortes, explained that there had been two competing political factions in Morocco. The Moroccan emperor upheld a belligerent stance with the tacit support of the British, although the rival party, led by Abbas, sought peace after seeing the initial successes of Spanish arms in 1859. O'Donnell realized that the emperor's policies would take precedence and broke off the talks at the end of February. By June 1860 O'Donnell had gone as far as to publicly ponder the notion that Spain use its resources for internal, rather than external, development, such as the construction of roads, the rehabilitation of ports, and other public works.[84] In light of the ongoing conflict in Algeria and the costs of a thirty-year war for the French, O'Donnell emphasized that conquest in Morocco could take years. In some ways the Treaty of Wad-Ras displayed Spanish ambivalence and dissension over the spoils of imperial warfare.

The Taking of Tetuán

The revelry and self-congratulatory rhetoric that marked Spain's victory in Tetuán quickly dissipated. Nationalists and supporters of the war had taken to the streets demanding a bigger push into Moroccan territory. One student banner, displayed on February 14 in Madrid, read, *"Tomando a Tánger, Fez y Rabat, la paz."*[85] In this view peace should only come following deeper incursions into the heart of Moroccan territory and the seizure of key cities. But generals never deployed their troops in significant numbers past the gates of Tetuán. Debates in the Cortes in the summer of 1860 dissected the military operation as well as the treaty, and many publicly denounced the role played by the British in the negotiations with the sultan. Deputy Luis González Bravo challenged Calderón Collantes, claiming the latter had essentially bowed to British pressure and accepted their marching orders, creating a predetermined course of warfare and of peace. On the floor of the Cortes he questioned the idea that a Spanish occupation of Tangier would be a barrier to free trade, or what the British called "freedom of navigation through the Strait." Moreover, he stated that O'Donnell had known from the minute he arrived in Tetuán that the war was over. Calderón Collantes, for his part, contextualized his arguments by referencing two distinct historical events: the negotiation of the 1829 Treaty of Adrianople and preparations for war by the French in Algeria. He spent considerable time describing the Gallic "enterprise of Christian sociability [in North Africa], whose objective of eliminating piracy did not include any kind of spirit of conquest." Despite this, Calderón Collantes emphasized, the French had found it difficult to win over Africans, "and above all to make them accept a civilization founded on Christian principles contrary to a religion that has fatalism at its core."[86] After disparaging the Muslim faith, he warned against exaggerated expressions of religious intolerance that hearkened back to the Reconquest and hatred between the two races.

Rivero, a member of the Democratic Party, forcefully maintained that Spaniards were unique in incorporating their religion, laws, and customs into their imperial ventures. Furthermore, he added, Spanish culture had deep roots in a "liberal spirit" at this point in history. By shoring up their African frontiers and renewing the nation's glorious past, troops in Morocco were going to "complete a civilizing mission, and should be applauded by Spain and by humanity." Following a discussion of the diplomatic correspondence between Lord John Russell, Andrew Buchanan, and the Spanish government from September and October 1859, he concluded: "We have not achieved what we desired."[87] Indicative of the state of public opinion, Rivero's proclamations expressed the frustrations of many Spaniards who had seen their imperial ambitions thwarted.

In August 1860, Abbas was inspecting Spanish frigates and steamships docked at the port of Tangier as part of a diplomatic mission. On board the *Rey Francisco*, he reportedly paid a great deal of attention to new inventions—from the weaponry on the vessel to a photograph of Queen Isabel.[88] Such acts of diplomacy and additional exchanges yielded tangible results, with a Spanish correspondent stating that local residents in the vicinity of Ceuta were particularly "cheerful and friendly" after receiving news of a Moroccan delegation in Spain. One Riffian, speaking in broken Spanish, said that Abbas respected Spain and that the Christian "sultan" in turn was a friend to the people of the Rif. Then, according to the account, the "Moor" embraced him, shook his hand, and departed.[89] Cultural encounters took place on both sides of the Strait, and Moroccan delegations visited Spain on multiple occasions while Tetuán was occupied.[90] In 1861 the press covered an Abbas trip closely and described the curious crowds of onlookers who greeted him, even at events like the circus and dances.[91] Received by the queen and royal dignitaries at the palace, he delivered a "magnificent and elegant" discourse in Arabic, with an interpreter translating into Spanish.[92] Prominent local families hosted gatherings in his honor in Valencia, and women even covered themselves in his presence. One particular event generated a great deal of interest among journalists as the prince, speaking through his inter-

FIG. 10. "Solemn reception of the Moroccan ambassador Prince Moulay
El-Abbas by Her Majesty the Queen, 5 September 1860," José Vallejo.
Reprinted courtesy of the Biblioteca Nacional, Madrid, Spain.

preter, asked a young woman who had arrived with a black veil
to uncover herself.[93] In sum, he seemed to respect certain European mores and value European technology and know-how
while at the same time retaining his cultural heritage. During
the ceremonies marking the return of Tetuán to Morocco, the
prince recalled Spain with fondness in conversations with officials, noting specifically the attention he had received in Madrid
and the respect the queen had shown him (figure 10).[94]

The narrative of conquest justified by a particularly Catholic vision of the civilizing mission underpinned Spain's war
efforts under the administration of the Liberal Union. Ideas
on race, religion, and gender allowed metropolitan Spaniards
to envision an empire based upon difference rather than egal-
itarian principles.[95] They believed, like the anonymous author
of *The War of Africa and the Taking of Tetuán*, that the progress
of civilization would overcome barbarism. The brief play, written in five acts, provides a romanticized rendering of the "War

of Africa" replete with cultural stereotypes and a melodramatic corollary to the taking of Tetuán. Clearly torn from the pages of playwright Juan Eugenio Hartzenbusch's work, the drama unfolds as both a love story and a conversion narrative, with the antagonist a wrathful Muslim father rather than a vindictive Moorish queen, as in *Los amantes de Teruel*. The main character, Zulima from Anghera, had fallen in love with an archetypal Spanish soldier, Pedro. But she faced the ire of her father for acting on her passion, and Pedro adamantly maintained that she convert from Islam and embrace Catholicism before they married. As Pedro fled from the family's compound, he was taken prisoner by Zulima's father Abul. At the moment he is to be executed, he is rescued dramatically by a valiant comrade. Fighting ensues, and in a climactic denouement, Pedro wounds Abul, the father of his bride-to-be, in a quintessentially masculine act. Just then a local man arrives ruefully announcing the taking of Tetuán, and Abul dies of his wounds. Zulima, at first, is horrified to find out Pedro had killed her father. But soon she forgives him, agreeing to renounce her faith and to marry her "beloved Christian."[96] As an allegory for a sexualized form of conquest and the defeat of a patriarchal tyrant, the play portrays empire building as a process of both moral and spiritual penetration. Similar to the principles embedded in the storyline of *The Martyrs of Cochin China*, martial and Christian values were entangled in this civilizing mission (see chapter 1). Unlike Pedro's ultimate success, however, Spain was not able to best the British. Spanish forces were withdrawn from Tetuán in 1862, with Britain loaning Morocco money to pay off the indemnity of 400 million *reales* (the equivalent of 4 million U.S. dollars in 1861) that was the centerpiece of the 1860 peace treaty.[97] The most visible symbol of Spanish conquest, the city of Tetuán, had to be abandoned.

The rhetorical edifice of Spanish identity in many ways continued to hinge on historical legacies and religious symbolism. Spaniards referred to the peoples of northern Morocco—Arabs and Berbers alike—with the catchall term "Moors," a throwback to an earlier age. They defined their overseas wars as a continuance of Isabel la Católica's Reconquest. The Ayuntamiento of Havana, praising the Spanish-Moroccan War in a letter to Her Majesty Isabel II, succinctly applauded the triumph of "the Cross over the . . . faded power of Islam."[98] Castelar wrote that Spain, as the "missionary of nations," bore the weight of destiny in civilizing peoples submerged in barbarism.[99] Spaniards certainly sought to "civilize Africa," but few in Spain embraced a particularly secular conception of the "civilizing mission." Appropriately, the concrete symbol of conquest, the Church of the Immaculate Conception in Tetuán, outlasted the short-lived occupation by Spanish forces. Foregrounding the historical and religious context to the Spanish-Moroccan War thus challenges the prevailing notion that material and secular considerations alone informed imperial narratives in nineteenth-century Europe.

THREE

The Visual Culture of Mid-Nineteenth-Century Spanish Imperialism

The city of Barcelona commissioned the artist Marià Fortuny (1838–74), born in the Catalan town of Reus, to accompany General Juan Prim, the Count of Reus, on the campaign in Morocco, and he returned two years later to compose his masterpiece, the unfinished painting *The Battle of Tetuán*. The work, almost ten by thirty-two feet, is a panoramic view of an epic struggle between Spanish forces in the center and Moroccan troops in the foreground. Prim leads the charge toward the enemy encampment, and the wounded stagger among the dead. Resting camels look tranquil and a bit out of place in an otherwise chaotic scene that captures the flight of routed Muslim soldiers on agitated horses. Almost half of the painting is a vast blue sky with scattered clouds that morph into the smoke of gunfire below. Even amid the violence and destruction, with Spanish and Moroccan soldiers almost indistinguishable as they grapple, some engaged in hand to hand combat, there are figures that appear to languish in the middle of the composition. A man with a whitish gray beard, covered partially by a striking blue garment, points toward a Spanish contingent of cavalry in a dramatic, melancholy gesture. His mouth is closed and he does not utter any words, appearing to exhibit despair at the brutal incursion of foreign troops. Artists used figures of languorous "Moors," stretched out across their canvasses, to characterize the supposed passivity and weakness of Arab cultures and peoples as Europeans attempted to carve out imperial domains in

North Africa.[1] From a variety of perspectives this chapter will explore the visual culture of mid-nineteenth-century Spanish imperialism and imagery that represented a counterpoint to the militarized, bourgeois masculinity of nineteenth-century European states.

Some of the techniques Fortuny would hone over his short but influential career had been developed in Rome, where he had worked as a young man.[2] There, he struck up a friendship with an aspiring painter from Seville, José Villegas y Cordero (1844–1921), who would later become the director of the Prado Museum in Madrid. Fortuny and Villegas not only were friends but also traveled to Morocco in the early 1860s, providing an important spark for their artistic production and aesthetic sensibilities.[3] Fortuny returned to Rome for a brief period and immediately painted *The Battle of Wad-Ras*, the precursor to *The Battle of Tetuán*. Similarly, in 1871 Villegas drew on his experiences abroad in drafting a Moroccan expert in weapons, a slight male figure, with shoes off, who carefully inspects a rifle. His head covered, he dons brightly colored clothing, and his chest remains exposed, a signifier of the exotic Orient (figure 11). To a nineteenth-century European viewer, the figure in Villegas's *Marroquies examinando armas* would not have appeared physically imposing or particularly masculine. Villegas presented a fundamentally different sensibility in *Acción de 25 de noviembre*, a sketch of the Madrileño Manuel Matías Membrado from 1859. The levelheaded and decisive army chaplain, in the wake of four companies of soldiers having lost sight of their commanding officers, had grabbed a gun and ordered them forward in the heat of battle in Morocco. Membrado raises his hand and looks off into the distance, seemingly without fear, displaying the valor that purportedly typified a Spanish soldier.

Depictions of the Orient and of non-Europeans almost always stood in stark contrast to men like the disinterested Membrado. Public monuments, especially in Europe and Latin America, immortalized men on horseback, heroic soldiers like General Arsenio Martínez Campos. In sacrificing for his nation Martínez

FIG. 11. José Villegas y Cordero (Spanish, 1844–1921), *Moroccans Inspecting Weapons*, 1871, oil on panel, Joslyn Art Museum, Omaha, Nebraska. Bequest of Francis T. B. Martin, 1995.47.

Campos had defeated men like the Moroccan expert in arms. A Beaux-Arts statue placed in Madrid's Retiro Park in the early twentieth century honors the service of Martínez Campos in multiple overseas wars, including the 1859 campaign that inaugurated modern Spain's expansion into Morocco. Europeans were beginning to define an inverse relationship between their colonial subjects and archetypal European males through art as well as public discourse. They did so with photography too, capturing realistic scenes that forever changed conceptions of "materiality, experience, and truth."[4] As Andrew Ginger has recognized, the "1850s and 1860s have habitually been seen as a crucial turning point in cultural modernity."[5] Both fine art and crude caricature from the time exhibited the characteristics and symbols of imperialism. While late Romanticism gave way to realism in terms of artistic aesthetics, images retained elements of both as Spaniards established themselves as mythic conquerors of the exotic other in Africa and in the Americas. Photographs displayed a similar dynamic to Orientalist works of art. Artists using different media consciously presented figures in repose, dressed in traditional garb, as a point of contrast to the industrious and modern European subject. Yet Christianity also retained a central position in Spanish visual culture as a marker of European civilization.

Art and literature, as Edward Said has shown, offer a window into the mentality of the age, and Orientalist art in particular demonstrates a radical shift in European attitudes toward the East.[6] Earlier, for example, English scholar-officials such as William Jones advocated rule with a minimum of interference and with a certain adherence to tradition. He argued that the British should help Indians recover their ancient literary and cultural heritage and revitalize their Hindu faith. However, colonial policies changed significantly over the course of the nineteenth century. In 1817 James Mill, an employee of the East India Company, decried Indian social practices and customs as backward and ill-suited for the demands of the modern age. He and his son, John Stuart Mill, insisted that only illiberal, dictatorial rule could bring about a healthy government and economy. Progress had to be exported to peoples in the East, with their underutilized resources and unexploited lands. Thomas Babington Macaulay famously theorized the degenerate Bengali as inferior and unintelligent: "There never perhaps existed a people so thoroughly fitted by habit for a foreign yoke."[7] Thus, non-Western peoples were essentially unfit for self-rule, autonomy, or liberalism.

Considered a land of backwardness and fanaticism by many Europeans, including luminaries such as Victor Hugo, Spain also had been portrayed as a retrograde state, burdened by the weight of its long history and complicated interactions between Christian, Muslim, and Jewish communities.[8] The French artist Henri Regnault expressly wrote of his desire to "find and study the living traces of the vanquished Moors of late medieval Spain in North Africa."[9] After visiting the Iberian Peninsula and Morocco, he painted a realistic and haunting scene of a decapitation titled *Summary Execution under the Moorish Kings of Granada*, perhaps an imaginative rendering of a judgment under the last sultan of Granada, Boabdil. With the Alhambra in the background, its classic architecture a representation of the Orient, an imposing figure completes the bloody task without remorse. María DeGuzmán provocatively interprets Regnault's oil painting as a depiction, through French eyes, of Spanish identity, comprised of "a volatile 'Oriental' mixture destined to violently implode or languorously putrefy."[10] While Europeans certainly contrasted themselves with Asians and Africans, some denigrated Spaniards as "half African," in the words of Hugo, and put forward exotic stereotypes that lasted well into the twentieth century.

Within the paradigm of Orientalist art, the Oriental other is portrayed as an artifact of the past, living in a culture untouched by the progress of modernization. Some artists even went as far as to claim people outside of the West were living more like their ancestors in ancient, biblical times.[11] Lazy figures with seemingly nothing to do often litter their canvases, tacitly attesting to the unquestioned ideals of European racism and a faith in the superiority of their civilization. The 1874 Villegas oil painting *Siesta* illustrates this otherness with a muscular man lounging on a chair, pipe in hand, and a topless woman, perhaps an odalisque, playing an oud on his lap. He looks dreamily away from the viewer, with a flintlock pistol placed casually on a table next to him and fabrics tossed to the side over an unused Qur'an stand. A bejeweled case holds a dagger at his side, and the smoke from incense burning lingers in the air. Such images convey the sense that the mythical Orient and its various cultures were fundamentally different from and inferior to those of Europe.

As noted in earlier chapters, the French occupation of Algeria served as a paradigm of empire building for Spaniards eager to avenge losses in the Americas and reclaim the mantle of imperial glory. Prior to the 1830s many in France had pined for great military victories abroad that would provide a bridge to the Napoleonic age and simultaneously help them compete economically with Britain. They also hoped to open up new markets for their nascent industries. Perhaps most important, Charles X, the restored monarch of France, was looking to suppress internal dissent and reestablish tenets of an absolutist state. The government carefully prepared a plan of attack, received assurances from other Great Powers that their conquest would be respected, and sent over a massive force of 635 ships and over thirty-four thousand men.[12] Hussein Dey, the Ottoman governor of Algiers, assembled a larger force, equipped with inferior artillery but better rifles, although they could not defeat the French.[13] On July 5, 1830, the French took the city. Just as in the case of Napoleon in Egypt, the French came with large numbers of pamphlets in Arabic assuring the people of Algiers that they had come to liberate them from the tyranny of the Turk. By 1834 the French had declared their possession a military colony under the authority of the Ministry of War, a status Algeria would retain until 1848. Between 1830 and 1871, only the year 1861 passed without major armed resistance against the colonizers. In conducting operations against the last remaining resistance leader, 'Abd al-Qadir, the French employed a scorched earth policy, burning crops, killing livestock, and forbidding the populace to plant crops or tend to their animals. In at least three cases troops burned alive or asphyxiated communities seeking refuge in caves, killing up to a thousand people at a time. This was a total war, engaging over one hundred thousand French soldiers by 1846. Famine and hardship certainly went hand in hand with four decades of unremitting violence and dislocation begun by the invasion. Despite this bloodshed and loss of life the French pushed to the west in the 1840s, bombarding Tangier and Essaouira (Mogador) in 1844. Spanish commentators praised the effort, in addition to the struggle against 'Abd al-Qadir, as a model of a "noble drive to glory."[14]

Artists like Eugène Delacroix and Jean-Léon Gérôme, as well as politicians and intellectuals such as Alexis de Tocqueville, traveled to Algeria to experience the empire firsthand. Tocqueville visited twice in the 1840s and wrote extensively about the people and their interactions with French colonizers. He reflected on the disconnected nature of relations between Europeans and Africans and between emergent democratic norms and the engine of imperialism driving expansion. Yet he remained torn between racist theories of natural progress, emphasizing stages of development among civilizations, and a kind of cultural amalgamation between the races. Much like Castelar, Tocqueville argued, at times, for religious tolerance and a move toward common laws for all groups.[15] He advocated winning over the Kabyles through art and commerce rather than by force. In his 1841 *Essay on Algeria*, however, he emphasized differences with Arab speakers, stating, "The Arabs have fewer needs than the civilized nations of Europe."[16] Later on he embraced a more militaristic vision of French colonialism. According to Jennifer Pitts, "Tocqueville's early impressions recall the more Romantic responses to North Africa of Gustave Flaubert and Eugène Delacroix."[17]

With an emphasis on the natural world, Romanticism dramatically captured landscapes and imbued them with a sense of solitude and escape from the growing industries taking over urban centers. Vividly painted Orientalist works of art overlapped in terms of theme and content, expressing a desire to see and experience the wide-open spaces and distinctive features of lands far from northern Europe that also remained emblematic of the putative divide between East and West. Eugène Fromentin's 1859 *Bab-el-Gharbi Street in Laghouat* renders a parched desert town in Algeria as a place of inertia—men languishing in the heat of the day, unable or unwilling to work and produce like their counterparts in industrializing Europe. The first important artist to travel to the French colony after the defeat of 'Abd al-Qadir, he spent an extended amount of time in Algeria. In both *Bab-el-Gharbi Street* and his 1869 painting *The Land of Thirst*, no outward signs of upheaval betray the French colonial presence. Laghouat had been sacked in 1852, and Fromentin visited the town the following year, after the French claimed it had been pacified.[18] Algerians simply appear to be dying under the oppressive summer sun. Other artists presented Maghrebis in the exact same way in the context of the Spanish-Moroccan War, with limbs splayed out and heads propped up by elbows. Fortuny includes a man lying down in the center of his 1860 drawing of a Moroccan café. A lithograph of the entrance of Spanish cavalry into Tetuán on February 6, 1860, includes a bearded man on the ground facing the men on horseback as they ride through a city gate. On the cover of an 1860 book by Victor Balaguer, a larger-than-life Spanish soldier triumphantly places a flag over a defeated man. Dressed in a traditional white robe, he lays in repose, his sword having fallen from his grasp and his red banner crumpled on the dry desert soil. With a forlorn gaze, the man looks hapless in the face of the Spanish onslaught.[19]

While the Spanish press contextualized this kind of Orientalist imagery with the backdrop of war and violence in the early 1860s, many works of art elided the defining historical context of the age—the advent of a new kind of imperialism. The German painter Adolf Schreyer also traveled to North Africa, visiting Algeria in the early 1860s. By then there were more than a hundred thousand French settlers in the colony. Vast quantities of land had been appropriated for different reasons—punishment for resistance, acquisition through conquest, or the expropriation of supposedly empty land. Much of the latter was in fact traditional communal grazing lands for villages and seminomadic or nomadic peoples. Schreyer's painting *The Oasis* shows an open landscape, an image reminiscent of impressionism as well as Romanticism. But perhaps, as one art historian has noted in reference to Auguste Renoir, if we attach his work to the Orientalist tradition, "his impressionism [is] a secondary matter."[20] There are obvious parallels to other works from the time, with a relaxed figure leaning against a tree, unconcerned that he has placed his weapon at a distance. The blurry figure in the background may be one of those recently displaced by war and the upheavals of the French occupation.

Like his contemporaries in Europe, Pedro Antonio de Alarcón chose to visit North Africa on the cusp of his nation's victorious military campaign. Alarcón, just as he decided to enlist in the Spanish army, commissioned the Málaga-based photographer Enrique Facio to travel with him.[21] Facio took more than fifty photos and was the first Spanish photojournalist to work in a conflict zone, according to Antonio David Palma Crespo. His images, coming shortly after his peers had shot the Mexican-American and Crimean wars, are among the first photographs of a battlefield.[22] Alarcón's war testimonials were published in the periodical *El Museo Universal*; he claimed to have sold fifty thousand copies.[23] The pictures, however, were not incorporated; newspapers in Spain only began to print photographs in the 1890s.[24]

Artists, among them Alarcón's friend José Vallejo, likewise drew scenes to bear witness to the unfolding events of modern war, many of which replicated the photos taken. Emilio Castelar's *Chronicle of the War of Africa* published a large number of the sketches. Vallejo had ingratiated himself into a regiment from Zamora and subsequently joined a guerrilla operation at

Castillejos. He even served in the Battle of Tetuán, taking fire from the Moroccans, and received the Cross of San Fernando from O'Donnell for his actions.[25] Spanish drawings and photographs showed Morocco in much the same state as Orientalist artists presented Algeria—a place haunted by death, locked in the distant past.

Aesthetic differences emerged in the 1860s as defenders of realism began to stake out a position more akin to xenophobia and photography challenged the preeminence of the fine arts. One critic of Orientalism insisted that palm trees and camels would "never produce the sweet and peaceful emotion given me by the sight of cows in a meadow edged with poplars."[26] Verity and beauty had become contested and relative notions. Castelar went on the offensive and claimed that his publication, the *Chronicle of the War of Africa*, was the only one to have contracted with an artist to "give its subscribers absolutely the truth."[27] Yet Alarcón also insisted that his main intention was to provide "a true and exact idea" of what the military campaign looked like in Morocco. For a later edition of his *Diary*, he referred to the book as a type of photography that captured the essence of the war.[28] His photographer Facio shot, with an eye toward objectivity, a series of pictures of Spanish soldiers and their encampments. In one photograph from 1860 a regiment from Mallorca poses for the camera with weapons proudly displayed, as a chaplain in the center of the group tightly grasps an open Bible in both hands. Meeting the gaze of the cameraman, some men place their hands on their hips, while some have a hand on their swords (figure 12). Their martial sensibility, paired with visible traits of European masculinity and modernity, contrasts with the vulnerability of Moroccan men depicted in paintings, drawings, and photographs.

Vallejo reaffirmed to readers his desire to capture the truth in his images and described his work as, in part, an effort to provide his compatriots with a vision of the distinctive "social classes of the Moors." To portray the conflict accurately, however, he needed greater access to enemy soldiers. He lamented

FIG. 12. "An encampment during the campaign of Africa, 1860. A group of officials from Mallorca," photograph by E. Facio. Reprinted courtesy of the Archivo General de Palacio.

the fact that he had been at the front in almost all of the military actions through December 1859. But he had not been able to see Moroccan troops amassed and ready for battle, as they too often "disappeared like ghosts" when they came into contact with Spanish forces. Therefore, he took the opportunity to draw prisoners of war instead, who in turn signed the images as proof of authenticity. Vallejo described one prisoner who had been held as a slave, according to an interpreter, as a stupid, "miserable Moorish mendicant captured in the action of 30 December begging for his life and for bread" (figure 13). In the drawing a bedroll made from "the skin of a dog or a cat" hangs from the man's head.[29]

From the Spanish hospital in Ceuta, Vallejo came into contact with other prisoners at the end of December as well. The *Chronicle* covered one man, Buselejam Beljileli-el-Amori E-Bene-Susi, with an in-depth story. Hailing from the coastal region of Beni Amar near Tangier, he was a widower with a young wife and three children. A sharif, he engaged in agriculture and could

Visual Culture

FIG. 13. "Chronicles of the War of Africa: The Moorish slave prisoner," José Vallejo. Reprinted courtesy of the Biblioteca Nacional, Madrid, Spain.

read and write, qualities that set him apart from the majority of the local inhabitants discussed by Spanish soldiers in northern Morocco. The article's author even noted with surprise that the prisoner had composed a letter to his sons while in Spanish custody, writing, "'Allah has decreed it, and I am under the power of the Christians; but Allah wanted me to fall into Spanish hands; they treat me well and help me to recover." According to Spanish observers, the man had excited a great curiosity in the army: "His dress consisted of a traditional brown robe with a hood, white pants to the knee and a shirt: on his feet straw-colored slippers. . . . His beard, partly gray, revealed a ruddy face and a flat nose: his countenance, however, is not disagreeable. He walks with admirable serenity, flanked on one side by a civil official and on the other by his [Algerian] interpreter." The article appeared with a sketch drawn and signed by both Vallejo and the "Moor" as a testament to its veracity. Despite the origins and education of Beljileli, Vallejo disparagingly said that "he was found so unkempt, that the last beggar in Spain is clean compared to him."[30]

The Spanish press presented other prisoners in a more positive light. According to the *Chronicle*, "the most notable [of the Moorish prisoners] is named Saled, and they say he is the governor of Larache. . . . He is young, dark-skinned, with a thin black beard, beautiful eyes and a strong gaze. His pleasant physiognomy reveals intelligence and audacity."[31] This rhetoric reproduced emerging scientific racial theories that postulated a correlation between physical appearance, even aesthetic qualities, and character traits. While Vallejo repeatedly spoke to the importance of exact depictions in his work, his subjects, like most non-Europeans analyzed in Spanish print media, remained largely inscrutable. In the portrait titled *Esclavo moro prisionero* (the Moorish slave prisoner) there is almost nothing in the background to indicate why he might have been captured.

Vallejo, unlike the subjects he drew, became a protagonist in many of the events he covered. Furthermore, he openly criticized reporters who holed up in Ceuta, which was the equivalent, he wrote, "of being in Madrid or even worse" in terms of access to news from the front.[32] Apart from some of his compatriots, he presented himself as a man of action. About to sketch a scene, he heard O'Donnell shout to the troops, "¡VIVA LA REINA!" He was so inspired that he threw down his pencil, mounted his horse, and joined the charge against twenty-thousand cavalrymen. On the road to Tetuán, with regiments from Cuenca, Arápiles, and Vergara, among others, Vallejo felt as if they were replicating the march of Hernán Cortés as he approached the imperial city of Tenochtitlan.[33] A sense of time travel and of the power of Spain's history pervaded both the journalism, art, and literature of the time.

The French painter Georges Rochegrosse also visited Egypt and North Africa, and his realistic works transported the viewer back to parables from the Bible, reproducing the notion that traveling to the Orient was akin to traveling back to antiquity. In the words of Fromentin, the Orient was the "living effigy" of biblical times.[34] A Spanish travel account of a voyage down the west coast of Africa in 1864 likewise suggested that the so-called Gold Coast might in fact be the land of Ophir, mentioned in the Bible as the source of King Solomon's gold and ivory, used to construct his temple in Jerusalem.[35] Not only did Orientalism allow for the fantasy of time travel, placing non-Europeans well behind the West along the historical continuum known as progress, but Orientalist art also permitted Westerners to travel voyeuristically into the realm of the forbidden, into absolute decadence and unrestrained pleasure.[36] According to Fromentin, "It might have been possible for me to enter the mosque, but I did not try. To penetrate further into Arab life than is permitted seems to me misplaced curiosity. This people must be seen from the distance at which it chooses to reveal itself: men close up, women from afar."[37] Thus the painting *Entrance to a Mosque, Delhi*, by the American Edwin Lord Weeks, depicts the outside of a mosque, showing only the shoes of those who have entered.

FIG. 14. "Panoramic view of Tetuán," photograph by E. Facio.
Reprinted courtesy of the Archivo General de Palacio.

In a comparable way Facio's visuals maintain a critical distance from the centers of Muslim religious life. Likely resid-
ing in Tetuán for a period of time after the war ended, he took
a series of pictures of the skyline and the city's architecture,
including multiple photographs of many of the striking mosques.
One lucid image captured two of the most prominent minarets
in the city, including al-Jami' al-Kabir (the Great Mosque) in
the medina (figure 14). Quiet and still, the structures rise from
the desert landscape with few indications of modern technology and without people in sight. He also photographed a min-
aret that seems to touch the sky on the right side of the shot.
Located on the street renamed Calle Iberia during the occupation, the mosque and the structures below betray no signs
of life. The city is largely quiet and still, with no one visible in
the background. A Vallejo sketch, looking toward the city from
outside the walls, offers a different window into daily life in
Tetuán, with death featured prominently. Gravediggers in the
foreground prepare for a body to be interred in the Jewish cemetery.[38] A Spanish flag flies high above the activity below, but

FIG. 15. "Chronicles of the War of Africa: View of the citadel and cemetery of Tetuán," José Vallejo. Reprinted courtesy of the Biblioteca Nacional, Madrid, Spain.

the cause of the person's death is not apparent (figure 15). In Gérôme's *The Muezzin (The Call to Prayer)*, painted in 1866, Cairo similarly appears desolate, and a haze hangs low. A dog is sleeping on a rooftop, and only a single solitary individual is pictured. Other Vallejo sketches portray the lonely streets of the medina and the deserted marketplace of Tetuán. One, *Calle de la alcaicería, en Tetuán,* includes a Spanish soldier with an arm placed comfortably on his hip, appearing to chat amicably with a local resident in a djellaba. These images offered a striking contrast to industrializing Europe with its bustling cities and crowded streets.

On the other hand, many European artists vividly portrayed the interiority and exotic allure of Orientalism—images involving the sexualized female other. Specifically, they projected their fantasies onto Oriental women and the harem. In spite of the fact that women in Ottoman harems were likely to be the most educated, trained in the arts, able to speak European languages, and active in court life, the harem represented forbidden pleasure, a sphere of female activity to which men were

E. Facio fot

FIG. 16. "The Moorish woman Hatima of Tetuán," photograph by E. Facio. Reprinted courtesy of the Archivo General de Palacio.

denied access.[39] Therefore, artists imagined seminude slaves as a commonplace feature of Oriental life, a perfect contrast with European ideals of freedom and equality. Orientalist artists also portrayed dancing girls serving and performing for Eastern despots languishing on their thrones. Many images from the Spanish press reinforced such stereotypes. For instance, sketches from *El Cañón Rayado* from 1859 and 1860 depict the fantasy of dark-skinned women sensually rewarding Spanish soldiers for their service. One has the title "The women of Tetuán appreciative of our troops," while another is called "The dream of a cadet."[40] The latter's scene of half-naked women and Black

Visual Culture

slaves serving a victorious Spaniard is structured like the Paul Bouchard painting *Les Almées* and others that portray the subjugation and sexualization supposedly characteristic of the East.

Facio photographed male and female residents of Tetuán, including Muslim women. Although he did not offer decadent visions of Oriental sexuality on display for his Spanish audience, pictures such as his "Mora Hatima" evoked the history of al-Andalus and romanticized notions of an imagined past. With her head covered, Hatima stares intently into the camera, her head resting confidently on her left hand (figure 16). Vallejo, in his sketch "Jewish types of Tetuán," presented a Jewish woman, head covered, breastfeeding a baby, with another older child next to her left shoulder. She looks straight at the viewer with self-confidence (figure 17). Two men of different faiths stand to the side, appearing to converse. One is Jewish; the other is covered head to toe by a traditional North African white robe, with a longer beard, seated cross-legged in a merchant's produce stand. The periodical *El Mundo Pintoresco* (The picturesque world) published similarly realistic drawings of street scenes and marketplace activity. In one, *Aspect of a Tetuán Street*, a bearded man smoking a pipe engages the child seated next to him while a vendor looks to hawk the wares he carries on his back.[41] Commercial activity and daily life do not appear to have been entirely disrupted by the Spanish military presence in the city.

Not all artists took such a dispassionate view of non-Europeans. A defining aspect of Orientalism showcases the effeminate man as the binary opposite of the militaristic yet calculating and thoughtful European male. In Villegas y Cordero's rendering of a Moroccan arms expert, his right breast and nipple remain exposed, like female slaves in paintings such as *La esclava* by Antonio María Fabrés Costa. Flowing robes do not fully cover the man's body, and he wears no shoes, unlike European soldiers clad in dark uniforms and knee-high leather boots. Other portraits show Moroccan warriors in states of repose and lethargy, almost like female nudes in the sensuous

renderings of odalisques. Fabrés Costa's *The Rest of the Warrior* centers on a Black man, his torso uncovered, resting next to his sword, a hookah at the foreground in front of his lavish bed. Like the man in Villegas's *Siesta*, the decadent warrior in no way appears threatening or dangerous to a European audience.

Satirists approached their subjects with an arsenal of ridicule and scorn, taking Orientalist imagery to an extreme. Over the course of its two years as a publication, Manuel Angelón's *El Cañón Rayado* (The crazy cannon) consistently caricatured Moroccan peoples in derisive terms drawing on racist stereotypes in both articles and illustrations.[42] In the first issue an entire page lays out the "Precedents to the War of Africa" in nine obscene and biting cartoons (figure 18). The first sets the stage for the conflict, as menacing dark-skinned tribesmen savagely attack the Spanish coat-of-arms, mounted on a stone marker, with the butts of their rifles. The tongue-in-cheek caption explains that although this was a demonstration of their bravery and valor, the provocation ultimately precipitated a war. The artist then renders Spain as a lion dressed in the finery of the age, standing on two feet while confronting a deferential Moroccan emperor

Visual Culture

over the skirmishes. The lion later swims over to Africa as the Gallic cock, an English bulldog, and a Portuguese rooster watch, admiring the bravery of Spain. The fourth image portrays the death of the emperor, 'Abd al-Rahman, described as prudent in a subsequent caption. Yet the artist shows a scrum to seize the throne, a parody of the violence between rival candidates that had on occasion accompanied such maneuvering in the past. A dozen men, many with limbs hacked off or decapitated, fight as a cloud of dust and disorder swirls around their bodies. The comical struggle between wild-eyed men continues in the next frame, as an "Octavian peace" descends upon the dustup and an ultimatum sent by Spain explodes amid the brawl like a bomb. The final series of cartoons represents Moroccans as simultaneously impulsive and repulsive. Nine men squat together, about to defecate uncontrollably. The drawing parallels a similar sketch of Mulay al'Abbas, presented in the same position, crouching with stomach problems.[43] In *El Cañón Rayado*'s version, the caption plays on the words "to fire" and satirizes the idea that they plan to unleash an unusual weapon. The penultimate frame has the men holding their noses or covering their faces as they gasp for breath, exasperated as they inhale the smell of "African gunpowder."[44] The completely absurd images incorporate condescension, farce, and crass visuals, unlike an earlier bourgeois culture and Orientalist tropes. Nevertheless, each style of art served to dehumanize and marginalize the peoples against whom the Spaniards had fought in North Africa.

These characterizations also came to denote those who could be potentially disloyal. A caricature by Felipó from early 1860, with the title "Moroccan spies," shows two men, one standing on the back of the other.[45] They deviously attempt to engage in a fool's errand of espionage. The man on top has his hand to his ear as he listens intently to the recently installed telegraph wire. As the Spanish audience knows, they will not be able to decipher the messages.[46] A drawing signed by Moliné from the same year depicts a perturbed man trying to stay balanced while standing atop Morocco, while archetypal Spanish soldiers haul

FIG. 18. "Precedents to the War of Africa." From *El Cañón Rayado* (The crazy cannon) no. 1 (December 11, 1859), 3.

away pieces of the empire below him with the names of the cities Tangier and Tetuán scrawled on them.[47] The artists of *El Cañón Rayado* had from the beginning moved away from presenting "Moors" as human beings, instead drawing monkeys with turbans on their heads.[48] This type of imagery perfectly captures the European belief that a vast gulf separated East from West and Islamic tradition from Christian culture and technology.

As they paired soldiers against the passive or laughable Muslim subject, Spanish artists did at times show their compatriots resorting to extreme violence, as depicted in lithographs from the Spanish-Moroccan War. In two drawings that appeared in *El Cañón Rayado*, a man looks to behead a Moroccan soldier while another brutally places an enemy combatant into a cannon he is about to fire.[49] The message sent to Morocco in effect demanded total surrender after the humiliating defeat of the emperor's troops. Short of the complete submission of the Moroccans, Spaniards would use any means necessary to ensure compliance—yet they also could be capable of empathy and acts of humanitarianism. In the nineteenth-century European imagination it was an absolute necessity that aid be provided from benevolent powers to support supposed lesser peoples crying out for help. In Alarcón's *Diary*, published in 1859, a realistic sketch of the hospital in Ceuta appears under the title "Injured Moors," while a similar image from a different publication highlights a Spanish soldier reaching out to two defeated people. The caption reads, "Do not fear: The Spanish official never injures his defenseless enemies."[50]

Such tensions reveal a paradoxical vision of the Orient. While many Spaniards did have sympathy for the defeated Moroccan forces and appreciated their historical contributions to Andalusian and Spanish culture, they also perceived North Africans as exotic and racially distinct from the European Spaniard. Ginger captures this duality in describing the work of the artist Eugenio Lucas Velázquez and his 1859 painting *Flight of the Moors from Spain*. He writes that, from a Spanish perspective, "[Moors] needed at once to be removed from and to be integrated into national life."⁵¹ Accordingly the styles of both Lucas and Villegas "could oscillate between incorporation and rejection" of an Islamic heritage, according to Sarah Tabbal.⁵² This correlates with the Enlightenment ideas of the Marquis de Condorcet, who had suggested that progress naturally would lead to the elimination of many "tribes" and "hordes" that, "reduced in number as they are driven back by civilized nations . . . will finally disappear imperceptibly before them or merge into them."⁵³ Romantically casting the "Moor" as a type of noble savage, liberals and even republicans like Lucas could lament their demise while at once celebrating European Christian civilization. Victory in Africa had realized the goal initially set out by Consul-General Juan Blanco del Valle prior to the start of the war in Morocco, in which he expressed his desire for "the magnificent triumph that civilization is ready to achieve over barbarism."⁵⁴

Documents from the time explicitly connect Spanish expansionism in Africa to territorial acquisition and conquest in the Americas, the subjects of the following three chapters. The queen's name and image frequently served as a shorthand reference to both past and present, tying together Isabel II's reign and that of her predecessor, who vanquished the last of the caliphates in Iberia, the Nasrid city-state of Granada, and spearheaded voyages across the Atlantic that established a foothold in the Caribbean. In Havana, Cuba, in 1859, an official letter from the *ayuntamiento* lavished praise on "Isabel I, [who] through her faith and love of the Patria, contributed to the discovery of America; [and] Isabel II, [who] through her faith and love of past glories and of her children today, contributed to civilizing Africa!'"⁵⁵ The veneration of progress, and the march of white civilization, brought Spaniards to America in the fifteenth century and would carry them there again in the mid-nineteenth century. These ideals, grounded in historical and religious themes, served to justify a global program of imperialism. For example, in the painting *Oath of the Governor and Captain General of Santo Domingo, Don Pedro Santana*, Salvadoran-born artist Wenceslao Cisneros realistically depicted the Dominican president, his hand on a Bible placed next to a wood carving of the crucifixion, swearing an oath of loyalty to Spain under a large portrait of Queen Isabel II.[56] Composed in 1862, the ceremony had taken place the year before. A priest stands to the left of the captain general of Cuba, Francisco Serrano, presiding over the all-male audience, the vast majority of whom were white. Officials such as Brigadier Antonio Peláez Campomanes and José Malo de Molina, analyzed in chapter 4, look on solemnly, seeming to approve of the political process that would devolve power away from the island's people and return it to the metropole. The canvas symbolically marks the end of Dominican sovereignty and the beginning of a tumultuous period of Spanish rule in the early 1860s.

FOUR

Order, Progress, and Civilization

The Annexation of the Dominican Republic

José de la Gándara y Navarro was charged, as the governor and captain general of Santo Domingo, with pacifying territory that had only recently been reincorporated into the Spanish Monarchy. Having served previously on the West African island outpost of Fernando Po, he faced a seemingly unprecedented large-scale rebellion, especially strong on the porous border with Haiti. A Spanish commission sent over to assess the situation in 1864 concluded that peninsular troops could not defeat the guerrilla bands operating throughout the island.[1] In addressing the Dominican people that spring, however, Gándara reassuringly stated the protective forces they sought would not be withdrawn due to an uprising of "blind partisans of insurrection." The unjustified resistance to a noble nation would be met with strength, and Spain, he promised, would bring "the element of progress and civilization" to a downtrodden people. Much like those who flew banners and shouted slogans on the streets of Madrid during the Spanish-Moroccan War, Spanish nationalists couched their presence in the Dominican Republic as an ongoing campaign of civilization against barbarism. Spain's most important diplomat serving in the Caribbean at the time plainly declared, "The black [faction] represents barbarism and African traditions."[2] According to Gándara, "the rebels have arms in hand, but they do not have reason in their [collective] conscience." He ended with the rallying cry of the war, proclaiming his cause to be "order and justice."[3] This chapter explores

EL TENIENTE GENERAL,

Dⁿ. JOSÉ DE LA GÁNDARA.

FIG. 19. Lieutenant General Don José de la Gándara. From José Muñoz Gaviria, *África: Islas de Fernando Póo, Corisco y Annobón* (Madrid: Rubio, Grilo y Viturri, 1871), 17.

how Spain, much like other European colonial powers, blindly approached divisive issues of class and racial identification and relied mainly on military force to entrench rule from Madrid.

The civil war and ensuing War of Restoration (1863–65) in the Dominican Republic reveal the tenuous nature of what Benedict Anderson describes as a precocious conception of Creole community in Spanish America.[4] A collective attachment to the idea of a Dominican nation remained fragile through the 1860s, as many Hispanic residents continued to identify with Spain whereas those with African ancestry often felt a strong solidarity with Haiti. In fact, many insurgents fought with and received direct support from the Haitian government. Yet the idea of a light-skinned peasant—the *campesino cibaeño*, an important element of nationalist mythology in the Dominican Republic—fed the ideology of *antihaitianismo*, premised on the supposed threat of dark-skinned people from the west of the island. Thus key contradictions weakened a "national consciousness of the Dominican people [that] was far more developed than that of the elites," according to Ernesto Sagás in his work on Dominican political history. He found that a "Creole culture" had taken root among Black Dominicans and those with mixed race ancestry that differed substantially from the emergent identity of the urban middle classes.[5] Religiosity also separated Dominicans. Luis Martínez-Fernández has noted that a majority of the clergy in both Mexico and the Dominican Republic during the mid-nineteenth century held pro-Spanish views, verging on what he calls Europhilia.[6] These scholars, among many others, have undercut Anderson's synthetic notion of a Creole consciousness emerging across Spanish America, pointing instead to divergences between white and Black Creole identities and class differences as they supplanted previous loyalties to the Spanish Monarchy.

The History of a Divided Island

Nineteenth-century Dominican history cannot be untangled from the concomitant struggles for independence and freedom in Haiti. Whereas Haitians fought for and won independence from France in 1804, Dominican independence from Spain led to a long-lasting Haitian occupation beginning in 1822. It is not surprising, therefore, that Haitians more often than not appear as the racial and religious Other in narratives from the period. A case in point is a document commissioned by the captain general of Cuba Francisco Serrano and written by the jurist José Malo de Molina in 1861. Malo de Molina described the Haitian occupation from 1822 through 1844 as one of "brutal despotism," in which the white race was prohibited from owning property, the Spanish language was proscribed, and Dominicans lost their laws and customs. Dominican independence was declared in 1844, pushed forward by the separatism of a secret conspiratorial group called the Trinitarios, led by the staunchly Catholic Juan Pablo Duarte.[7] The "Dominican Christian family" that emerged consciously defined an identity in opposition to that of the "fetishist" and "sacrilegious" Haitians to the west.[8] Even today the flag, originally designed by Duarte, prominently features a cross, an open Bible, and the motto "Dios, Patria, Libertad." But Malo de Molina decried the fact that, although formally separated, Dominicans adopted only slightly modified French imperial laws, and some leading figures promoted religious tolerance. At the same time he lauded the abolition of slavery and recognized that all of the estimated two hundred thousand Dominicans on the island "were equal, enjoying the same civil and political rights."[9]

Independence from Haiti became a sacrosanct historical signifier for many nineteenth-century Dominican nationalists, and some said God had defeated the Haitians.[10] Yet tensions on the border, including skirmishes and battles, continued unabated for years. Many within the government therefore sought the protection of a foreign power, and some openly advocated bringing the Dominican Republic back into the Spanish fold.[11] As early as 1846 the biracial statesman Buenaventura Báez held a meeting at court in Paris petitioning European diplomats for help. Having once said that Europe "is the center of civilization," he disparaged "the cruelty and the incursions of the black race," a blunt reference to Haiti.[12] The Spanish diplomat Javier Istúriz recounted meeting Báez in 1846, describing him as a "person of talent, of sound judgment and business knowledge, with many supporters in Santo Domingo." According to Istúriz, Báez and his diplomatic coterie "wanted to put the island of Santo Domingo under the protection of Spain." They represented "the opinion of a great number of Dominicans, tired of the disorganization that reigned in their patria, but also concerned that they might fall under the dominion of the United States due to the proclivities of President Pedro Santana, who was favorable to that republic." No one took these issues lightly, and the idea of a protectorate remained controversial for decades. Istúriz, writing in the 1860s, claimed that Báez had always been a partisan of annexation, with his "adhesion to Spain made clear during his mission to Madrid in 1846."[13] The increasingly authoritarian Santana ultimately pushed Báez out of the presidency and out of the country in 1853, as the rivals openly displayed their differences over politics and church-state relations. Their antagonistic relationship was magnified by rumors swirling over annexation, with Santana favoring the United States over a European power.[14] By 1857 factions loyal to Báez and Santana had escalated their feuding, with Santana forced into exile.

As a solution to the political instability and turmoil on the island, exacerbated by conflict with Haiti, reincorporation into the Spanish Monarchy began to look like a more appealing option in the late 1850s. Spanish protection of a Caribbean territory that had definitively abolished slavery opened up the possibility that racial divisions in all of Spain's Antillean colonies might be mitigated. Statesmen like Mariano Álvarez and Gabriel Tassara underestimated reports of social and political tensions in the Dominican Republic, believing that diplomats and politicians like Santana had the situation under control. According to official correspondence from 1858, the fighting that had engulfed the island "has been happily ended due to the intervention of the Consuls of France, England, and Spain," and Santana had been able to unite the various competing forces.[15] Santana himself validated such views in a letter sent directly to Queen Isabel in Spain, saying that he was "the personification of sentiments to strengthen the ties that unite all of the people and the towns" of the Dominican Republic.[16] In addition, between 1858 and 1860 Santana began to warm to the prospect of Spanish, rather than American, annexation.[17] Tassara, in a suggestive private diplomatic note, issued a positive assessment of "things that have been put in place to precipitate the possession, not only of Santo Domingo, but also later of other important points in the Gulf."[18] He did not spell out the specifics, but Captain General Serrano, who would receive the letter, surely knew what he meant. Surreptitiously, the government in Madrid began to increase its military presence in the former colony. In the early summer of 1860 after the conclusion of a peace treaty in North Africa, Calderón Collantes directed "some warships" to the Dominican and Haitian coasts to support General Santana and to defuse the conflict. He hoped to prevent a civil war from breaking out and to counter the machinations of the British and French.[19]

The Spanish government also sent a military adviser from Cuba, Brigadier Antonio Peláez Campomanes, to write a report in advance of a possible annexation of the Dominican Republic. In 1860 Peláez traveled around the island for twenty-seven days, attuned to the nostalgia some older residents felt for the days of Spanish dominion. Highlighting the fact that the Spanish flag still flew alongside the Dominican standard, he mentioned that the taking of Tetuán had been celebrated with a twenty-one-gun salute. He described the abundance of forested areas that produced exports such as wood, tobacco, and some coffee. A peninsular newspaper report similarly presented a romanticized portrait of eternal greenery, tropical sun, picturesque mountain peaks, and unknown riches. It was a fertile paradise, producing three harvests a year seemingly without any work, that had inspired the intrepid adventurers of the fifteenth century.[20] Other observers, traveling to Samaná in the east, wrote of the potential of the island economy as well. The land was described as "virgin," much like the landscape encountered by the Spanish conquistadors, and the population as "scarce." Likewise, industry and commerce were largely unknown in these areas, and there was an inertia that seemed a great obstacle to progress. So, Spain was encouraged to take up the "noble, humanitarian work that is traditional in our country," such as setting up a telegraph line between Samaná and Santo Domingo and constructing roads.[21] Peláez also took on politics and denigrated the previous government, led by "the pardo Báez," as a bad administration with poor financial practices. Finally, he included a hagiographical description of the president. General Santana treated his subordinates like sons, according to Peláez. He spoke simply, without eloquence, seeming perspicacious, noble, and generous. Certainly this type of propaganda, circulating among governing officials, must have contributed to Spanish support for Santana's cause.[22]

Correspondence within the Overseas Ministry and the Ministry of Defense painted a rosy view of annexation as well. One letter stated that the Dominicans generally "held no animosity toward the Spanish."[23] Other reports indicated the potential positive impact Dominicans could have in augmenting the Spanish military, possibly adding up to 35,000 men to their forces.[24] Eighty percent of the population of approximately 250,000 people came from a racially mixed ancestry, and the rest were Spaniards and Creoles.[25] Furthermore, the Spanish diplomat Álvarez commented on the religious sensibility of the majority of the inhabitants, writing, "the Dominican people are very devout." Yet he lamented structural deficiencies as well, including the fact that no coherent educational system existed in the towns or the countryside.[26]

Álvarez made an economic case for annexation, tempered by an understanding of regional variation and the upsurge of political factions. He emphasized the fact that the populous north-central region of the Cibao relied heavily on tobacco, a

Order, Progress, Civilization

crop of disproportionate importance, especially in the markets of Hamburg and Bremen in northern Europe. The Cibao valley constituted the most productive area of the country. However, the region had been the epicenter of political discontent and a growing federalist movement inspired by the United States. Benigno Filomeno de Rojas, a representative from the Cibao, received a congressional rebuke and a chastising from the president for espousing a federal system. Nonetheless, the issue had the potential to drive people apart along regional lines, establishing "a difference between 'Dominicano' and 'Cibaeño.'" Furthermore, according to Álvarez, American "propaganda" and "el Yankismo" promoted federalism, a program that would move forward with support from or annexation by the United States. A myriad of competing factions converged on the regional hub of Santiago de los Caballeros. Partisans of the president, the Santanistas, often clashed with the Baecistas, followers of Báez. Powerful landowners and merchants from the Cibao, known as the Julistas, had risen against Báez on July 7, 1857. But they also vied against groups amenable to collaboration with the United States or Haiti. Álvarez feared a "Haitian party" the most because of the assistance they could rely upon from the Haitian government in the event of a conflict. By comparison the mercantile interests dominant in the "American" party based themselves in Puerto Plata and tended to focus on the guano islands of Alto Vela and Beata in the province of Azua.[27]

This complex landscape of political and economic forces created chronic instability on the island, illustrated by the fact that Santana and Báez had alternated in the presidency over a period of more than ten years prior to 1861. While many intellectuals had supported a more democratic system, symbolized by an abortive constitutional movement in the Cibao in 1858, the state had veered toward authoritarianism under both Santana and Báez. In theory, Spanish reincorporation promised to bring an end to factionalism and political polarization under the guise of a moderate brand of liberal constitutionalism.

In important ways diplomats and statesmen drove the process of bringing the Dominican Republic under Spanish control in 1861. Backed by a behind-the-scenes effort led by Álvarez, Santana spearheaded a plebiscite in March 1861 to justify Spanish rule.[28] Queen Isabel II formally accepted annexation in May, and the Cortes ratified the decision later in the year. By September 1861, at the time Malo de Molina was writing, the Dominican Republic had been ushered back into the imperial Spanish Monarchy, and Spain had extended its influence in the Americas. Regarding jurisprudence, Malo de Molina lauded the fact that "in Santo Domingo, there aren't differences in political and civil rights despite the diversity of races and social conditions." He suggested that "Antillean political legislation should disappear and that peninsular civil and criminal legislation should be applied" across the board, because Spain had accepted reincorporation with a promise to guard and respect Dominican rights.[29] The implications were important, as this program could have brought an end to Caribbean slavery.

Questions of Race, Nation, and Order

Spaniards, eager to recolonize, consistently cast Dominicans as backward and ignorant, unable to benefit or profit from the products of their fertile lands.[30] Álvarez, who served at different times as consul in Santo Domingo and Port-au-Prince, exemplified such attitudes and assessed matters of state through the prism of a racial hierarchy. He maintained that government in the hands of Black men was condemned to tyranny, although he tempered his racism with the idea that those of mixed ancestry might one day enter the pantheon of civilized peoples.[31] Spain had not extended full diplomatic recognition to Haiti, and Álvarez argued that France should have reconquered its former colony decades earlier.[32] Others, like Malo de Molina, posited the logic that racial mixing had impeded the development of the state, particularly on the island of Hispaniola.[33] In addition, fear of the "gente de color" permeated Spain's military culture. When Coronel Francisco Fort, a hero

Order, Progress, Civilization

of the Spanish-Moroccan War and leader of the Catalan volunteers, arrived in Puerto Plata in 1860, he noted that he had been received with proper courtesy. But he immediately fired off a letter to Captain General Serrano in Cuba expressing serious reservations: "There are incendiary proclamations circulating that are prejudicing the people of color against Spain."[34] Racial and social divisions haunted Spanish officials as they debated the administration and economic development of their former New World colony.

On May 22 and 23, 1861, less than a week after the queen had formalized the annexation of the Dominican Republic by Spain's monarchy, *La Discusión* ran back-to-back cover stories on Morocco and Santo Domingo, respectively. Juan de Dios Mora penned the first editorial, in which he subsumed the work of empire under the umbrella of Comtian positivism and science. Reminiscent of Giuseppe Mazzini in formulating natural divisions between the great European nation-states, he insisted that natural laws, rather than peoples and nationalities, determined history. He declared, "The rational laws of history remain immobile and fixed like the polar star."[35] In line with Mazzini's thinking, he maintained that each nation had its own mission and played a unique role in upholding the equilibrium demanded by providence and history. Of course, certain nation-states that had moved forward on the path from the theological age toward modern civilization bore a greater burden than others in propagating their values to inferior peoples. Therefore, he called for a pan-European imperial presence in North Africa. Castelar drew on the same themes in his explication of the Spanish-Moroccan War. While Africans remained "enslaved by their own ignorance," the Latin and Germanic races had to serve as beacons of liberty and progress in the march of civilization across the Mediterranean.[36] Justified by references to history and to French successes in Algeria, Mora criticized the tepid imperial policies of the government and pointed to the necessity of establishing a permanent Spanish stronghold in the area between Tangier and Tetuán and beyond.[37]

The following day *La Discusión*'s Victoriano Martínez Muller entered into the debate over the Dominican Republic with a cover story titled "The Question of Santo Domingo."[38] Martínez Muller believed that Dominican president Santana, in many ways a quintessential nineteenth-century caudillo, had been at the forefront of the movement for annexation to Spain. Yet Álvarez, the Spanish consul in Santo Domingo, arguably had played a much more important role as a protagonist in the unfolding events. In close contact with Cuban authorities, he had portrayed Santana as a sympathetic figure to superiors in Madrid and repeatedly asserted that Dominicans had retained their historic loyalties to the *madre patria*. He was so successful that British and French diplomats agreed with him in their private assessments of the situation, emphasizing the supposed fact that the majority of Dominicans had "remained Spanish."[39] Furthermore, consuls such as Álvarez intimated that the Dominican people supported annexation "without regard to race."[40] Although Martínez Muller concurred that "the reincorporation of Santo Domingo [was] a fortunate event for Spain," he expressed strong reservations about the government's actions.[41] First, he contested the language of Santana's proclamation relinquishing sovereignty to Queen Isabel II as anachronistic. Martínez Muller objected that the Spanish people, not the monarch, remained sovereign (even though this was in fact contradicted by the Constitution of 1845, which he did not mention). Significantly, he noted that the process of annexation should have been sanctioned by the will of the people through a referendum.[42] And with the legalities still to be ironed out, Martínez Muller wondered whether the Dominican Republic would be considered a province or a colony. Even if constitutional liberties were offered to Santo Domingo, he proceeded to explain, the same guarantees likely would not be extended to Cuba. For Martínez Muller, this was proof of the hypocrisy of Spanish overseas policies. If the claim was made that Cuba would be lost if given new rights, it then followed that Spain was ruling through oppression. As an ardent liberal Martínez Muller disavowed such cynical views

Order, Progress, Civilization

and advocated constitutional governance for all of the over-seas territories, regardless of the consequences. Yet his stance failed to address the most salient difference between the two island states—the status of slavery. Although legalized enslave-ment had been abolished in Santo Domingo in 1822, it thrived in Cuba and (to a lesser extent) in Puerto Rico. Martínez Muller did not touch on the subject, but many articles from the time treated slavery in the context of Cuban affairs and the bur-geoning antislavery movement in peninsular Spain, separate from the question of Dominican annexation.[43] Other writers highlighted the importance of special laws as palliatives to be crafted for each of the overseas territories.[44]

Race underpinned events on the island of Hispaniola in other ways. Both Santana and Álvarez consistently hit on racial themes in private letters and in public pronouncements. They insisted that they were working to uphold order and progress because of the imminent threat from the west—Haitian barbarism. In diplomatic correspondence prior to annexation Santana adroitly expressed concern over an incident in which rebels "seduced" the discontented and began to "Haitianize this part of the island."[45] Álvarez wrote of his frustrations as Haiti con-tinued to have a presence in the contested borderland between the two states. He worried that southern areas like Las Matas, San Juan, and Neyba, with economies based in part on live-stock, had seen increasing trade with Haiti rather than with Dominican regions like Azua. Álvarez felt that the strength of these commercial ties provided propaganda value for a Hai-tian regime with revanchist tendencies. In his view this also "served to agitate the terrible question of race," as Haitians slowly and deliberately prepared the ground for an invasion of the east.[46] Álvarez had suggested that Santana would per-severe in his military campaigns against Haiti "to maintain order and the consolidation of the Dominican Nationality."[47] Akin to Hegel's Orientalism, their conception of the Domini-can state, with strong Hispanic roots, was juxtaposed against a racial other in the form of a renegade regime unfettered by

Western values. Santana pointed to the successful containment of ongoing skirmishes with Haiti, sustained since independence from Haiti in 1844, as evidence of "the valor that typifies the noble Spanish race." General Antonio Abad Alfau said that Santana, in his role as the nation's liberator, "had salvaged order this time, just as in others he had saved our independence."[48] Santana concluded that resolving the conflict would usher in "a new era of progress" for the country, perhaps presaging annexation.[49]

Sporadic negotiations between the two island nations never bore fruit. Justifying his claims based on an armistice agreement that had been mediated by the British and French in 1859, Álvarez pressed for an indemnity of 400,000 *pesos fuertes* for expenses related to the mobilization of troops at the border and demanded the return of prisoners held by the rebel Domingo Ramírez in Haiti.[50] He suggested that the British might again get involved, although diplomats later conceded that foreign secretary Lord John Russell remained quite indifferent to events in the Dominican Republic.[51] Alfau, drawing on racialized tropes, warned that the Haitians had "seduced" various officials and generals of the Dominican army, "individuals that all pertain to the colored race" who proclaim the indivisibility of the island's territory. He openly worried about "the horrors of a Caste war."[52]

Between August and October 1860, diplomats and politicians laid the groundwork for a legal path toward incorporation with Spain. Álvarez held meetings with Santana and all of the key officials in his regime, including the vice president and the president of the Senate. He warned Santana that Spain did not want to see a military dictatorship established and pushed him in the direction of constitutionalism.[53] Geopolitical concerns certainly shaped the discussions. Just as Britain looked to check Spanish territorial aggrandizement in North Africa, the United States appeared poised to become the dominant power in the Caribbean and Central America. American newspapers denounced Spanish "designs" to conquer the Dominican Republic, a tactic that supposedly had been relegated to the dustbin of

Order, Progress, Civilization

history.[54] Álvarez responded to the contrary, insisting that the invasive Anglo-Saxon race actually had a "vast plan," hanging like the sword of Damocles, to seize Spain's former territory.[55]

The United States employed a variety of strategies, from appropriating sources of guano to spreading false rumors about enslavement in the Dominican capital, to undermine a renewed Spanish presence in the Caribbean. Tassara suggested that the United States might even provoke a conflict through a commercial dispute, as there is a "tendency among many of these politicians to look for a diversion through a foreign war."[56] U.S. agent Jonathan Elliot, known for his erratic and scandalous behavior, was accused of "inciting the blacks to rebel saying that the Government has encouraged White immigration in order to make them slaves." Santana immediately wrote to Washington asking that Elliot be removed from his post. Álvarez insisted that such declarations, similar to other stories circulating across the island, had no tangible effects on "the blacks and the other colored races," although he noted that they "could produce questions of race."[57] Despite such prescient asides, Spanish officials more often than not deliberately elided the "question of race" as they pursued their policies in the Americas. The facile denigration of non-Europeans, accompanied by a dismissal of their historical agency, allowed Spaniards such as Álvarez to casually ignore the implicit association between the Spanish government and the institution of slavery.[58]

Just as the consul Blanco del Valle pursued risky diplomatic strategies in North Africa, Álvarez pushed the envelope in Santo Domingo. He consistently brushed aside the cautionary language of Calderón Collantes, who wanted to "slowly prepare" for annexation, and made dramatic appeals for metropolitan intervention.[59] In September Álvarez wrote from the Dominican Republic that he was "convinced that only the protection of Spain can save the country."[60] Santana echoed these claims, bluntly stating that Spain had to rescue "the country from the growing intrigue and propaganda of the Americans and Haitians."[61] By the middle of October, annexation looked to be a fait accompli. One Spanish diplomat warned against continued Haitian depredations that were bringing the Dominican Republic closer to ruin, because the country "was going to be a prisoner to a race that neither speaks our language nor professes any religion."[62] To combat this eventuality, he encouraged Spain to establish a strong military presence in Santo Domingo, to preserve individual liberties, and to uphold the abolition of slavery.

A delegation from Santo Domingo arrived in Havana, Cuba on October 29 to discuss annexation and whether protectorate status should be provided under the Spanish Monarchy. Debates over whether to consider the Dominican Republic a province of Spain or a protectorate glossed over contested issues of race, national identity, and cultural hybridity. Álvarez clearly recommended annexation, an easier option in his opinion, taking into account religious, economic, and political matters while largely eliding race. He realized the Dominicans needed a new archbishop, but in terms of economics, he concluded that they were in good standing without any significant foreign debt.[63] Álvarez wrote in private correspondence that despite that fact that Santana was quite old, he was a "man of action" and was popular. He was strong enough to govern and maintain domestic order with Spain's help.[64] The peninsular press drew on similar themes, and one article asserted, "Every day enthusiasm grows among Dominicans for annexation to Spain."[65]

Like Calderón Collantes, Captain General Serrano had been proceeding with caution, and he did not issue a formal resolution on the matter. In diplomatic assessments from 1860 Spanish officials opined that France would not oppose the move and that England "would be limited to manifesting its discontent as in the War of Africa." They understood that the United States, preoccupied with its own affairs and with the question of slavery, would not be able to play a significant role. Some even predicted that the election of Lincoln would "have fatal consequences for the Union." Coupled with the extreme opinions of the fire-eaters, epitomized by those who vocally espoused

Order, Progress, Civilization

secession, actual violence likely would be unleashed, as armaments and munitions had been stockpiled in South Carolina.[66] Fortunately for Spain, the resulting war would leave the United States unable to pay much attention to the politics of neighboring states in the Americas.

Gabriel Tassara, Spain's consul in Washington, closely monitored events in North America, confirming that most Americans believed a renewed Spanish presence on Hispaniola was inevitable. He analyzed the situation as a partisan of realpolitik, convinced that Britain would like to see the United States annex the Dominican Republic, whereas France wanted to establish hegemony over the entire island itself. Dominicans even captured a French diplomat who had been sent to the island to foment dissent with pamphlets describing Santana as treasonous and tying Spain to a history of slavery.[67] But overall, Tassara opined, Britain and France were interested most in maintaining "a general equilibrium in America."[68] Both Álvarez and Tassara, Spanish consuls in the Americas, presented distorted reports to Spanish Foreign Ministry officials. Each man held President Lincoln in low esteem—a man lacking energy and character, Álvarez noted. He doubted that northerners would fight to liberate Black southerners in a protracted conflict.[69] Tassara disparaged the "negrophiles of the North" and expressed concern over a possible American intervention in the Gulf of Mexico.[70] While all of these claims proved to be false, they created a sense of urgency around matters in the Caribbean that put pressure on Spanish political and military officials to act.

On the other hand, in a December 1860 note to Captain General Serrano in Cuba, Prime Minister O'Donnell argued for a delay in plans to seize the Dominican Republic. Although key figures such as Álvarez were pushing for annexation, O'Donnell plainly "did not believe" that the moment had arrived for the Dominicans to "return and form part of the Spanish nationality." In other words, the circumstances were not propitious to launch such an ambitious and serious action. While he felt that Santo Domingo was a "precious pearl" and he wanted "the three islands [Cuba, Puerto Rico, Santo Domingo] to form, effec-tively, an Empire of inestimable worth," he was not convinced that support for annexation was unanimous. He doubted San-tana's claims to the contrary, reminding Serrano that there were parties opposed to the president who could rise up and undermine the entire venture. Even Santana admitted to Ser-rano that there was a strong Haitian faction along the bor-der region where few were in favor of Spanish control.[71] Spain was not quite strong enough to overcome these kinds of struc-tural disadvantages. In addition, the United States continued to exercise a great deal of influence in the region. Understand-ing the resonance of the Monroe Doctrine, O'Donnell worried about filibusters and offered a subsidy of a half a million *reales* to dislodge any North American who unlawfully took Domini-can territory. With the prospect of a Haitian invasion looming as well, O'Donnell authorized the same amount to suppress any hostilities on the border. Yet he did waver on immediate annexation if it constituted "a peremptory necessity" and if it would appear completely spontaneous. The failed attempt to invade Mexico in 1829 and "the bad fortune of the expedi-tion of [Brigadier Isidro] Barradas" certainly weighed heavily on his mind. Ultimately Spain's "noble enterprise," he urged, should be put off for at least a year. Preparing the way forward, albeit in secret, he wrote that Serrano should open an account for advances that his office could use to support the Domini-can government. It was all a question of timing, and O'Donnell wanted to wait for the United States to fracture along regional lines. Once divided into two opposing camps, one would be a natural ally of Spain.[72]

Despite the prime minister's private stance, President San-tana met with all of the nation's top officials in the town of Los Llanos, proclaiming his desire to bring the country under the fold of their former patrons. He looked to ensure a smooth transition to Spanish rule. Diplomatic cables helped, as some said in private that "the actual state of the Republic is one of the most complete tranquility. . . . The name of General San-

Order, Progress, Civilization

tana . . . is a true guarantee of security for the conservation of order."[73] But the reincorporation of the Dominican Republic began as his supporters and detractors claimed the mantle of liberty. Santana praised the Spanish nation, the heirs of Christopher Columbus and Isabel I, that "gives us the civil liberty that its people enjoy [and] guarantees us natural liberty."[74] Assuring the nation of property rights, he ended with *vivas* to Isabel II, the Catholic religion, the Dominican people, and Spain. On March 18, 1861, notables throughout the Dominican Republic signed petitions on behalf of dozens of municipalities pledging adherence to the Spanish state. Proponents felt that the celebrations hearkened back to Dominican independence from Haiti in 1844, when the mantra "Dios, Patria, y Libertad" resonated around the country.[75] One peninsular newspaper speciously announced the "spontaneous annexation" of the Dominican Republic, claiming that Spain's government had not been involved in any meaningful way.[76] Other journalists reported that Spanish troops were embraced with enthusiasm in all parts of the country.[77] Less than a month later, in a proclamation issued from the rebel stronghold of Las Caobas, on the Haitian frontier, José María Cabral echoed Santana's original statement. But he concluded with a eulogy to Dominican independence rather than to the *patria* of Spain and accused Santana of betrayal for "selling" the country to its former colonial ruler.[78]

Rebels published political manifestos airing their grievances, and an armed uprising appeared imminent. According to one broadside from early 1861 the former independence leader Francisco Sánchez "conspired against the independence of our Country with the Haitians to invade Dominican territory. . . . We know that General Sánchez is in contact with [Haitian] General Geffrard . . . and that he is in communication with Domingo Ramírez, who will be at the Dominican border in a few days. It has been said that a revolution will break out in the next month."[79] Subsequently there was serious unrest in Moca, a town in the Cibao, and in Las Matas, close to the Haitian border.[80] In June the official press reported that correspondence and papers of the "traitor" Ramírez had been discovered, allowing the government to admonish rebel complicity with Haiti.[81] Álvarez had damning evidence that linked Ramírez with General Valentín Alcántara, a key Haitian military figure, proving to the Spanish that Geffrard's government had sent money, arms, and other supplies to fuel the uprising.[82] Insurgent successes were few, and Santana proudly pointed to the town of El Cercado, its residents having risen up to defeat rebels without the support of Dominican or peninsular troops.[83] Sánchez was captured and killed in the invasion that took place in June, and government troops quickly suppressed Cabral's abortive uprising by the fall of 1861.[84] Other Dominican liberals, like Ulises Espaillat, chose to stay out of the fray, initially supporting annexation. He took a more pragmatic point of view early on but later joined forces with armed insurgents.[85]

Agitation on the Haitian border proved to be a useful foil in conversations with U.S. officials. Just ten days before the first shots were fired at Fort Sumter, South Carolina, Secretary of State William Seward condemned Spanish intervention for having violated U.S. policy and undermining the Dominican government. Apparently, President Lincoln could not believe that these "proceedings" had been authorized by Madrid, and he threatened armed intervention in response.[86] Two days later Tassara reassured the U.S. government, insisting that the menace of a Haitian invasion had precipitated a call from the Dominican Republic to Cuba for help. Therefore, forces were sent to protect Spanish subjects on the island.[87] The Americans tentatively found this to be "acceptable." Shortly thereafter they questioned "whether Spain accepts or expects to accept the dominion in San Domingo offered to her by the revolutionists who have seized upon it in her name and for her benefit."[88] By the summer the United States had viewed Spanish actions as "prejudicial to the interests" of their country.[89] The *New York Times* spoke out strongly against Spanish involvement, as reports detailed men of color, fighting for their personal and political

Order, Progress, Civilization

liberty, in danger of being "exterminated in mass" by occupying forces.[90] Amid civil war, cabinet-level officials in Washington continued to fret about Dominican politics.

At the same time, Spanish policymakers discussed which laws would be applied in the Dominican Republic. The British wanted concrete assurance from Spain that the institution of slavery would not be revived:

> Her Majesty's Government is fully convinced that the Government of Spain is far too generous to give their Sanction to so cruel a measure as the restoration to Slavery of a number of persons who are in the actual enjoyment of Freedom; but in order that no doubt may remain on a subject of such importance, I have been instructed by Lord John Russell to enquire of the Spanish Government whether all persons residing in the Territory of the Dominican Republick, at the time of its annexation to Spain, will be secured by Law in the possession of the Freedom which they actually enjoy, whether they were formerly Slaves or were born Free.[91]

Asked for advice on jurisprudence by the captain general of Cuba, Malo de Molina traveled to Santo Domingo and wrote an extended piece on the subject, as discussed in the beginning of the chapter. He found that all Dominicans historically had enjoyed the same civil rights, regardless of race, and therefore should be entitled to the legislation in effect across the peninsula.[92] By October peninsular legal codes had replaced the modified French imperial laws that had been in effect since the 1840s.

The end of 1861 represented a high-water mark for Spanish imperial ambitions, as Spain occupied portions of northern Morocco, forces had been sent to reinforce the British and French positions in Veracruz, and Dominican annexation had proceeded according to script. Yet their overseas ventures quickly collapsed from Mexico to Annam, and atrocities had tarnished a growing conflict in the Dominican Republic by 1863. How did a seemingly peaceful annexation in the name of liberty and equality so quickly devolve into scenes reminiscent of French attempts to put down Haitian rebels in 1802? While the arch-bishop of Santo Domingo blamed libertine behavior and the seductive capacity of rebellion, Dominican advocates of independence decried Spanish rule that had been characterized by barbarity and tyranny instead of adherence to the principle of liberty.[93] Rather than forge alliances with political and social groups across the different regions of the republic, Spain relied on the military to eliminate resistance. The 1863 Acta de Independencia, signed by dozens of Dominican statesmen, singled out two particular generals—Manuel Buceta and Juan López del Campillo—for opprobrium.[94] Even internal government correspondence recognized that the "revolution" was due in large part to the "public hatred" provoked by Buceta's actions.[95] Significantly, Buceta had been the military governor of the key Spanish fortress in Melilla prior to receiving a commission in the Dominican Republic (see chapter 1). In sum, brutalities committed during pacification campaigns, along with rumors that continually swept across the island claiming that Spain would reinstate slavery, undermined Spain's stated commitment to liberal, representative government.

FIVE

Anatomy of an Uprising

Race War and Dominican Independence

In many ways Madrid governed its former territory as a colony run by the military. O'Donnell organized the captaincy general of Santo Domingo into six military districts—Santo Domingo, Santiago de los Caballeros, El Seibo, Concepción de la Vega, Azua, and Samaná.[1] Manuel Buceta had been commissioned by the queen on October 5, 1861, to serve in Samaná at an annual salary of 4,500 *pesos*, with his command enlarged to include the entire Cibao by 1863. Under this type of rule President Santana quickly tendered his resignation as captain general and retired in 1862, frustrated with his declining influence within the government.[2] Yet diplomats apprehensively reported about rival powers' claims that Spain had not deployed enough resources to Dominican port cities. Even though generals ruled the island, critics believed the Spanish were preoccupied with Mexico and could not be counted on to dispatch any more ships or soldiers to Hispaniola.[3]

Border issues and racial strife continued to bedevil policymakers as well. In March 1862 Álvarez petitioned the Haitian government to withdraw its troops from frontier regions in recognition of the 1777 Treaty of Aranjuez between France and Spain.[4] He even attended a parliamentary session in the hope that Spanish protests against Haiti's border incursions and occupation would be discussed. Yet disturbances continued, and tales of foreign support helped to sustain anti-Spanish sentiment in the frontier zone. Diplomats reported hearing a story of the imminent arrival in Monte Cristi of twelve American steamships loaded with troops and supplies that would ostensibly be cementing an alliance with both the United States and Haiti against Spain.[5] The Spanish consul in Port-au-Prince, Haiti, Álvarez, privately lamented the fact that Black men and women populated the western half of the island, expressing a torrent of extreme prejudice in his letters sent back to Madrid. Conceding that Haitian president Fabre Nicolas Geffrard, a biracial statesman, was "the most reasonable and discreet of all the politicians in Haiti," he nonetheless worried about the racial dynamic of the postcolonial state.[6] Álvarez speculated that because the "civilized" people of color were relatively few in number, they could easily become victims of exterminating masses of savages on the island in the event of a revolt that could bring a "ferocious black" leader into power.[7] He espoused a kind of Spanish liberal racism: "The memories and savage instincts of Africa constitute the base of this nationality, which Geffrard, inclined toward civilization, does not dare to attack openly."[8]

Racial tensions insidiously divided the majority mixed-race population from peninsular Spaniards on the eastern side of Hispaniola. Many Dominican military officers faced relegation and were denied use of Spanish uniforms in the reserves.[9] Soldiers shipped in, including some who had fought in the Spanish-Moroccan War, degraded their fellow Black and biracial enlisted men, and even generals like Gregorio de Lora faced backlash for the color of their skin. Other problems plagued the new Spanish administration as well. Troops requisitioned animals that served as the most important means of transporting goods locally, especially in economically significant regions like the Cibao. The new archbishop, Bienvenido Monzón y Martín, attempted to root out immorality and ensure that formal Catholic practices would take the place of tradition and informal arrangements. Arriving in 1862, he brought a group of like-minded peninsular clerics who shared his goal of reinvigorating the country's traditional Catholic values. He quickly saw that "the institution of the family . . . was being degraded and

Anatomy of an Uprising

illegitimized by the remnants of the so-called civil marriage of the French code."[10] Cohabitation was widespread, and he railed against heresy. Monzón argued that order, progress, and civilization would not be possible without obedience, respect for the church, and the sanctity of marriage. Otherwise, libertinism and sin would run rampant. Taken together these shortsighted policies had the effect of alienating the very people the new administration supposedly served, including Dominican-born priests; a lasting armed insurrection, the subject of this chapter, began in February 1863.

Yet commentators in Washington DC continued to downplay the potential for violence and upheaval in the Dominican Republic. One newspaper editorial stated that "in the town of Seybo [El Seibo], which is in the northeastern part of the island, a few persons got up a *pronunciamiento*, and cried '*Viva la independencia*,' whereupon troops were sent to that district from the city of St. Domingo, and, as a matter of precaution, reinforcements are going from Havana." The author went on to claim, "The parties who have kicked up that row in Seybo are said to be friends and partisans of ex-President Baez, and I will bet a Dutch cheese that the whole affair ends in smoke."[11] Stationed in the American capital, Tassara likewise noted in March, 1863, "The insurrection in Santo Domingo is concluded."[12] Other correspondence showed signs of serious concern within Spanish diplomatic circles. Stationed in Port-au-Prince, Álvarez revealed that his government had asked Haitian counterparts to issue a declaration in their official gazette, *Le Moniteur*, calling on the public to reject the Dominican rebels.[13] By May, however, tensions had subsided enough that Captain General Felipe Rivero issued a decree acknowledging the extent of the violence that had befallen the countryside. With the exemplary punishment of eleven people sentenced to death as well as nineteen additional "fugitives" executed, he essentially announced the turmoil had come to an end.[14] Plus, he lifted the state of emergency in effect since February due to the return of "public tranquility" and the continued "loyalty and patriotism" of the people.[15]

In a separate decree from the same day Rivero announced the imminent dissolution of the military commission established on February 28 to investigate and report on the abortive revolt. Finally, the Overseas Ministry announced a general amnesty on May 27.[16]

In the northern coastal city of Puerto Plata, with a vibrant merchant population that included Dutch and German residents, a more damaging uprising took place at the end of August that exposed the deep fissures within Dominican society and served as a microcosm of what became known as the War of Restoration. A high-ranking officer in the military as well as a local curate had been encouraging dissent, much of which built upon existing tensions that were exacerbated by the Spanish military presence. The city had burned in July with dozens of structures seriously damaged, a foreshadowing of the violence to come. Buceta and López del Campillo took the lead in counterinsurgency operations in the countryside, while General Juan Suero guarded the military fortifications in the port city.[17] Although one of many rebel actions, this particular episode led to a military tribunal and the collection of evidence and oral testimony by Spanish authorities, who accused conspirators of treason. The scripted questions and responses reveal a carefully orchestrated plan to outmaneuver the Spanish garrison and ultimately declare independence.

To begin, the peninsular district attorney Andrés Prats, a member of the *ayuntamiento*, swore to tell the truth about the events to the hastily formed military commission. He immediately implicated General Lora, who had been one of the most important leaders charged with the city's defense, as a major figure in the "revolution."[18] Suero castigated the "traitorous" General Lora as well as others under his command on the days of August 26 and 27. As enemy troops were advancing, Lora had ordered the men to refrain from firing and instead shouted, "We are Dominicans."[19] All of the accused were asked the exact same questions: "What were the rebels saying, and what was the object of the revolution?" A twenty-five-year-old witness succinctly recounted, "I didn't hear anything but vivas to the Dominican Republic whose reestablishment should be without a doubt the object of the revolution." He stated that he had nothing else to say and that he had told the truth.[20] The script was repeated over and over by those caught up in the tribunal's proceedings, and few improvised or departed from the same rote questions and answers. A captain emphasized that he had heard "'long live the Dominican flag, long live the Dominican Republic' and . . . that the object of the revolution was to reestablish the republic." He maintained that he had told the truth "on his word of honor."[21] All subsequent testimony essentially repeated these claims.

The tribunal record demonstrates how racial conflict and fear drove the unrest in what was described as a tight-knit community. Throughout the procedures, many of those interrogated implicated others whom they knew personally, and dozens were held and questioned. According to witnesses three to five thousand rebels had fought, some armed with rifles and blunderbusses, many with only five shots each, eagerly awaiting munitions from Santiago, the ostensible rebel capital. Within their ranks, however, only a thousand or so were armed with guns, the rest with machetes. In spite of the paucity of arms they had significant rations, including fruits and meat.[22] In Los Mameyes, an area of Puerto Plata, one accused man, signing his statement with a cross, admitted that he had been with a group of women who had been taken prisoner after they were discovered killing a pig alongside suspected rebels.[23] While most of the accused were not identified clearly by race, the commission singled out one conspirator, Mamado Samí, as a Black man well-known throughout the community.[24] Rafael Leandro García elaborated, offering a more nuanced picture of racial division and the fear stoked by persistent rumor: "People spoke out against the whites and the Spanish, making the ignorant believe that they were going to brand and enslave them, making them work day and night, putting iron collars on them . . . with other fairy tales of this type to infuriate them and make them fight until the death." This answer was repeated verbatim in subsequent responses, such as in the testimony of Pedro María Leandro García, likely Rafael's relative. It appears that those recording, those testifying, or both drew upon a common template and were not extemporizing.[25] Significantly, rumors of enslavement and a return to brutal plantation labor undoubtedly fanned the flames of this rebellion against Spanish forces.

Speculation and palpable fear over reenslavement had such a significant impact on Dominicans that Archbishop Monzón felt compelled to respond. His pastoral letter from March 1863, composed amid the growing rebellion, forcefully denied that Spaniards planned to reinstate the institution of slavery. He urged the faithful to hate the high crime of treason but not to hate "your brothers" who had been deceived by the insurgents. Speaking directly to his "beloved Dominicans," Monzón beseeched them to understand that "neither their enlightened Government, the dignified Captain General of the Island, their Archbishop, nor any Spaniards want to enslave you, nor degrade you, exploit you nor dominate you with injustice and tyranny, as some ill-intentioned men maliciously and falsely have claimed." They simply wanted to bring order, integrity, and justice to the towns and countryside of the island so that peace and prosperity would reign, allowing all to enjoy the fruits of their labor. Then, all Dominicans would recognize the queen as their mother and Spain as their beloved *patria* once again.[26]

The Cibao Insurgency

The initial unrest spread from the border with Haiti into the heart of the Cibao, and Buceta appeared to spark an uptick in the violence from the start. With lessons learned from his defeat in Melilla, he went on the offensive instead of relying on defensive measures to stave off a simmering insurgency (see chapter 1). In mid-August, he dismissed the "criminals" and "bandits" operating on the Dominican frontier who, he claimed, dedicated themselves to the revolution because they realized the Spanish government would not permit their activities to

Anatomy of an Uprising

scandalize "civilized towns." He accused the Haitians of protecting these "evildoers" and argued "the violation of territories is a legal cause of war." He warned that the moment could arise in which the Spanish "would have to employ force to reach their desired result [the maintenance of order]."[27] Buceta was deployed to Dajabón, a town on the border between the two states, to stem guerrilla activity. He soon heard that the garrison of Guayubín, not far to the east, had been attacked by "an armed horde," and he immediately looked to engage the insurgents. Realizing Guayubín had been "burned and taken," he headed to Santiago, farther to the east in the central northern region he commanded. In Navarrete his small contingent of cavalry was dispersed. According to Spanish sources Buceta had to flee on foot into the forest, where he hid for three days "with one soldier and a corporal." Three battalions set off to avenge the mounting losses and to find Buceta. On the way they also met resistance, and a veteran commander from the Spanish-Moroccan War was killed along with several others. Many Spanish troops were wounded. The companies traveled through Navarrete on their way to Santiago, and Buceta, "hearing the bugle played, marched out of the forest where he had been hiding." Although he survived, important towns like Moca continued to fall to the rebels.[28]

American news disparaged Spain's efforts to hold the Dominican Republic and offered firsthand stories of the violence and upheaval. One letter to an editor, published in the *New York Herald*, contained a divergent account of Buceta's exploits, claiming an elderly Black man had saved his life. The writer explained:

> In the middle of August a general and just indignation against the Spanish government arose to the point of outbreak. In the small towns of Guayubia [sic] and Savanette [sic] an open revolution broke out against the Spanish authorities, and was so far successful that the Dominican colors were hoisted and the Spanish garrison expelled from there, who retired partly to Hayti . . . and partly to Santiago de los Caballeros, the cap-

ital of the province of Cibao. Different battles were fought on the western frontier, which resulted all more or less in a complete victory of the revolutionary arms. The commander of the Spanish forces, Brigadier General Buceta, a most tyrannical and cowardly hearted man, was only saved from the Dominicans by an old negro, who, although a native of the island, was noble enough to hide him during three days, and to conduct him back to Santiago by hidden paths.[29]

A third version of the story asserted that "General Buceta, after seeing several of his companions shot down at his side, was enabled to escape to Santiago de los Caballeros, arriving there with only a few orderlies of his old command. It is said that he blackened his face and passed for a negro."[30] While significant details varied between the different reports, the picture of Buceta remained the same. He faced withering criticism in most foreign news outlets that exposed the ramifications of his brutal and callous counterinsurgency campaign.

Guerrillas continued to operate in the countryside, and they pushed into the city of Puerto Plata. According to documents, by eleven in the morning on August 21, Buceta's forces had been defeated and his cavalry scattered. Within three days Captain General Felipe Rivero decreed that the island was in a "state of exception." Due to the "siege" faced by the authorities, he put Santo Domingo under military rule, with Santiago de los Caballeros to have a special military commission charged with rooting out the causes of "conspiracy, disloyalty, and rebellion against the state."[31] One mason described families marching out of Puerto Plata en masse with news of rebels approaching on August 26.[32] A forty-four-year-old cobbler explained that he was given a rifle at five in the afternoon. After hearing the rebels enter the town at dawn on August 27, he was directed to the fort by General Suero. There, the mayor ordered residents to work on the fortifications in advance of the assault. Sailors, day laborers, and artisans, ranging in age from their early twenties to early fifties, worked as carpenters, in storehouses, and

Anatomy of an Uprising

on one of the fort's wells.[33] Others had slightly different experiences. With a lengthy explanation a local man recalled how General Suero had called all men to present themselves at three in the afternoon on August 25. He then fled the city the following day, returning only after the fighting had ceased days later.[34]

The interrogations reveal a complex network of conspiratorial generals, such as Lora and Benito Martínez, who allied with liberal dissidents headquartered in Santiago de los Caballeros, such as Benigno Filomeno de Rojas. One man testified that Manuel Chivo led the rebel troops from Moca, José Salcedo headed the government that had been established in Santiago, and Baldomero Regalado lent weapons, including a machete, to rebels like the accused Federico Scheffenberg, one of the signers of the 1863 declaration of independence.[35] The latter witness noted that two emissaries had been sent to Haiti to procure arms. Scheffenberg claimed the provisional government had not only declared independence but sent a letter to the queen, purporting to represent the will of the people, which had not been consulted in the process of annexation.[36] The letter insisted that Santana had deceived her and the Spanish Monarchy as a whole. Another man said he had overheard the rebels say that if they took Puerto Plata, they would have a republic composed of fourteen thousand men.[37]

Rebels managed to circulate and publish the text of their letter addressed to Queen Isabel II demanding liberal reform, religious tolerance, and independence from Spain. Rojas, the author and one of the key independence leaders, had strong words for Buceta: "Fit as he might be to be Governor of the penal settlement at Samaná, he was quite unfit to direct the destinies of what had been one of the most advanced provinces of the Dominican Republic." Rojas put forward a vision of an independent, rather than colonial, government: "The forty years of civil and political liberty, the toleration in religious matter which the people enjoyed under the republican government, together with numberless other advantages, not the least of which was a national representation and a participation in public matters, an indispensable right in a democracy, could not be well reconciled with the monarchical system, and worse still with the Colonial."[38] Likewise, the declaration of independence, signed on September 14 in Santiago de los Caballeros, emphasized natural rights and, in an attempt to coopt the vocabulary of Spanish history, the "reconquest" of liberty.[39] The proannexationist periodical *La Razón*, on the other hand, portrayed the insurgent liberals as criminals and as enemies of order. One writer decried the guerrilla rebels who upheld rights and freedom as they perpetrated crimes and massacres, destroying the Cibao and leaving few resources for the population to survive on. Ultimately, they had abused words and language itself, the editors insisted, because all Dominicans had enjoyed the same rights as *peninsulares* under the Spanish Monarchy.[40]

Severe reprisals faced those convicted by the Spanish, as the tribunal gathered evidence to prosecute rebels for betraying Spain. By the end of the month the inquiry got underway, and Spanish officials attempted to determine the causes of the violence. To avoid punishment, the accused crafted a straightforward response repeated throughout the proceedings: they claimed to have been sick on the day of the uprising. When asked where he had been on the days of August 26–28, forty-three-year-old Juan Antonio del Rosario stated that he had been sick at home. Prodded to name people who could corroborate his testimony, he insisted that all of the residents of San Marcos, his hometown, would verify his whereabouts, but those in Puerto Plata probably could not.[41] While the fates of all the individuals questioned are not always laid out clearly in the documents, with some later pardoned and others freed by rebel bands in the fog of war, the resistance grew after August and continued to gain strength over the next year.[42]

Press coverage highlighted the racial dimensions of the fighting in Puerto Plata on August 27. One writer decried the tactics of General Suero, who, with reinforcements arriving from Cuba and Puerto Rico, staved off an attack of eight hundred men: "The Spaniards behaved as in a foreign conquered town, pillaging and

Anatomy of an Uprising

even murdering innocent colored people. Among the killed—we ought to say butchered—were many foreigners." Accordingly, the Spanish "treated every one as an enemy," while the insurgents behaved in an "honorable" fashion. When the besieged Suero reached Santiago, the city was burning and lacked supplies due to the fact that Buceta had "entirely neglected to provision the fort." Approximately four thousand Spanish troops marched back to Puerto Plata under extreme conditions, but no more than three thousand made it, having been harassed the entire way by Dominican guerrilla fighters. Upon their return they essentially were confined to the city limits. Another article, originally published in the *Turks Island Standard*, presented Spanish actions in an extremely negative light, reminiscent of the Black Legend:

> If anything were wanted to complete our contempt of the course pursued by the Spanish authorities, we have it in their detestable conduct toward the colored people of Puerto Plata. . . . The worst passions of the human soul were let loose, and the cry was, blood! blood! blood! and not until two or three days had elapsed did the officers make any efforts to mitigate these cruelties. . . . the bodies of those who had been murdered were thrown into the public streets, and basely insulted after death. . . . Such is the ruthless and savage vandalism which civilized Spain has sent to St. Domingo.[43]

The author plainly emphasized the hypocrisy of the "civilized" brutalizing the so-called savages for a readership eager to condemn Spanish imperial war efforts.

Other articles reproduced a vitriolic racist view of people of color, disparaging Dominicans and caricaturing rebel soldiers. A *New York Herald* editorial contrasted the nation of Spain, which "represents progress and liberality," with "Dominicans . . . a degraded, ignorant and decaying race. . . . The white race, under the auspices of Spain, is, in my humble judgment, destined to occupy this evergreen island of the tropics, enriching and gladdening it with the triumphs of science, industry and art."[44] Under the headline "The Entire Spanish Province in a Blaze," an American writer compared the Dominican insurrection to a wildfire spreading from "its cradle" in the Cibao outward in all directions. Irregular bands of fighters were best suited for this struggle: "For a guerilla [sic] war no country is better adapted, being traversed in every portion by ranges of hills and mountains, some of which rise to the height of six thousand feet." Without taking into consideration the aspirations of liberal Spanish imperialists back home, the journalist rhetorically asked, "Is it worth [Spain's] while to conquer Sto. Domingo?" He lamented the economic situation of the country while seeming to suggest slavery as an alternative to the current system of free labor: "Never while the sun shines will the Dominicans be induced to develop the resources of their country by voluntary labor." A large-scale process of immigration from Europe would be necessary for true development and progress. Without it, the writer continued, "I am convinced it would be a useless conquest." He concluded with a disparaging note and a play on the concept of natural rights: "The real kernel of Dominican hostility to the Spaniards is their constitutional dislike to earn their bread by the sweat of their brow. . . . [The Spaniards] have no business whatever in St. Domingo. The people of that country have a 'natural and inalienable right' to go to the devil on their own road."[45]

Articles from the *New York Herald* continuously mocked the inhabitants of the Dominican Republic in derisive racist language. One journalist issued a blistering, satirical report on the dire situation: "The Spanish portion of St. Domingo is at the present writing the theatre of one of the very funniest revolutions of this age of topsy-turvy revolutions. . . . It is simply and entirely an uprising of the native Dominicans against the Spanish military officers. What is the basis of the difficulty? Of what do the Dominicans complain? you will naturally ask. That is impossible to say. Nobody knows what the fight is all about." The article made light of the fact that the Dominicans had burned Santiago to dislodge the Spanish, while the Spanish had done the same to Puerto Plata to prevent rebels from taking refuge there.[46] The writer, and the diplomat Tassara—who included the news clipping in his diplomatic file—blamed American agitators for the increasingly bloody conflict. Tassara, writing to his superiors in Madrid, agreed with the American correspondent that "foreign abolitionists of the Congo-Sumner school are trying to provoke a race war, sending arms to the black savages on the frontier with Haiti." Tassara worriedly passed on news that he had heard of an association in Boston putting together an expedition of twenty "adventurers" to support the Santo Domingo rebellion with "arms and funds."[47] Of course, Tassara adamantly denied that a war between the races was on the horizon.[48] Many Spanish diplomats believed that they had uncovered a fledgling conspiracy in the Caribbean among U.S. abolitionists such as James Redpath in Boston, Lucius Chandler, the consul in Matanzas, and Thomas Savage, the consul in Cuba. Spaniards asserted that the Americans aimed to repatriate free Black men and women to the Dominican Republic.[49]

Most foreign reporting described a complete breakdown of Spanish authority by the fall of 1863. Americans pilloried the state of affairs in the Dominican Republic, although they could not intervene because of their own civil war. One observer called it a major mistake and concluded that it was a dangerous political miscalculation to continue the fight.[50] Puerto Plata burned again in October. The consensus appeared to be that the Dominicans were "in complete possession of the whole country" with the exception of the forts of Puerto Plata, Samaná, and the city of Santo Domingo. One article painted a grim picture of the aftermath of rebellion:

> Of about ten thousand Spanish soldiers assembled in the island two months ago, scarcely seven thousand remain. . . . The Spanish part of the population is, as may be expected, in a state of the utmost consternation and alarm. We are informed that lately Captain General Rivero, accompanied by his lady, spent an entire night in prayer at the church of La

Merced. . . . The creoles, in joke, say that it was a great mistake, as the virgin of La Merced is, and always has been, the decided patroness of the Dominicans. The lady of the Captain General, together with the families of . . . many other officials, have since left for Cuba or Puerto Rico.[51]

Buceta was demoted in September and given command of the reserves.[52]

Turnover within the Spanish military took place at an alarming rate, and few successful campaigns impeded rebel actions. Carlos de Vargas took control in Santo Domingo for Rivero on October 23 after having sent a classified communiqué to Madrid asserting that pacification could not take place without reinforcements.[53] The official replacing Serrano in Cuba, General Domingo Dulce, bitterly criticized the entire venture as a campaign dominated by terror: "The people neither desire not want to be ruled by their former metropole. . . . Because the Dominican nation was not able to oppose the 1861 declaration, they protested with a savage war" sustained ever since. This "forced annexation," he intoned, must cease.[54]

Other challenges included illicit arms smuggling, as in the case of two Dominican men who purportedly procured weapons and gunpowder from Nassau, Bahamas, in late 1863. The Spanish blamed the Americans and Germans for aiding the shipment, disguised as a commercial vessel loaded with wheat headed to Cap-Haïtien through the Turks Islands. Spain increased its naval presence in the area, as its forces cruised the coast between Puerto Plata, Monte Cristi, and the Haitian border to try to intercept such smuggling operations.[55] In spite of attempts at a blockade of the entirety of the Dominican coast in October, and again in November, one reporter opined that "there is very little hope of ultimate success."[56] British officials scoffed at news of a major Spanish naval operation: "Nothing which can be regarded as an effectual Blockade of all the Ports of Santo Domingo has in fact been established by . . . Spain; that there are no more than three Spanish vessels of War at three places

Anatomy of an Uprising

immediately off the Port of Santo Domingo . . . the whole coast, and every Port is under the command of the insurgents."[57]

Spanish diplomats countered bad press with a bit of dissimulation and rosy assessments of counterinsurgency victories. One riposte, reprinted in the *London Gazette*, responded to British pronouncements: "The Blockade in question is maintained at the present moment by twenty-three vessels of war, frigates, and schooners, a number of which, besides being sufficient for the purpose, could be increased by the squadron anchored at Cuba. On the other hand, the insurrection is now limited to the province of Seybo, the coasts of which are so strictly watched that all vessels endeavouring to aid the rebels have been captured."[58] Álvarez argued that the chaos sowed by the insurgents would be their undoing: "The revolutionary Government is unable to prevent the excesses" of the various guerrilla factions, headed by men like Chivo, that "continued to rob and assassinate unarmed civilians." "If military operations were conducted with vigor," he predicted, the Cibao would no longer be engulfed in a state of anarchy, and Santiago would be back in the hands of the Spanish army. Yet he was aware that the ongoing instability could provide an opening for the Americans to intervene were their civil war to finally come to an end.[59] Internal correspondence also addressed damaging reports by positing innate differences between Spaniards and Anglo-Saxons. One unsigned letter circulated within the Overseas Ministry insisted that the character of the Spanish people remained unchanged from the reign of Ferdinand and Isabel, and a Spaniard simply didn't think like an Englishman or an American: "Passion more than reason governs a Spaniard, and love of the self is more profound than their self-interest." Accordingly, to abandon Santo Domingo then would have constituted "too grave a wound to national pride." Only when "the treasury and the patience of the madre patria have run out" would Spaniards be able to consider leaving.[60]

The foreign press covered the financial aspect of the war as well. One English-language report compared the mounting expenses in the Dominican Republic to the French outlays during the first two years of the war in Mexico: "It appears . . . that the Spanish occupation of San Domingo has already cost the Madrid government upwards of six millions of dollars, and that heavy appropriations will have to be made to meet the deficit created by the expenses of the war now being carried on there. The invasion of Mexico has cost the French government upwards of seventy millions."[61] Political and financial instability contributed to Spain's growing inability to quell the violence.

The conflict worsened as entrenched bands of guerrillas controlled the Cibao and thwarted a planned march of Spanish troops from the northern port of Monte Cristi to Santiago. Tens of thousands of casualties marred the independence struggle, and disease ravaged soldiers. In Azua occupied military zones appeared to be depopulated, as people had fled to the nearby mountains of the Cordillera Central.[62] Santana had been recalled, as it became clear that an all-out war had begun, and, with a sense of melodrama, he stated that his honor was at stake. By this time Santana had attributed the rebellion to the "policies unfortunately pursued" by the Spanish administration, including the archbishop and military officials. He had the most contempt for Buceta, "a tyrant in the full meaning of the word, who provoked those honorable inhabitants of Santiago, accustomed to liberal treatment." Buceta's crimes "had no equal in the history of Christian peoples."[63] But in the end Santana could not break into the rebel-held Cibao, either.

Insurgents likewise suffered from internal divisions as competing factions vied for control within the rebel camp. For example, President Salcedo faced his ouster after mistakenly invoking the name of Báez in an infamous speech. One newspaper overview succinctly explained the situation in 1864:

> The people of San Domingo are heroically continuing their war of independence against their Spanish oppressors. The provisional President, Gen. Salcedo, not having given satisfaction to the people, has been deposed, and Gen. [Gaspar]

Polanco has been elected, in his stead, President of the Provisional Government. The new President has issued a proclamation to the troops and manifesto to the people, dated October 15, 1864, in which he announces his determination to continue the war until the expulsion of the Spaniards. . . . [T]he Cabinet of Marshal Narváez had unanimously resolved to abandon San Domingo, first on account of the difficulty experienced in carrying out its subjugation; and secondly, because England had recognized the insurgents as belligerents. . . . The ablest statesmen of Spain begin to find out that the war in San Domingo requires greater expenses than Spain is able to bear.[64]

Polanco, accused of the subsequent murder of Salcedo, ultimately fell from power when Rojas replaced him in 1865, invoking the ideals of the 1858 constitution written in Moca.

Latin Americans proudly linked the populist independence wars against the Spanish with the contemporaneous struggles in the Caribbean. In Venezuela lead editorials pushed for American unity against the imperial aggression witnessed in the Dominican Republic, Mexico, and Peru. From Caracas, Bruno González wrote that these Spanish incursions had caused the old liberators, "Bolívar, Sucre, Santander, Piar, Cerdeño and so many others, to turn over in their graves." But of course, their spirit animated the current generation and connected them directly to the heroes of Ayacucho. González did not mince words, contrasting "the treason committed by Santana in delivering Santo Domingo to the Columbian executioners" of the Old World with "Juárez's heroic fight in Mexico." He ended with a tribute to Latin American unity and to the Monroe Doctrine: "The Americas are one in theory, in language, in customs . . . they form one nationality—the American nationality."[65] Spanish bellicosity and racial animus exhibited in the Dominican Republic and in Mexico, as will be discussed in the following chapter, had the unintended consequence of bringing Latin American nations closer together as they confronted a common enemy. Peninsular diplomats downplayed such highfalutin proclamations as nothing more than Dominican propaganda. A handwritten note in the margins of an editorial published the following week, preserved in Spain's Foreign Ministry archives, dismissed González's message: "It is evident that some Dominican émigrés are taking part in the editing of this paper."[66]

Conclusion

Even after two years of open warfare between 1863 and 1865 that paralleled the devastation in the United States, many Spaniards clung to utopian visions of progress that would herald a new age of liberty and equality in the age of empire building. Proponents did not see their ideals as mutually exclusive. José López de la Vega, composing a paean to efforts to retain the Dominican Republic, intoned without a hint or irony: "Humanitarian Spain. . . . does not want to dominate anyone by force: we do not want anyone to serve us as slaves." He inverted the slogan of Dominican independence, "God, Country, Liberty," and called instead for "God, Country and Constitutional Monarchy." He implored the "the young people of modern Spain" to rally around the throne. Drawing on the language and spirit of both Hegel and Castelar, he posed the question of whether Spanish youth would witness the "triumph of the beautiful ideal of Progress." López de la Vega countered the claim that the conflict in the Caribbean had degenerated into "a race war," as he could not accept the idea that Spain would ever be the enemy of liberty. With the Laws of the Indies, he wrote, Spain had treated those of African origin better than others had treated the Irish and Polish, who were white. Like Gándara and many likeminded Europeans, López de la Vega equated hard work, generosity, and justice with civilization. While there was a faction opposed to these European values in Hispaniola, he avowed that "the American people love Spain and want European civilization."[67]

López de la Vega's apologist manifesto, published in 1865, urged Spain not to surrender and be humiliated. What is more, he firmly maintained that theirs had not been a fight against

Anatomy of an Uprising

the Dominican people but against its bastard sons, "the ille-gitimate children of the Island and a few hundred adventur-ers, men of color from Haiti, North America, Jamaica, etc." Spain had always supported the weak against the strong, and no American people had ever risen up against the *madre patria* so long as they had been endowed with a wise and paternal-istic administration. The nation must uphold national honor, "evoking the sweet memory of the heroes of our independence and the patriarchs of the year 12, that erected the first pillars of our political regeneration." He espoused unity to dispel the chi-mera of political fragmentation: "We are not democrats or pro-gressives, we are not the liberal union nor are we moderates . . . We are Spaniards."[68] Yet others conceded that the struggle had in fact morphed into a brutal war marred by a growing racial divide in the years 1863–65, challenging the fragile coalition in the metropole that had vocally advocated empire building.

And like the architects of the Constitution of Cádiz, who did not abolish the slave trade in spite of their liberal ideals and rhetoric, mid-nineteenth-century imperialists downplayed the significance of race and slavery in their quest to recreate an imperial monarchy. Tassara epitomized the myopia of govern-ment and military officials charged with overseeing Domini-can affairs. He believed that the institution of slavery was so strong that it would persist despite the ongoing civil war in the United States, and he claimed that the loyalty of southern slaves was assured for the time being. As a conscientious dip-lomat Tassara also presented the case that the war could have repercussions in the Caribbean, and he wanted Spain to be pre-pared for any eventuality. The viability of slavery, therefore, would not be the issue, but external threats would remain.[69] Diplomats such as Tassara displayed far greater concern about the prospect of Yankee imperialism than they did about slave unrest and racial justice.[70]

While many, including contributors to *La Discusión*, contin-ued to paint Spanish imperialists as "agents of progress," the periodical had substantially revised its positions by the fall of

1863. One unsigned article covering Spain's overseas territories called slavery a "horrible cancer that devours our national honor."[71] Regarding the Dominican question, a concise editorial posited only one solution: "abandon the soil that rejects us."[72] By early 1864 another journalist had called for an end to eulogies of Christopher Columbus and the Catholic Kings, saying "people don't live on and sustain themselves only through [past] glory." The author, José María Autran, criticized the tremendous cost of propping up a poor country populated by people harboring a growing "hatred of everything that Spain is and represents today."[73] In the same newspaper, *El Museo Universal*, however, the dominant sentiment remained proimperial and ardently racist. The front-page story the first week of February called news from Santo Domingo "satisfactory," as troops reportedly had begun to clear the country of insurgents. To solve some of the more intractable problems and completely pacify the colony, the writer Nemesio Fernández Cuesta opined, "We cannot find any other way except for white colonization on a large scale."[74] Racial fantasies centered on white emigration tempted those who did not want to give up on Spanish arms and overseas empire building. Many wanted to persevere.

Among those who favored white emigration to the Caribbean was the Cuban Calixto Bernal, who by 1864 had continued to push for Spanish dominion over Santo Domingo. Writing for the Madrid-based *Revista Hispano-Americana*, which featured a number of prominent liberals and abolitionists born in the Antilles, Bernal saw the Dominican Republic as the centerpiece of a strategic push for recolonization of the Americas.[75] He anxiously considered the ramifications of colonial success on Hispaniola: "If Santo Domingo had prospered with reincorporation, it was very natural, logical, almost certain, that other American republics . . . would have aspired to the same status. . . . Only the annexation of Santo Domingo would have allowed Spain to peacefully and honorably recover, if not all, at least an important part of their former overseas possessions." Bernal proceeded to delve into reasons for the insurrection and

Anatomy of an Uprising

why love had turned to hate. If, as so many commentators sustained, annexation truly had been spontaneous, driven by nostalgia for Spain and by the need for protection from the "yoke" of Haiti, then what had changed so quickly and so radically? He pointed to the mistreatment of the Dominicans, especially people of color, as the proximate cause and advocated granting autonomy rather than fighting to preserve domination.[76]

Many remained unconvinced that the rebellion could be tamed. The liberal intellectual Gaspar Núñez de Arce summed up the rampant pessimism that followed the fall of the O'Donnell government and the unraveling of Spanish imperial designs in the Caribbean. He concluded, "This project has been a humiliating declaration of impotence." Spain was particularly humbled, he wrote, as France "raised a new imperium over the ruins of the Mexican Republic. A thousand leagues from Madrid, caught between brutal and bloodthirsty blacks, Spain is not Spain."[77] The intertwined issues of race and slavery undermined liberal Spain's attempts to revive the glories of its former empire in the Caribbean.

SIX
....

Death to Spain!

Mexican Views of Spanish Intervention

The third act of Spain's drive to re-create its empire between 1859 and 1861 took shape in Mexico at the tail end of a civil war between competing political factions, leading to the French intervention in 1862 and the fall of the Liberal Union government in Spain by early 1863.[1] Both the War of the Reform (1858–61) and Spanish plotting in the Caribbean contributed greatly to the turmoil and chaos that descended upon Mexico. In 1856 assassinations of Spaniards at San Vicente, a sugar mill near Cuernavaca, aggravated tensions with Spain, although the criminals subsequently were put to death.[2] The 1859 Treaty of Mon-Almonte, signed in Paris between Spain and embattled Mexican conservatives led by Miguel Miramón, provided, among other provisions, indemnification for such losses. But the liberal Mexican press emphatically denied the validity of Mon-Almonte, signed during the conflict. Joaquín Pacheco, the Spanish ambassador and only diplomat to recognize Miramón as president, was expelled, complicating relations with Spain by the first months of 1861 as the liberal Benito Juárez marched triumphantly into Mexico City.[3] Miramón had committed himself to destabilizing Mexico and undermining Juárez by purchasing ships in Havana to bombard the port of Veracruz the year before. Although his attempt failed, it served to foreshadow a European intervention that could, according to one Mexican observer, change the destiny and fortune of Mexico.[4]

The tripartite alliance that became a reality by October 1861 and led to the French occupation of Mexico traditionally tends to be cast as a story of financial disputes and great power diplomacy spearheaded by Britain and France. As early as July 1861 the French minister in Mexico proposed that Britain, France, and Spain take Mexican customhouses so that Mexico would pay all outstanding debt obligations.[5] Ironically, France had few significant financial ties to Mexico prior to the invasion.[6] Spanish intentions have been glossed over, in part because the Liberal Union did not succeed in putting together an empire to rival those of its European neighbors by the mid-1860s. Yet, as this chapter shows, Mexicans rightfully feared a Spanish intervention, because ministers within O'Donnell's cabinet actively conspired with Mexican monarchists to seize territories in the Americas and establish Spain as a preeminent global power once again. While such plots dated back to 1854, with Mexican diplomats working covertly in the courts of London, Paris, and Rome, Spanish officials ramped up their efforts in early 1860, just as they did in the Dominican Republic.[7]

Prior to leaving for Mexico to fill his new post as Spain's ambassador, Pacheco stopped over in Paris and London to meet with diplomats in March and April 1860. He wrote back to Madrid with subtle references to plans seemingly crafted in conjunction with Spain's overseas minister, Saturnino Calderón Collantes.[8] In correspondence directed to the minister Pacheco referenced Miramón's abortive effort to take Veracruz, tarnished by European views that Spain was behind the entire venture. Had Spain in fact tacitly supported him? The letter does not provide a definitive answer. Pacheco airily dismissed any role to be played by the Spanish legation in London, and Javier Istúriz in particular, confidently stating, "I have spoken with him of things in Mexico, and I believe that there is nothing to do here, in this instance."[9] The suggestive references to Spanish plots in the Americas had started earlier in his letters from Paris. In one he described a terse meeting with Napoleon III, who appeared preoccupied with matters in Europe.

Pacheco insisted that "we don't have to wait for their support" now, while wisely using vague language and including no clear context for the proposed actions. Calderón Collantes most likely understood the message being sent. Pacheco lauded the great Spanish victory in Tetuán as a prelude to his grand vision. With Spain having made peace in Africa, he demanded boats for the Pacific: "This is and has always been my *delenda Carthago*."[10] Expressing his tremendous desire to destroy the analog to Carthage, imperial Rome's rival city situated directly across the Mediterranean, Pacheco sailed to the Americas armed with an arsenal of diplomatic subterfuge and Machiavellian plans to seize Mexico.

Colonization fit squarely within the parameters of mainstream intellectual discourse in Europe and in the Americas. In the periodical *La Discusión* Castelar pushed the notion that commercial and scientific interests dictated a pragmatic policy designed to increase Hispanic influence around the globe.[11] Liberal Mexican newspapers reprinted Castelar's editorials as his influence grew on both sides of the Atlantic, despite the fact that he overtly supported a new kind of Spanish empire.[12] Like-minded liberals in Mexico shared a similar vision. In an article titled "Colonization," one contributor to the periodical *El Siglo Diez y Nueve* (The nineteenth century) extolled the benefits of order and progress through internal colonization, a tool that would increase Mexico's domestic agricultural output without the use of slave labor. Due to the lack of a strong, hardworking population, Mexico consequently had to embark on such a program to build its economy and to ensure peace and stability.[13]

With Tetuán secured and negotiations proceeding apace for a Spanish sphere of influence in Annam and Hispaniola, recolonization became a touchstone for sentimental imperialists like Castelar. In addition, with the United States clearly moving toward a catastrophic civil war, Spain appeared to be well-positioned to enlarge its territories in the Americas. Castelar had spoken passionately about the possibility of a union between metropolitan Spain and its former colonies, especially Mexico.

Death to Spain!

Writing in *La América*, he insisted all Spaniards were brothers, connected as members of the Latin race that was called on to exercise "a ministry superior to that of the Anglo-Saxon race."[14] He described the Latin race as artistic and bellicose yet also disciplined and unified, consistently preaching the core values of its Christian faith. With a nod to the notion of racial fusion, he insisted that the Spanish could harmonize the individualism of the Germanic character and the sociability of the Latin character to forge a progressive future for all.[15] By contrast, Anglo-Saxons were calculating, focused on commerce, and tended to turn away from humanitarian principles. Thus America, for the benefit of civilization, had to repulse Anglo-American forces and embrace Hispanism. Even later in life Castelar wrote nostalgically about "the close ties between our Spain and the American peoples. . . . The citizen of Hispanic-American Republics is the son, like it or not, of old Spain; and our patria is the common mother of everyone without any distinction, all have the same names and share the same blood . . . in our veins, [. . .] all that constitutes the self." Having traveled widely, Castelar understood and appreciated "the fundamental idea of the unity of our race" that continued to bridge the divide between "the two Spanish families" in Europe and in the Americas.[16] The sense that union could be achieved without the ravages of war, a peaceful campaign in the aftermath of the Spanish-Moroccan War, symbolized the idealism of nineteenth-century democrats like Castelar. He simultaneously advocated progressive political causes, including antislavery, while putting forward an ideology of liberal imperialism emblematic of the postrevolutionary age.

Spanish intellectuals, such as the contributors to *La América*—founded in 1857 just after Spain's diplomatic ties to Mexico had been broken—tended to analyze Mexico through the lens of race. In 1851 Mexico counted approximately 7,661,000 inhabitants, with 1.2 million people of Spanish ancestry and 3.68 million with an Indigenous lineage. Close to three million Mexicans had mestizo roots. Juan Lorenzana, writing in *La América*, argued that only an infusion of white, Catholic Spaniards could save Mexico from racial decay. In 1867 *La España* even published material in favor of the elimination of Indians. These kinds of ideas legitimized and justified intervention in the Americas. Understandably, writes Romana Falcón, in Mexico a great deal of "hostility toward *peninsulares* was ostensible and public, and was driven by continuous attacks by the press." Almost all Spanish journalists, with the exception of contributors to the periodical *El Pueblo*, came to support intervention in Mexico, just as they had been cheerleaders for the Spanish-Moroccan War and Dominican annexation. Periodicals in Spain like the rightwing, ultramontane *La Regeneración*, as well as the moderately conservative *La España*, agreed that hatred between "the castes and the races" was to blame for Mexico's travails since independence. On March 24, 1858, with diplomatic ties between Spain and Mexico frayed, Castelar concluded in *La América* that the root of problems in Mexico was "the cauldron of indigenous passions." Falcón argues that in Spain "conceptions of race . . . permeated all classes and occupations," and ideas of racial superiority "merged" with Spanish nationalism.[17] These popular attitudes pervaded the culture of Spanish imperialism.

The Spanish in Mexico

Premiering for the first time in Madrid at the Teatro Novedades in February 1862, the play *The Spanish in Mexico* clearly distinguishes between European Spaniards and racialized Mexicans. The production presents a world turned upside down, as postcolonial Mexico has succumbed to radicalism and discord reminiscent of the French Revolution. Spain, alongside France and England as the arbiters of civilization, has to step in to prevent modern-day *sans-culottes* from enslaving the country. The curtain is raised as Guadalupe, married to a biracial man named Pancho, receives food for her young son from Don Diego, the Spanish *hacendado* (landowner). The archetypal colonial subject, Pancho has been a negligent and domineering father who left his wife Guadalupe and their children, who are in turn forced to rely on the patriarchal Spaniard. Amid an atmosphere of uncertainty and instability, the Spanish characters read aloud from a newspaper article describing the festivities celebrating Christopher Columbus and the annexation of the Dominican Republic by Spain. An elderly priest then questions the value of liberty—in a country like Mexico—that had come at the cost of a tremendous loss of life. He decries endemic violence, as one tyrant after another had relied on the force of arms rather than the rule of law. Diego replies that if true liberty existed in Mexico, the country would follow the path of Santo Domingo.

Don Diego becomes concerned when local authorities begin to round up suspicious people and tensions rise. As Spanish soldiers arrive on the scene, they are greeted with shouts of "death to the gachupines" and "death to Spain!" In the action that ensues, the Mexican characters, unsurprisingly, are shown to be "bandidos," fond of drink and money. Pancho, who had been enslaved on a Cuban plantation during his absence, now serves the Mexican Republic but acts like a petty tyrant. After a series of skirmishes and an episode of hostage taking, the aging priest rebukes Pancho for being a bad father. In the climactic final scene, Pancho repents and admits to Diego, his former owner in Cuba and symbol of the benevolent Spanish state, that Diego had been a generous father figure to him. In closing, the priest laments that these "poor Mexicans . . . didn't learn that people who were once brothers should live as brothers!"[18] Drawing on a familial metaphor of empire, the playwright demonstrates that Spanish forces must depose men like Pancho, who represent lawlessness and despotism. Such a rendering completely diminishes the horrific violence of slavery and erases the treachery of Spanish officials at the time. Courting conservatives, like the fictional landowner in the play, who remained deeply hostile to the Juárez regime, Spain flouted liberal values and a constitutional history dating back to 1812.

Mexican nationalists, of course, presented Spaniards as conquistadors and usurpers rather than as saviors. Celebrating the anniversary of independence from Spain on the night of September 15, 1861, in the National Theater of Mexico, the intellectual Ignacio Altamirano singled out the clergy, the heirs to a Spanish authoritarian tradition, as the root cause of the current crisis.[19] Accordingly, the country had faced instability and civil war, an inheritance he viewed precisely as "the last expression of Spanish tyranny in our country." Referencing the French Constitution of 1793 in his speech, he argued that Mexico must replace the old Catholicism with a "democratic evangelism" and the "divine religious liberalism . . . of the carpenter from Nazareth."[20] While some in Spain rejected radical politics tied to the legacy of the age of revolution, many liberals in Mexico actively embraced such a connection in putting forward their openly anticlerical policies.[21] Altamirano ended his paean to Mexico by citing the example of Lajos Kossuth and the Hungarian uprising of 1848. Just as Castelar had posited the ineluctable force of progress toppling Old Regime states, Mexican liberals likewise eulogized "the idea of democracy that would establish the foundations of progress" in Mexico.[22] At the same time they expressed serious reservations about the possibility of foreign intervention that might endanger the entire project.

For many in Mexico the prospect of Spanish occupation far outweighed concern over British or even French plots. Time and again Mexican journalists, politicians, and diplomats fretted over Spain's overseas policies, especially the annexation of the Dominican Republic. Santo Domingo figured prominently in both cultural productions and in government correspondence. As early as June 1861 the Mexican ambassador to Napoleon III's France, Juan Antonio de la Fuente, wrote that Spain's intentions "will be the ruin of our nationality." The occupation of Santo Domingo, according to Fuente, had served as the opening salvo in an attempt to reestablish Spanish influence in the Americas and nullify the Monroe Doctrine. Furthermore he believed there was truth to the idea that the Spanish consul Gabriel Tassara advocated a strategic alliance with the "dissident states" of North America, the kind of pact Juárez clearly rejected. As a diplomat and a Mexican nationalist Fuente pushed Mexico to adopt the Monroe Doctrine as well.[23] In talks with U.S. ambassador to Mexico Thomas Corwin, he mentioned that the old consensus, the idea that Spain was "absolutely a satellite of France," had begun to break down. Now Latin Americans saw that Spaniards had "an air of arrogance" because of "their easy exploits in Morocco and the acquisition of Santo Domingo, which had been even easier." Although Fuente saw the advantages of maintaining strong ties to Spain, he worried about the repercussions of a revived Spanish imperium and insisted that Mexico must have the army prepared for war. He pressed Mexico to cultivate closer relations with the United States and work toward eliminating the vestiges of European influence in the Americas. He forcefully argued that Mexico should support the North in the war against the separatists. In addition, he lauded the fact that European liberals and the print media recognized the ideological affinities between Mexico, with its history of freeing slaves, and the North, now committed to bringing an end to American slavery.[24]

During the summer and fall of 1861 Mexicans remained focused on the machinations of the Spanish government. In early September, press reports indicated Spain would be sending troops from Cuba to Mexico alongside French and British forces.[25] Fuente supposed hostilities were on the horizon, as reactionary newspapers in Spain were engaged in a polemic over which prince would be sent to reign in Mexico. He hoped Spain would unilaterally declare war, believing antipathy toward an old enemy would help their cause: "In Mexico, war with Spain would be eminently more national than any other conflict."[26] Although Fuente was stationed in Paris and realized that his country's lack of stability seriously concerned Napoleon III's ministers, he overlooked French designs on Mexico. He also put no credence in the rumor he had heard concerning Napoleon's desire to give Francis II of Naples the Mexican crown.[27] Behind the scenes, however, it had become clear that Spain and France planned to resurrect "the throne of Montezuma," as one British critic put it. He wrote that by September, more than a year after Pacheco's visit to Paris, French diplomats looked to prevent a U.S. payment to Mexico that would effectively forestall a naval intervention. This obviously showed that the economic justifications publicly espoused by the three powers simply masked an intention to seize power.[28]

Just as many Spanish diplomats were blind to the historical divisions caused by racism and slavery in the Caribbean, both Fuente and U.S. secretary of state William Seward failed to see that France, rather than Spain, might invade independent Mexico. Fuente was relieved when U.S. ambassador to France William Dayton solicited a declaration from French minister of foreign affairs Antoine-Edouard Thouvenel that "England and France did not aspire to territorial acquisition nor to a political upheaval in the interior of Mexico." Fuente, in his diplomatic correspondence, wrote that Spain would only become involved if admitted into a tripartite alliance by England and France. But first the latter countries would have to renounce political intervention and territorial acquisition as well.[29]

Despite such diplomatic reassurances Mexican officials prepared to defend their nation against Spain. Matías Romero, Mexico's ambassador to Washington, met with Edward Dunbar, a liberal antislavery activist who had expressed a great deal of interest in organizing a brigade, composed of five battalions, to help defend Mexico. Word spread within diplomatic circles that Dunbar had also met with President Lincoln and Secretary of State Seward to discuss his plans.[30] Mexicans actively pursued aid from the United States even as the civil war raged, working to negotiate a loan of between five and ten million *pesos* that would have been used to pay off the indemnities demanded by the Europeans. Romero suspected that it would not come to fruition, but officials, including Corwin, supported the proposal. Through the fall Seward continued to inquire about Spanish intentions; Romero had heard that Spain was sending a fleet to Veracruz to preempt the arrival of the combined Anglo-French contingent.[31] Some in the U.S.

media presented the issue as a return of Spanish conquistadors, and the conservative press likewise stoked Mexican fears of an imminent Spanish invasion.[32] The *Tribune*, an organ of the Republican Party, printed an editorial encouraging Mexico to establish a monarchy with a European prince. With evident sarcasm, the author suggested the Pope could serve as the head of the "Pontifical States." Accordingly, France and England should consent to having Mexico return to the status of a colony of Spain.[33]

Of course, the Spanish rejected such speculative fictions. Tassara, in a brief meeting with Seward, explained that Spain only wanted to prevent the United States from absorbing Mexico, and as that was unlikely under the circumstances, Spanish commercial interests and prosperity remained their top priorities. Speaking to the Mexican delegation, Tassara continued to deny that Spain wanted to reconquer Mexico: "Spain's natural expansion is into Morocco and Portugal." However, he tellingly advised Mexico to do whatever the triple alliance asked to avoid "fatal consequences." Yet the two men found common ground in reflecting back upon a shared history. Romero admitted a certain admiration for the Count of Aranda, the great eighteenth-century statesman. If Spain had followed through with Aranda's 1783 plan to carve America into three semiautonomous kingdoms, he noted nostalgically, "today we would have a king and would be like Brazil, prosperous and tranquil." Tassara agreed that he had always thought Mexico should have been a monarchy.[34] Although some news reports claimed Spain would declare war on Mexico, Seward admitted that the United States would not be able to formally oppose it. Seward also told Romero that the United States could not offer a loan to Mexico, as Corwin had urgently requested. In a formal meeting with Seward, Mexican ambassador Romero read aloud an unequivocal statement: "The Spanish Government believed that the time was propitious on account of the civil war in the United States . . . [Spain declared] that she does not make war upon Mexico for the purpose of conquest. But no one will be deceived by this: Spain purposes to repeat in Mexico the ridiculous and infamous scene enacted by her in San Domingo."[35]

Fuente, privately writing about his frustrated desire to return home and join the fight, predicted that Spain was going to begin its operations at the beginning of November 1861 and would not slow down its plans.[36] The end goal was the reconquest of Mexico. Internal political fissures concerned Fuente, especially the influence of Mexican conservatives who agitated against the liberal Juárez. He wrote that "the clerical-military party in the mountains of Querétaro had raised the flag of Spain" in an act of resistance to the central government. Reporting from his post in Paris, he passed along the news that British lord John Russell believed a Spanish monarchy could be established given the state of disorganization in Mexico.[37]

Outstanding debt obligations presented Britain, France, and Spain with a casus belli, especially after the Juárez government renounced its debt obligations, upward of 80 million *pesos*, in July 1861. Many in the Spanish press covered the "question of Mexico" as a simple issue of reparations. Far from seeking the ruin of an independent state, Spanish forces would help support a strong, stable government in Mexico, providing that amends were made for prior transgressions.[38] *La América* ran a series of editorials against interventionism in general, especially the pattern of substituting one prince for another. Looking at the recent events in Italy, Francisco Lozano Muñoz applauded transfers of power accompanied by the expansion of suffrage and liberalism. He argued that the principle of intervention had fallen out of favor in the modern world, based as it was on an abuse of foreign power against the voices of marginalized peoples.[39] As Falcón has noted, with the prospect of a third major involvement in an overseas military operation in as many years, Spanish liberals hesitantly endorsed the looming siege, cautiously hoping that it would help strengthen ties with the Republic of Mexico in the long run.[40]

By the end of October, with a treaty signed in London, the three European powers declared their intention to send naval

Death to Spain!

vessels to the coast of Mexico in a joint show of force. Russell insisted that all English demands be met, including remuneration of the money purportedly stolen from the British legation in Mexico.[41] The British press justified Britain's bellicose position by referencing their historical ties to Mexico, including monetary support provided during the independence struggle against Spain: "Volunteers from this country fought in the ranks of emancipation; and to aid the completion of its escape from Spanish bondage, £12,000,000 of English money was subscribed as a loan on no usurious terms."[42] O'Donnell, speaking to Queen Isabel and the Cortes, emphasized Spanish generosity and efforts to imbue Mexico with the values of civilization and order.[43] Meanwhile Mexican officials in Cuba continued to downplay the significance of the gunboat diplomacy. One report suggested that France and England still felt that it was premature to plan an occupation and that the collective endeavor might fall apart. According to the Mexican Consulate in Havana, the Spanish, however, had presented a plan to occupy Veracruz and Tampico.[44] In mid-November word spread that a Spanish warship, two English ships, and one French vessel had arrived in Veracruz.[45] The Juárez government began posting public notices that all Mexicans should arm themselves against the threat of foreign aggression and an impending "break" in relations with Spain.[46] Those who supported the peninsula would be considered traitors to their country.[47]

Even as Spanish forces sent from Cuba landed in Veracruz, Mexican officials and intellectuals expressed a certain naivety about European imperialism. From Washington the Mexican ambassador passed along the assurances of both Seward and Tassara that Spain was not going to reconquer Mexico. Seward could not imagine how three rival European powers would reconcile their divergent interests. Gunboat diplomacy did not necessarily lead to occupation and military action, he calmly explained.[48] As late as November 1861, in *El Siglo Diez y Nueve*, Francisco Zarco pondered what "political interests would move France to intervene in Mexico." He confidently wrote, "We have discovered none." In addition, he believed domestic political concerns exclusively drove the Spanish government to prosecute foreign wars: "Spain appears to use distant expeditions to calm internal unrest, that continues uninterrupted with the annexation of Santo Domingo." The periodical reprinted conflicting editorials from the peninsula. The Madrid daily *La Esperanza*, an organ of Carlism, stated that Spain had an absolute right to intervene. The opposition journal *La Iberia* dissented, lamenting the fact that "This story in Mexico is a copy of the one in Africa. Africa offended and insulted us for many years. . . . Mexico disrespected us [and] violated people and the interests of our compatriots for many years." The article concluded by ridiculing the "stupidity and ineptitude" of a regime that would recognize the legitimacy of the Dominican government in pursuing annexation while supporting a reactionary faction in Mexico that would topple the elected government.[49] Divisions in the peninsula fueled the optimism of those who dismissed Spain's imperial pretensions.

By early December twelve Spanish warships had arrived. A number of the vessels, such as the heavily armored *Princesa de Asturias*, had been used the previous year off the coast of Morocco in the Spanish-Moroccan War.[50] And just as journalists and artists had accompanied the army across the Mediterranean, peninsular writers embedded with brigades in Mexico. Describing his experience alongside the enlisted men, one reporter compiled his observations for a supplemental edition of Madrid's periodical *La América*. It included notes on the economy, geography, and local people. He wrote about a relatively vibrant market for local crops, including tobacco, sugar, and coffee. It seemed to him, after some tentative discussions with residents, that educational resources were scarce, and even religion appeared lacking. Parochial facilities were crumbling, and chapels were in disrepair. Despite myriad difficulties and illness, the expeditionary force remained disciplined and would assemble with precision, even after a long day's march into the interior. The journalist emphasized the silence with

Death to Spain!

which the brigade was received by local populations, a mix of quiet scorn and indifference. They would respond to soldiers' questions by turning and walking away.[51]

The Mexican military closely monitored the foreign soldiers arriving at its shores, paying the most attention to Spanish forces. They interrogated deserters, fishing for information about weaknesses and liabilities they might expose. Silvestre Alonso, a twenty-year-old second corporal from Asturias, stated that he had come over with ten thousand men commanded by General Manuel Gasset on December 1, followed by five thousand more shortly thereafter. But he had been disillusioned by his time serving in the armed forces, because he was treated like a conscript, as if after the war he would want to live as a "peasant." He disclosed that Spanish troops were disgusted with the bad treatment they received from their superiors. Plus, many were sick in the hospital, and some had already died, he explained.[52] A twenty-six-year-old corporal from the province of Burgos also arrived on December 1 and deserted because he was sympathetic to Mexican forces. He similarly told of being treated like a peasant and being "disgusted with the campaign," seeing that so many of the troops were often sick. Because many deserters offered the same rote responses, it appears Mexican military officials had asked leading questions and transcribed similar descriptions of poor treatment compounded by suffering from outbreaks of disease.[53]

In December, as troops began to occupy the port of Veracruz, journalists could no longer ignore the impending hostilities. Mexican diplomats discovered that the conspiratorial Miramón had traveled to Washington to visit Tassara prior to going to Havana. There, he would be charged with uniting the various "reactionary parties that still remained in Mexico with arms in hand to organize a simulacrum of a government that would be recognized and supported by Spain."[54] A state of emergency was issued in Puebla on January 4, 1862.[55] As Mexicans continued to present Spain as the protagonist of the entire affair, they demanded a formal declaration of war from Madrid, a tacit recognition of Mexico's status as a civilized nation.[56] Diplomats reported from Europe that Don Sebastián, the uncle of the queen, would be named king, while others indicated the Count of Trapani was being considered.[57] The uncle of the former king of Naples Francis II, the Count of Trapani had been a candidate to take power in the aftermath of the 1829 Barradas expedition.[58] Either way a Bourbon would be placed on a newly minted Mexican throne. By the end of January 1862, even though the press had exposed the fact that Mexican agents had ultimately offered the crown to Archduke Ferdinand Maximilian with French backing, Mexican diplomats continued to worry about Spanish troop strength on their soil.[59] Romero produced a letter, supposedly written by Calderón Collantes in late January, which described a Spanish plan to augment their forces in Mexico with three thousand troops mandated to march on the capital if necessary.[60]

Mexican officials pointed to the rise of Spain, with successes in Morocco and in the Caribbean, as a warning to all Spanish Americans. For instance, Romero welcomed a proposal put forward by a Peruvian diplomat for a defensive alliance with Mexico as Spain, he claimed, planned to "reconquer their old colonies."[61] Romero confidently predicted that all of the other Spanish American republics would join as well. Many agreed that Spain held imperial designs on their territories and painted their struggles in light of a history of conquest and exploitation. In a poem titled "Mexico and Spain," written in early 1862 in Lima, democracy is presented as the antithesis of Spanish aggression, symbolized by men like Cortés and Pizarro. Spain is cast as the villain fighting against a continent that is both unified and resilient. Toward the end, the author makes the striking claim that America is not Morocco, alluding to the defeat of the sultan in 1860. Armed with nationalist fervor, the author suggests, Mexico will not suffer the same fate that North Africa did. Significantly, neither France nor Britain is mentioned, as Latin Americans viewed Spain as the greatest threat to their hard-won liberties.[62]

Death to Spain!

Many writers, alienated by attitudes characterized by conde-scension and prejudice, spoke out against Spain publicly. For example, one Mexican theater production parodied the history of Spanish intolerance. The 1861 play, titled *Virtue Pursued by Superstition and Fanaticism, or the Moro Babú*, satirized Span-ish institutions and practices by importing a Mediterranean story to Mexico City's Teatro de Oriente. It begins with an exor-cism, then proceeds to the shadowy workings of the Inquisi-tion of Mallorca. With justice ultimately served, the fourth act renders Babú free, and the imperial Inquisition is destroyed.[63] The hero, in the figure of a persecuted Moor, had overcome the fanatical Spanish state, symbolizing a postcolonial world turned upside down.

For months, with the allies pressing their demands for finan-cial remuneration, Mexican journalists and officials remained incredulous. Rumors circulated that the candidate to the throne had apprehensively inquired about the will of the people. Accord-ing to sources leaked to the Mexican delegation in Paris, Max-imilian wanted to know whether Mexicans would support a European emperor and offhandedly requested that an army of occupation accompany him to the New World.[64] In Washington Romero still held out hope for American diplomatic and finan-cial intervention, as some predicted the U.S. Civil War could end within months. Seward expressed skepticism that the tri-partite alliance would establish a monarchy in Mexico without first consulting the U.S. government about their plans.[65] The Mexican press focused on divisions among the powers and on Spain's limited resources.[66]

In the city of Veracruz, Spanish forces repeatedly stated that they had not come to conquer and would abide by the stipula-tions of the diplomatic accord. While calling for all arms to be surrendered to him, General Gasset of Spain hoped to win over hearts and minds. He issued a proclamation intended to ame-liorate Mexican fears: "The Spanish troops that occupy your city have no mission of conquest. . . . They are led hither solely by the duty of demanding satisfaction for the failure to comply with treaties, and the acts of violence committed against our countrymen, as also by the necessity of obtaining guarantees that similar outrages shall not be repeated."[67] The following week the allies issued a manifesto spelling out their expectations. Spain included an ultimatum demanding "satisfaction" for the expulsion of Pacheco, fulfillment of the Treaty of Mon-Almonte, and indemnification for losses such as the murders at San Vicente. They insisted upon compliance "without humiliating the Mexicans."[68] Significantly, Spanish honor now stood at risk: "Spain can nowhere be insulted with impunity, and that distance there is none where honor is at stake."[69] This presented serious obstacles for the Spanish government, as imperial expectations in Spain had risen in line with successes in Morocco and the Dominican Republic. Rhetoric that justified the siege of Veracruz became more extreme. One image reproduced in a Spanish newspaper portrayed stereotypical Mexican bandits lynching Spaniards from a bridge late at night (figure 20). The article referred to the crime as a barbaric act committed by "thieves" on Mexican Independence Day, a brutal attack that threatened all those with Spanish heritage.[70] The sensationalistic coverage heightened expectations for an expedition that would exact revenge on former subjects of the monarchy.

The conqueror of Tetuán, General Juan Prim, had been named to head the Spanish expedition in the fall of 1861, arriving in Havana in December (see chapter 2). After much pomp and circumstance, he departed for the mainland on December 28, accompanied by a French contingent that included officers, troops, and warships. While estimates varied widely, the Mexican press steadfastly claimed that an army of up to 150,000 soldiers could be fielded to defend their homeland from European incursions.[71] They also chafed at reporting that indicated Gasset had already been collecting customs revenues in Veracruz to be split between the three powers. A British correspondent played up the difficulties Spain faced, presenting Prim as a lone warrior bent on achieving glory. Because "he already expresses his desire to settle the dispute for himself," the writer surmised, he

Death to Spain!

FIG. 20. "Barbarous attack committed in Mexico against two Spaniards. Sketch sent by Mr. Barrera." From *El Museo Universal* no. 52 (December 29, 1861), 413.

should be indulged. Otherwise, "Spain would never succeed in gaining a footing in the country, where she would have to fight every inch of her way, and find every man's hand turned against her." In addition, infighting undercut the Spanish leadership: "Prim writes vehement dispatches to O'Donnell, complaining of his . . . position"; Gassett "insists upon being replaced"; and "Serrano's indignation knows no bounds." This unflattering portrait led the writer to argue that "England and France have made a great mistake" in joining the Spanish. "Marry in haste and repent at leisure," he chided, firmly stating that "with the hated Spaniards Juarez . . . will enter into no compromise, no conciliation."[72]

Married to a Mexican woman, Francisca Agüero, Prim had deep ties to prominent Mexican liberal and conservative families. Yet his well-known political leanings gave pause to Mexican conservatives who had spoken out in favor of intervention. While Serrano supported a Spanish prince taking power in Mexico, Prim never favored an operation with the aim of placing a European monarch on a putative Mexican throne. By February the situation had begun to change with the arrival of additional French troops under the command of the Count of Lorencez. In March 1862 Prim expressed reservations directly to Napoleon III, writing from his inland bunker in Orizaba: "The arrival in Veracruz of General Almonte, of the old minister Haro, of Father Miranda, and the other Mexican émigrés, bringing with them the idea of creating a monarchy in favor of Prince Maximilian of Austria . . . is going to create a difficult situation for everyone, but it will be the most difficult for the Commander-in-Chief of the Spanish troops." He suggested that proximity to the United States and the creation of an independent Mexican state decades earlier "had created habits and customs and certainly a republican language that would not be easy to destroy. . . . [I]n this country the intensely felt public opinion is not and cannot be monarchical. . . . [T]he power of Your Imperial Majesty is not enough to establish a throne for the House of Austria in Mexico." Prim predicted that Maximilian would be received just as the conservatives, who found themselves dispersed and defeated by 1861 with the end of the War of the Reform, had been.[73]

Liberals in Spain split over the ramifications of the Mexican intervention and the possibility of a Habsburg prince being invited to the New World. Some felt that, with the support of the people, Prim could guarantee a strong new government for Mexico. One writer for *La América* sustained that monarchical government best suited the Mexicans, as opposed to the liberal constitutionalism that held sway in much of western Europe.

Death to Spain!

He lamented the decision taken by Spanish leaders in the early 1820s to deny Mexico a Spanish prince for their throne. As a result, he wrote, chronic instability had plagued the various republican regimes in power since independence. He insisted that Mexico traditionally had been antirepublican; the very word "republican" was synonymous with anarchy. Therefore, much like the periods after revolutionary turmoil in France, a democratic dictatorship had to be installed to regenerate the country. Published toward the end of March 1862, the editorial expressed confidence that Prim's expedition would succeed in establishing just such a regime in Mexico.[74]

But within weeks the French moved quickly to change the dynamics of the occupation. They rejected Prim's overtures to the Mexican government and the Convention of La Soledad reached in February, which amounted to a declaration of war. Napoleon maintained that Prim's diplomacy and desire to preserve Mexican independence, enshrined in the London treaty, represented a threat to French dignity. While Prim did not want to oppose France militarily, he likewise did not want to see his soldiers remain as bystanders. On April 12, 1862, as all Mexican men between the ages of twenty and sixty were called to arms, *El Siglo Diez y Nueve* led the day's news with the headline "War with France."[75] Spanish troops quickly began to pack up and return to Cuba, with the British navy departing to Bermuda. Spanish forces evacuated Mexico completely by the end of the month before the first major engagement in Puebla on May 5.

A mix of outrage and recrimination came with disengagement. As many newspapers castigated France for having violated the articles of the tripartite treaty and for reigniting the flames of civil war, and others criticized the actions of Prim, some intellectuals clung to a cautious optimism. After withdrawing, Prim himself emphasized familial bonds and the notion that Spanish Americans were brothers, strong enough to govern themselves independently. Speaking in New York to an array of representatives and officials from Central and South America, he said, "We want nothing more than your happiness, such is the hope and the desire of your mother."[76] Proud of Spain's moderation in Mexico, Spanish journalists envisioned an increasingly influential foreign policy that would reconnect Spanish America with the motherland. One editorial foresaw a "Spain that could be a nation of the first order," reaching a new level of importance on the international stage. Spain would exert a kind of soft power over an area of land "twenty times bigger than that of France, three times larger than that of China, and whose population surpassed twenty-four million souls." Anticipating turn-of-the-century Hispanism, this kind of rhetoric romanticized transatlantic ties that had been broken with the wars of independence. The writer confidently predicted that Spanish Americans would not distrust peninsular Spaniards but "will look at us like brothers," as "we constitute one people," one race.[77]

On the other hand, a wave of Latin American nationalists decried the nascent imperial drive of European states that had culminated with intervention in Mexico. In an editorial simply titled "America," one of the many anti-Spanish jeremiads from the period, a Venezuelan implored fellow citizens to defend "the independence and the liberty of America." He stressed that "the occupation of Mexico . . . was for us an attack . . . it was clear that the invasion was a revival of our past slavery . . . and the horrible chains" that represented the burden they had borne as colonies of Europe. The Dominican Republic, accordingly, had not been annexed but stolen in an act of piracy, and Spain now threatened Peru's Chincha Islands. Written in 1864 and published in a Caracas newspaper, the editorial implicated Pacheco as a danger to all of the former Spanish American colonies. National honor, intimately tied to masculinity and symbols of pride like the flag, certainly was at stake. The Americas had to band together and form a union to resist European powers and the rise of a new imperialism. They could not have any illusions: "The secret councils of France and Spain will divide our rich territory" if no actions were taken to oppose them.[78]

Liberal Spain attempted to reconstruct its global empire of

Death to Spain!

old, but the entangled issues of nationalism, race, and religion frustrated their efforts. As the metropolitan public increasingly pressured the government to fulfill the promise of overseas ventures, active resistance, paired with international diplomacy, thwarted Spain's efforts to carve out a new empire. Akin to the ways in which British diplomats frustrated Spanish incursions into North Africa, French strategists successfully halted Spain's reentry into Mexico. Although the Spanish troops had arrived first, the French had committed to breaking the tripartite pact and to installing a European dynasty in the New World. Some in the peninsular press insisted that French domination had caused the immediate ruin of Spanish influence in America.[79] A deputy in the Cortes spoke of the "great shame" felt across the nation in the aftermath of the disastrous expedition.[80] While peninsular cultural productions between 1859 and early 1862 glorified the missionary nation of Spain, with its religious martyrs and valiant soldiers, imperial successes, and the Liberal Union government that supported them, were short-lived.

SEVEN

The Traveling Society of La Exploradora

Imperial Enterprises in the Río Muni

B y the end of the nineteenth century the remnants of a global empire had crumbled following what many peninsular Spaniards considered a disastrous Spanish-American War. But so-called Africanistas continued to push for a colonial policy to acquire land as European powers scrambled to carve up Africa. The Spanish-Moroccan War still remained popular among many liberals, including veterans of the conflict, while other failed military actions, such as the pacification campaigns in the Dominican Republic, received scorn in the press.[1] In the early twentieth century Spain established a formal protectorate over the area around Tetuán, its North African capital, that lasted from 1912 to 1956. And Spanish Guinea remained a colony from the mid-nineteenth century until its independence in 1968.[2] Spanish colonial rule lasted longest on Atlantic islands like Fernando Po, to the north of the Río Muni estuary and the Portuguese colonies of São Tomé and Príncipe. Spain also devoted some of its scant resources to settlements on the outlying West African islands of Annobón, Corisco, Elobey Grande, and Elobey Chico, located immediately adjacent to the mouth of the river, with no concerted attempt to move onto the mainland until the voyages of Manuel Iradier (1854–1911) in the 1870s and 1880s.[3] Iradier, in this final act of nineteenth-century empire building, added a veneer of scientific racism to the nascent ideology of National-Catholicism. And similar to the occupation of Tetuán, Spanish efforts centered not only on commercial development but on the edifice of a Catholic civilizing mission.

The last gasp of liberal imperialism, with roots in the early 1840s, came on the heels of a radical revolutionary experiment in September 1868 that ushered in universal manhood suffrage and popular sovereignty in the peninsula. Called the "Glorious Revolution," many of the protagonists of Liberal Union adventurism—Nicolás María Rivero, Emilio Castelar, Miguel Morayta, Juan Prim, Domingo Dulce—were involved. They advocated expelling the Bourbon monarchy from Spain and the establishment of a true republican tradition to replace the moribund Constitution of 1845. Castelar, even with public demonstrations of support, had lost his professorship at the Universidad Central in 1865, and the military suppressed the protests.[4] Living in exile, he did not participate directly in the 1868 uprising, though he received accolades as he reclaimed the university position that had been stripped from him.[5] Students and militia members gathered at the train station when he returned in October.[6] The liberal press unapologetically cheered the regime change and expressed relief that the country had embraced its heritage. No member of the Bourbon monarchy, accordingly, was fit to rule.[7] One journalist wrote at the top of the day's edition, "Thanks to God. We now have the freedom to write; now we can provide the news to the public; now we have neither preliminary censorship, nor fines, nor horrible mutilations of the newspaper." The author ended by saying that they could now achieve their modest journalistic aspirations. Other articles extolled the Spanish people, who had manifested their love of liberty with unanimity and enthusiasm.[8]

The celebratory tone of the coverage contrasted greatly with reports of a conspiracy, originating in the eastern part of Cuba, that began to appear in the press soon afterward. Spanish nationalists presented the insurgency, which had started with Carlos Manuel de Céspedes liberating the slaves on his plantation, as a fundamental threat to the "good Spaniards" on the island who remained fervently loyal.[9] The dichotomy between the good and bad Spaniard, steeped in a rhetoric rooted in polemics over the rise of constitutionalism and liberalism in the early nineteenth century, had overtly racial overtones by the late 1860s.[10] Some members of the Spanish press presaged the arguments of public figures like the French premier Jules Ferry, who in 1883 forcefully stated that "superior races have rights over inferior races. . . . because they have a duty. They have the duty to civilize inferior races."[11] In the periodical *La Época*, one journalist strongly warned against granting liberty to "the blacks," which would give the Cuban rebellion of 1868 a "formidable, terrifying, and invincible character." At the same time, the author presented the revolution of September in peninsular Spain as the natural culmination of the liberal tradition. In this context Spain must hold on to its Caribbean possessions, he intoned, so that the slogan "Long live Spain with honor" would be upheld and not substituted by a cry of "Long live independent Cuba."[12] Even Castelar did not outwardly sympathize with Cuban freedom fighters. In response to an American journalist's question on the subject, he said, "I am first a Spaniard, and then a Republican."[13] Within this dominant worldview, and as repeated in popular news forums, liberalism and republicanism in no way precluded ideas of racial supremacy and imperialism cloaked in Spanish nationalism.

A Brief History of Colonizing Fernando Po

Writing from the settlement of Santa Isabel (Malabo) three years later, the Spanish governor Antonio Vivar outlined a plan to settle and transform the island of Fernando Po, goals that had yet to be achieved a decade after the Spanish-Moroccan War had been waged expressly to enlarge Spain's flagging imperial possessions in the northern reaches of Moroccan territory. The 1871 document covers some of the same ground that officials such as José Malo de Molina and Antonio Peláez Campomanes had surveyed as they assessed the potential viability and profitability of colonial ventures in the Dominican Republic (see chapter 4). Spanish colonists struggled to maintain a presence in the African outpost, established on the heels of English settlements from the 1820s and 1830s. The history of the colony dated to voyages in the 1840s. The first, headed by Juan José de Lerena, furthered Spanish claims to sovereignty in the region. But Spain established a stronger foothold on Santa Isabel among an African population influenced by Protestantism and English mores with the 1858 expedition of Carlos Chacón. Brigadier José de la Gándara, later sent to work on pacification campaigns in the Dominican Republic, became governor the following year. He named José Muñoz Gaviria, who narrated his trip in several publications, as a key administrator charged with tax collection. In many ways, Vivar's account laid out a vision of Spanish colonialism in clearer terms than those of Malo de Molina and Peláez by definitively prescribing both methods and a practice. What did Spanish imperialism consist of, and how was it to be constructed? Vivar asserted that three issues were crucial: "health, colonization, and cultivation." First, a team carefully had to "prepare studies"; then after a time of deliberation, the plans would be put into action.[14]

Royal orders from these years allocated an annual stipend to missionaries who built schools to foster religious education. Much of the construction from the period did not last due to poor materials being used, but the church and the English consular residence were exceptions. While they benefited from early studies and grammars of local languages, including Kru, the churchmen maintained the supremacy of Spanish and used their native tongue in most instruction and preaching. The Jesuits hoped that they could minister to the largely Protestant populace, but they had few if any converts over the first eleven years of colonization (their mission lasted from 1858–72).[15] One observer noted that despite the vigorous efforts and religious instruction, only eight Africans had converted to Catholicism.[16] Vivar, expressing some liberal sentiment, highlighted the fact that the "revolution of 1868" and "freedom of religion" had changed the situation, allowing many who had been "unjustly deprived" to practice their own faith.[17]

Vivar described a number of ways to colonize, including building a penal colony and transporting Asians to populate the island, noting the possibility of bringing in "Coolies" as the English had done in Australia. He recognized that the two major voyages that had been launched with settlers had failed: one in 1859 with approximately 125 people, and another in 1869 with 82 prospective colonists. Despite these efforts only three of the people from both expeditions remained living on the island. There had been efforts to bring in prisoners as well; an 1866 Cuban ship brought 166 "repugnant men," but only eight remained (200 "Congos" also arrived in 1862 from Cuba).[18] Vivar plainly stated the obvious—the results of all of these projects were completely "negative." Yet he offered hope with a vision that involved utilizing slave labor. Although the slave trade definitively had been abolished, and the 1870 Moret Law had freed all children of slaves and enslaved people over the age of sixty in the Caribbean, Vivar advocated purchasing slaves from the African littoral in Cameroon to work and help populate the island.[19] He bluntly stated that these "wretched beings," given the right conditions, could be redeemed and rescued. They would become free with the stipulation that they remain on the island for a period of at least ten years. His idea correlated with other initiatives in the nineteenth-century Atlantic World, such as the contractual obligations of slaves in the British Caribbean, forced to serve as apprentices even with the abolition of slavery in 1833, and similar plans advanced by French liberals such as Alexis de Tocqueville. Regarding cultivation, Vivar mentioned commodities that might be profitable, such as cotton, cacao, coffee, sugar, and tobacco. But an outside workforce was needed immediately: "It is proven that the indigenous people flee and there is no way to attract them" to this kind of labor.[20]

His anthropological insights differentiated between ethnic groups in the region, such as the Fangs (known as the Pamues at the time) and the Bubis, a Bantu people who predominated on the island.[21] In the late 1850s Spanish colonists counted 824 Africans living in and around Santa Isabel, and the six resident

The Traveling Society

Europeans maintained a contract labor force of "158 Krumanes [Kru] for work and domestic service."[22] One travel account, penned in 1864, described the Kru, originally from the Liberian coast, as a race of strong men without whom Europeans would not be able to conduct any kind of commerce in the region.[23] In addition to African laborers, one contemporary source counted twelve members of a colonial infantry among the population.[24] Vivar dryly showed the state of desolation on the island. He said that, although surrounded by fertile lands, six houses "could be called as such."[25] Most people lived in small huts with bamboo roofs. Tropical fruit trees abounded, providing pineapples, mangos, bananas, tamarinds, oranges, bananas, and guavas.[26] Fish and seafood provided needed protein to supplement a diet that largely consisted of yams as the principal source of nutrition, while coffee and cacao were cultivated on twenty hectares of land. One peninsular producer cultivated 170 hectares with cacao, cotton, and rice. At least one African landowner also grew his own crops, and one Black woman, an English-educated widow, ran a notable commercial enterprise.[27] Sugarcane was favored by some of the Cuban deportees instead of cotton or cacao, but Vivar advocated exploiting palm oil, found in abundance, for export to English markets. Without a study, he cautioned, Spain's "sons and riches" would be consumed by this colonial venture.[28] He would have been well-aware of a government report that estimated that fifty million *reales* had been spent on Fernando Po during the decade 1858–68.[29] On the other hand, he lauded the great benefits of the recent political revolution and the "enormous" economic upswing that accompanied it, so the metropole might be better situated to provide funds for economic aid. He supposed the colony would be self-sustaining with a concrete plan in place to develop its potential (an index at the end listed annual expenses, not including naval costs, at 265,806 *pesos fuertes* annually).[30]

While Vivar planned for an agricultural takeoff premised on slave labor, many of the early colonists complained bitterly about extreme conditions while traveling and on the island. English steamships, departing on the twenty-second of each month and arriving in Fernando Po on the twenty-sixth of the following month, regularly plied the route from Plymouth carrying goods, people, and correspondence from Spain. For new visitors the climate felt enervating and insalubrious, with extreme heat and humidity both day and night; umbrellas were recommended to avoid direct exposure to the sun. Seasonal rains of up to six months in duration followed the hot months. The Indigenous people of Fernando Po did not appear to suffer from some of the serious maladies and parasites common on the coasts, such as elephantiasis, hydrocele, and guinea worm. But once on the island almost all Spaniards came down with fevers and sickness, with the most extreme killing even healthy individuals in little more than twenty-four hours.[31] Muñoz Gaviria found that the most effective preventive measure was quinine. He and Governor Gándara, over the course of three years, "consumed a fabulous quantity" of the medicine. He would take it twice a day, in the morning and again in the afternoon, whether he was feeling ill or not, in addition to other "tonics" such as coffee. While he reported avoiding any major bouts of illness, malaria devastated the colonial population, and fevers constituted a serious threat to public health.[32] Health concerns precluded most bourgeois women from the settlement, and there were few if any white women in Santa Isabel. Even Governor Gándara's wife retired to the Canary Islands after having remained aboard a ship for two months rather than risk contracting a serious contagion.[33] Muñoz Gaviria proclaimed that whites simply had to acclimate to the heat and the depleting effects of miasmas.[34] More than three dozen colonists on Fernando Po disagreed, signing an 1859 protest letter that described a "fatal climate." On the island a mere six months, they wrote that they "have not enjoyed one single day . . . [being] attacked constantly by fevers and by dysentery, which has resulted in enough deaths." Although they initially could count on supplies from the peninsula, including bread, garbanzo beans, and wine, many of the colonists expressed a clear desire to return immediately to Spain, their true "patria."[35]

Accounts from the time, such as that of Muñoz Gaviria, reproduced the racism that had been propagated in the context of the Spanish-Moroccan War and the War of Restoration in the Dominican Republic. He wrote a series of dispatches for the newspaper *El Museo Universal* and took photographs in the early 1860s while traveling down the coast of West Africa, later publishing a book based on his experiences. He departed on an English vessel and resided on the island of Fernando Po for upward of three years, depicting local peoples in vivid detail. He classified the peoples he came into contact with along the way according to a racialized logic: "the blacks of Dahomey are bellicose . . . they only think of the present moment, they are inclined to rob." He concluded that their barbarism emanated from a profound ignorance perpetuated by their kings, who acted as if they were gods. Superstitious behaviors and worship of fetishes characterized their religious traditions. Muñoz Gaviria began one of his columns with a tale of martyrdom upon the death of a king, as twenty-four women chose to be buried alongside the fallen monarch to assist him in the afterlife with duties such as burning incense every day in his honor. Prior to being interred they had to have their legs broken with hammers, he claimed. Furthermore, the people of Dahomey publicly venerated mountains, trees, birds, sharks, and snakes, reputedly holding the serpent god "Dahoé" in the highest esteem. Private objects of worship included "the bone of an animal, the spine of a fish, a stone, a feather," perhaps reminiscent of the ancient civilization of Rome, he declared.[36] And each fetish had the ability to see and speak.[37]

Muñoz Gaviria presented the Bubis of Fernando Po similarly. The name, he suggested, simply meant "man" rather than a strictly demarcated ethnic group. He introduced the Bubis with detailed physical descriptions, highlighting their flexibility, strength, musculature, and skull shape, a nod to the emerging science of phrenology. To clearly differentiate them from Europeans, he emphasized the use of scarification and the yellow ochre they used to paint radiating lines on their skin

FIG. 21. "Island of Fernando Po—The king of the Bubis of Basupu and his family. (From photography.)" From *El Museo Universal* no. 52 (August 7, 1864), 253.

and sometimes in their hair. Although they generally would be found in a state of complete nudity, he noted, the Bubis decorated themselves with shells and the vertebrae of snakes. An aristocracy adorned themselves with necklaces, made in part with the intestines and fat of animals that apparently repelled mosquitos to set them apart from the rest of the population. For Muñoz Gaviria their pomp and regalia typified "the savage life."[38] Their government included a significant role for assemblies of elders that formed an advisory structure within a patriarchal society, headed by a hereditary monarch.[39]

Religion became the prime signifier that set European cultures apart from African traditions. Muñoz Gaviria emphatically stated that the Bubis had no beliefs, creed, or recognizable spiritual practices, and they could not comprehend the Christian idea of an immortal soul. They did not even have a word for religion, he maintained, nor did they worship idols. Muñoz Gaviria imagined that they held secretive ceremonies under the

The Traveling Society

cover of dense forest canopies, "where the European gaze has not penetrated." He also bemoaned the idea that missionaries on the island had "to live the life of the savages" in an attempt to spread their Catholic faith. The use of imperialist rhetoric and tropes came naturally, with all Bubi behaviors categorized definitively as superstition.[40] Press accounts from the time inadvertently would juxtapose scenes of urban life in Europe next to images of people viewed as inferior and fundamentally different. In a summer issue of *El Museo Universal* from 1864, editors included a depiction of bourgeois Spanish families promenading down the newly completed Recoletos boulevard under the heading "Modern Madrid." The following page featured a sketch of a Bubi royal family wearing little clothing, demonstrating a stark contrast between ways of life (figure 21). Although recreated from a photograph—which represented an additional technological bridge between Europe and sub-Saharan Africa—the drawing included no background details.

Muñoz Gaviria captured a dramatically different aspect of modern West African culture in a picture he took of Bonkoro II, the king of the Benga people who resided in Elobey. Bonkoro I had received a signed nationality card from Lerena in 1843 and guarded it carefully before passing it down to his son.[41] Bonkoro II, in a still from the early 1860s, presented himself to the photographer in a completely different manner than the royals appearing in *El Museo Universal*. Wearing European attire, a white collared shirt, and a fitted waistcoat, he stares intently at the camera with a look approaching scorn. His arm rests casually on a three-legged wooden table next to his wide-brimmed hat. The stark scene contains no additional items or decor in the foreground, and the monochrome background appears to be a sheet or a curtain. Of the photos Muñoz Gaviria took, including a panoramic view of Santa Isabel, twenty-five remain today. Yet this particular image of hybridity, of a proud African king in nontraditional garb, contrasts with other portraits that displayed African styles of dress and culture to a bourgeois public eager for the exotic.[42]

Muñoz Gaviria continued, in subsequent issues of *El Museo Universal*, to focus on the distinctive aspects of Bubi culture that separated their customs from European mores. They certainly appreciated gifts, including clothing, and enjoyed tobacco and aguardiente. Bubis would demand military service of all adults, regardless of sex. They used wooden spears and shields to protect themselves from the arrows of enemy warriors. Yet conflicts rarely occurred, and few transgressed the norms of the seemingly tranquil society. Muñoz Gaviria lamented that nothing, neither "money, promises, nor punishments would move them to work and to cultivate the land." The burden of caring for crops such as yams and fruits seemed to fall on the women. Men practiced polygamy and demanded marital fidelity of all spouses. A woman caught in the act of adultery, Muñoz Gaviria asserted, would be punished by having an arm amputated. Other aspects of their culture proved to be disconcerting to Europeans as well, such as "lascivious" music and dances. Overall, from a colonizer's perspective, the Bubi people simply did not need much, as they wore little clothing, resided in small huts, and lived more like animals than men. Therefore Muñoz Gaviria condemned them as "the most idle and slothful race in all of creation."[43] His assessment certainly presented Spaniards with a fundamental problem as they attempted to develop the colony and profit from its people's labor and the fertile tropical climate.

By the late 1860s funds became scarce, and the government scaled back ambitious colonial development plans for Fernando Po.[44] Yet across Europe and the Americas, newly established scientific and economic societies began a push into tropical Africa that morphed into a veritable race by the 1880s. According to Edward Berenson men like the journalist Henry Morton Stanley, who consulted with Manuel Iradier in the 1870s, "contributed, wittingly or not, to a colonial enterprise that expressed and reinforced Europe's racial stereotypes about Africa and Africans and inflicted considerable suffering in what Stanley dubbed the 'Dark Continent.'"[45] Iradier began his account of the voyages he undertook to the Gulf of Guinea with a conversation he reportedly had with Stanley while he covered the Carlist Wars in Spain. Stanley advised the twenty-year-old that his age was well-suited to a project that, even though it was on a grandiose scale, was realizable.[46] Iradier, however, had to self-finance in large part, as the desired funds had not materialized by 1874 when he began preparations.[47] He undertook the trip on a budget of 8,000 pesetas, while the Frenchman Pierre Savorgnan de Brazza, for example, began with a scant 10,000 francs the same year. Both were born in the early 1850s, and they departed to the same region of West Africa receiving few accolades and little attention from the media.[48]

Iradier's views epitomized the emerging scientific consensus of the age and were comparable to those espoused by Muñoz Gaviria. For example, distinguishing between the civilized and savage worlds, he maintained that many of the "savage" peoples of Equatorial Africa did not have a religion, nor did they worship God. He found no evidence of altars, orations, idols, sacrifices, or even sacred trees, but rather encountered a kind of simple spirituality. They had mediums rather than a class of priests and believed in the mesmerizing powers of arrows, hidden blows, and unknown noises. In turn, these could cause instant death, the growth of new organs, paralysis, or the augmentation of predictive abilities.[49] Iradier, however, understood that other ethnic groups, such as the Bengas, could have heartfelt religious sentiment and did believe in a supreme being.[50]

Based in part on scientific and ethnographic observation, Iradier's memoir described the isolated coastal peoples of the Río Muni as patriarchal, with agricultural work done by the women. The men engaged in hunting and fishing and also served as warriors.[51] The king of Corisco, Combenyamango (r. 1859–83), in Iradier's derisive words, showed no "signs of valor nor of intelligence" and, by his demeanor, looked like a poor man. Accordingly, he appeared more equipped to be led rather than to lead.[52] Iradier stated that his guide, Elombuangani, also from Corsico, struggled to understand the rudiments of science because of his "fetishistic ideas" and "limited" cranial capacity.[53] Even worse in European eyes, the Pamues, considered a separate race by Iradier, reputedly ate the flesh of human cadavers and on occasion would purchase the dead to consume from other nearby peoples. Iradier offered a gruesome description: "the king ate the head and the testicles; the nobility the chest and the arms, and the people all the rest." This showed Iradier that they organized their society in a hierarchy familiar to Europeans, albeit accompanied by savage acts such as cannibalism. He tempered the fear this might inspire in fellow Europeans—white flesh, the Pamues opined, had a bitter taste and was not as pleasing as its Black counterpart.[54]

While these crude stereotypes did not prove to be true, the accompanying images and narratives pervaded nineteenth-century texts. And by the second half of the nineteenth century, scientists claimed they affirmed what generations of white Europeans had suspected—the inferiority of African peoples. Therefore racism in many ways determined Spanish views of the Indigenous peoples of West Africa, from the kingdom of Dahomey and the Bight of Benin south toward Fernando Po and Corisco. In the conclusion to his travel account, Iradier reproduced the idea that Black people were the degenerate descendants of the superior races, which comported with the notion that Africans, as the children of Ham, had lived in the same state of barbarism and savagery for centuries. This echoed Orientalist imagery of primitive peoples stuck in the annals of time, unable to cope with the demands of modernity. "Rationalists" insisted that "physiological reasons emanating from divine law" had condemned Black spirits to "progress" so slowly that they required many more centuries to catch up to white men.[55] Regardless of the reason, Iradier concurred that Black people had been relegated to a lower position on the evolutionary scale. While eighteenth-century intellectuals, including Thomas Jefferson, had suggested that science might one day prove European racial dominance, nineteenth-century thinkers and policymakers could look back upon decades of experiments and scholarly

The Traveling Society

texts that appeared to irrefutably demonstrate racial difference based upon biological makeup.[56] For them, Jefferson had been correct all along. Measuring facial angles and the capacity and shapes of skulls became paramount tasks for scientists who continued to propagate racial science, and Iradier traveled to Guinea prepared to measure, classify, and quantify the Black bodies he encountered.

Iradier traveled to the Gulf of Guinea twice but began critical scientific experiments on the people of the region on his first trip in 1875.[57] This occurred at an important juncture in Spanish scientific history, as Madrid's National Museum of Anthropology and organizations such as the Spanish Anthropological Society and the Basque Traveling Society, La Exploradora, had been founded in the previous decade. The Anthropological Society had been created expressly to analyze "the classification of the races" and to study "the progress of individual freedom" in art and literature.[58] Ángel Pulido, one of the earliest proponents of studying race and craniometry, had been introduced to Pedro González de Velasco, the founder of the Anthropological Society, by Emilio Castelar, who had written extensively on the idea of human progress and freedom (see introduction). Pulido believed that these anthropological undertakings would help Spaniards come to terms with "the origins, viability and sociability of nations."[59] In addition, he argued that racial difference might be determined and shaped by cultural attributes, including religious practices. Unlike Gobineau, who emphasized the principle of inequality, Iradier forcefully drove home the idea that the African should be improved: "The perfection of the inhabitant of Africa depends on the united forces of religion, science, commerce and agriculture . . . it is necessary to widely disseminate them among the tribes and between the States in a manner that results in knowledge and influence extended to all parts to triple their productive value and benefits." In other words, missionaries, explorers, merchants, and colonists all needed to work together, "harmonizing ideas of exploration and civilization in Central Africa with the prosperity of Spanish colonies in the Gulf of Guinea."[60]

A Swedish scientist, Anders Retzius, had developed a cephalic index to gauge the percentage of width to length of a skull, which would in turn point to intrinsic characteristics and traits.[61] General classifications indicated whether people had long heads, called dolichocephalic, or narrow heads, brachycephalic. While the pioneer of phrenology, Franz Joseph Gall, did not advocate racial classification based on skull measurements, later scientists generally came to agree that superior peoples were dolichocephalic. Spaniards like Federico Olóriz, a medical doctor at the University of Granada who avidly studied craniometry, at first expressed ambivalence toward claims of Germanic superiority emanating from luminaries in the field. But he concluded that due to the complex history of race in Iberia, the Spanish people had become more dolichocephalic through the process of racial fusion and shared the attributes of the German race, who also were dolichocephalic. His analysis of the cephalic index received the approbation of none other than Marcelino Menéndez y Pelayo, who wrote that such quantitative scientific findings mirrored those of his qualitative history of Spanish Catholicism.[62]

In a chapter titled "Anthropology," Iradier explained his own phrenological experiments on skull shape and size. Similar to Samuel Morton, who had published work on the subject in the United States in 1839, Iradier measured the longitudinal diameter, parietal diameter, frontal diameter, vertical diameter, intermastoid arch, intermastoid line, and occipital-frontal arch. He also calculated facial angles and commented on the shapes and sizes of African ears, thumbs, fingers, and hands, which supposedly differentiated them from his own people. Ultimately, he determined that the people of Corisco were dolichocephalic, with sharply defined facial angles, but the number on the index fell just below that of a typical European. No mention is made of specific reactions to what must have constituted an intrusive kind of medical procedure. But he bemoaned that only six complete measurements were taken, because he had to "fight the superstition of the blacks" who feared the instruments he used as a form of magic. In addition, he warned, a traveler should avoid digging up skeletons, which would unleash the fury and hatred of the savage heart. He therefore provided extensive data for one skull, concluding that the cephalic index correlated to that of a Stone Age man. The numbers also approximated the skull measurements of the Guanches of the Canary Islands or the Gauls of the Iron Age. Iradier dismissively noted that the villagers he encountered "actually" lived like people from Stone Age societies. Lamenting his lack of subjects, he postulated the idea that the blood of the Benga circulated more slowly and their hair grew more slowly than that of a European, perhaps due to the effects of climate. While he did not feel confident in his hypothesis regarding circulation, he authoritatively stated that their "cool" blood was fundamentally different from his. Reinforcing the idea of a sexualized and dangerous Black male, Iradier contended that "the penis is larger and thinner in the African. The act of coitus lasts longer." Finally, he declared that the Africans he tested had better memory, vision, hearing, and sense of smell.[63]

Spaniards drew on a paternalistic rhetoric to characterize their views of the inhabitants of the Río Muni. Because he surmised coastal peoples tended toward mendacity, Iradier stressed that shame and remorse, a language common to Europeans, did not exist among the groups he interacted with, and it was necessary to speak to an African like a child. He summarized the difference: "The white man with his intelligence has dominated nature. The African with his wisdom and malice has deceived nature."[64] In this discourse the archetypal tribesman represented the inverse of the industrious, modern white man. The primitive savage, upon learning of civilization, had to be encouraged to work hard to effectuate a change in circumstances. The European would say, according to Iradier, "Hunt the elephant and you will exchange the ivory for arms. . . . Extract oil from the palm, sap from the rubber tree, and you will be compensated." Despite the promotion of a strong work ethic, Spanish colonizers would retain the trope of the African as childlike, deceitful, and thieving.[65]

Iradier presented his readers with a multidimensional portrait of the coastal peoples of the Río Muni, who, despite their failings and their retrograde culture, could feel and love just like European men and women. He saw firsthand as they shed tears of sadness, expressed horror and indignation, and displayed love. With little formal education they accordingly evinced more imagination than intelligence. Continuing to present their societies as Stone Age, in terms of both development and sophistication, Iradier placed two drawings side by side in the text. One is a mammoth sketched by an early human; the other depicts an elephant drawn by a contemporary African. He clearly wanted to show stagnation or even retrogression—that their level of artistry had remained the same for millennia.[66] The chapter ends with a conversation between Iradier and one of his servants, who told the explorer that, above all, he wanted to grow old so that he could be in charge in his home and in his community and "command" rather than "obey." When asked if he envied Europeans, the more intelligent race that also had more material possessions, the man definitively said no. Instead, he lambasted their lack of hygiene and responded, "We want to be blacks. . . . The whites . . . deceive us and we are more than they are."[67]

Without much fanfare or front-page coverage, the periodical press buried Iradier's return home in the general notices of the day. Items such as news of a fire on board the vessel *San Joaquín*, forcing it to limp into the port of Cádiz, preceded the one-sentence statement: "The voyager Manuel Iradier, coming from the interior of Africa, has arrived in Vitoria, and plans to give some conferences in that capital."[68] By contrast, Brazza would be giving a lecture to an overflow audience of ten thousand people at the Sorbonne by 1882. He had become arguably the most celebrated French man or woman of the time. His "pacific conquest" of lands along the Congo River and his well-known rivalry with Stanley had made him a national hero.[69] In the spring of 1881 at least one Spanish paper, the Madrid-based *El Globo*, published a front-page story extolling the benefits of African colonialism and mentioned the promise of figures like Iradier. Much like press coverage during the Spanish-Moroccan War, the journalist began by lauding French successes and the profits they enjoyed from their colonies. Of course, commerce with Algeria featured prominently, in addition to their wise acquisition of Senegal and Gabon. While "all the nations of Europe vigorously defend the rights to the possession of extensive territories on the African coasts," he wrote, Spain remained largely apathetic, the only European nation not to utilize and benefit from their colonies to the south. The article's author did not equivocate on the absolute necessity of building an empire in Africa, because "this colossal movement . . . so clearly demonstrates the level of civilization and the well-being of the nations that sustain it." Spaniards proudly justified expansion overseas by appealing to a universal civilizing mission. This ideology did not belong to the Spanish, French, or English, but brought together European rivals. He posited that only the most enlightened, wealthy, and free people would dedicate themselves to such a worthy enterprise.[70]

The article, titled "The Exploration of Africa," ended on a positive note, as the indifference previously seen in Spain had begun to subside with the emergence of a new dialogue centered on the prosperity of colonial endeavors. The author attributed the change to an unnamed learned entity, perhaps the Anthropological Society, or more likely the association that had supported Iradier's first voyage, La Exploradora. The organization promoted two different initiatives—economic development in Morocco, such as the establishment of a commercial fishery or factory on the coast, and a great expedition to central Africa to explore from Corisco Bay all the way to Lake Tanganyika. Written prior to the Berlin Conference, which carved Africa into spheres of European influence, the author mistakenly believed Spain held sway over many of the territories in between, and that another trip by the "distinguished" explorer Iradier would help to cement their claims. With enough provisions and a solid base of operations, the trip would be simple because, "for a bottle of aguardiente, the indigenous chiefs are capable of selling an entire kingdom."[71] As many scholars have argued, however, West African notions of land ownership and possession contrasted a great deal with the laws and customs of Europeans.[72]

Akin to press descriptions of Brazza, the article characterized Iradier as a highly intelligent man grounded in the pursuit of science to the point of disinterest in worldly matters.[73] And as the association La Exploradora pointed out in a message to Spain's overseas ministry, "civilization can only be brought to a country through peaceful and tranquil means," such as commerce and education.[74] Just as Brazza presented himself as a hero who would resist the sexual temptations of near-naked African women, as Berenson shows, Iradier likewise epitomized an ideal of prudence and pragmatism. And much as Brazza conquered without war yet did not shy away from threats of violence, Iradier's party did not hesitate to convey a casual ruthlessness: "He [Iradier] can burn the village in a moment and leave everyone dead in the forest."[75] El Globo's story dutifully captured this combination of traits that they hoped would help to sell Iradier's venture to the public, especially to those who might fund a second voyage to follow up on the perceived successes of the first.

Iradier did mount a second expedition to the Río Muni, but the scramble for Africa largely had passed by Spanish business and political interests. While numerous French and British delegates had been welcomed to Belgian King Leopold II's inaugural meeting of the International African Association in 1876, no Spaniards attended, and Iradier had been in Africa that year. By 1882, just a year after the story had appeared in a Madrid headline pitching a return to Africa, Brazza completed a second mission to the same region, the French annexed a part of Congo, Britain established an informal protectorate over Egypt, and

The Traveling Society

the Belgians could count years of work on their behalf by Stanley, whom they sent over once again to secure the vast lands of central Africa for Leopold II.[76] Even the Germans had started to exploit the rich and productive lands of the Río Muni basin.[77] Iradier, departing on a second expedition in 1884, would arrive too late to make any difference, as the Berlin Conference was underway in the fall of the same year.

The Lessons of Modern Spanish History

In 1881 the forty-eight-year-old Castelar, reelected to the Cortes as a deputy from Barcelona, gave a wide-ranging speech on the scope and future of democracy in Spain. In some ways it represented an addendum to some of his earlier writings from the 1850s and 1860s (see the introduction to this volume). Castelar presented a dialectical history of action and reaction, hinging on the revolution of 1868 as a turning point and the Constitution of 1869 as a watershed moment in modern Spanish history. Accordingly, the revolution had its origins in the six years prior, but a reactionary period followed between 1874 and 1881 in which politicians walked back democratic gains. Castelar delivered the address as a corrupted system of power brokers ushered in a liberal government through manipulation and fraud under a system called the *turno pacífico*.[78] Despite the king's role in bringing in a new representative assembly by decree, which he did not mention, Castelar portrayed the Democratic Party as the apogee of progress. The party's success heralded "the end of the reactions" and a vital new age epitomized by the virtues of stability and humanitarianism. He declared with certainty, "For European democracy in general, and for Spanish democracy in particular, revolutionary times have passed. . . . Revolution has been succeeded by evolution."[79] For Castelar, this organic process had a dual nature substantiated by the systematic logic of science and mystical notions of spirituality.

Castelar assessed the situation overseas as well and, staying true to his abolitionist principles, praised the gradualist *patronato* system introduced in 1880, which phased out the institution of slavery in Cuba. Yet he made no reference to the horrors of the Ten Years' War or to the fragile pact that had brought it to an end. Significantly, he advocated greater autonomy for the Antilles and for peninsular provinces, such as the Basque Country, which he expected would bring about the reconstitution of the Latin race and a brand of colonization without conquest or war.[80] In sum, his reliance on positivism, premised on the inexorable march of progress, continued to blind him to the true violence required to maintain colonial and racial domination, described in the preceding seven chapters.

At this point, a new generation of intellectuals had emerged to trumpet the cause of imperialism, putting forward economic and racialized arguments and seeking to build on extant territorial claims. Joaquín Costa, one of the defining thinkers of the age, promoted state-sponsored empire building in his 1882 tract *Spanish Commerce and the Question of Africa*. Living during what he viewed as an epic struggle between the Latin and Saxon races, he helped to organize a national conference on the subject the following year—the Spanish Congress of Colonial and Mercantile Geography.[81] Such efforts ultimately did not yield the results that many ardent nationalists sought. Spanish overseas possessions did not rival those of the British, the French, or even those of Belgium, and the Berlin Conference showed Spain to be in a weakened position on the international stage. Yet the imperial ideology popularized by the likes of Castelar, Vivar, Iradier, and so many others not only informed a nascent Hispanist movement but also influenced the advent of National-Catholicism and the Africanistas who would spearhead colonization in North Africa during the early twentieth century.[82]

Epilogue

This book begins by asking what race and empire meant to people living in the mid-nineteenth century. It ends by proposing to reconsider what imperialism signifies now. Specifically, what do the men and women who worked on behalf of a fraught institution mean to us living today? And how can we better understand the anticolonial struggles that emerged to contest growing European power and influence? Amplified by the rise of the sensationalist media in the later 1800s, the exploits of charismatic heroes of empire seemed to "expand the limits of human possibility and broaden everyone's horizons."[1] They were celebrated and commemorated then, and many still are revered. Nationalist historiographies in the Americas, by contrast, tend to eulogize anticolonial freedom fighters while glossing over the complexities and contradictions of their actions and ideologies.[2] Alongside cultural shifts and decades of historiography that have decentered earlier imperial narratives and emphasized postcolonialism and subalternity, the legacy of this defining period in modern history remains unclear. I can't help but think about Spaniards as they drive or walk through the Plaza de Castelar, in the center of the Paseo de la Castellana, Madrid's main artery, and see the turn-of-the-century statue dedicated to the Spanish statesman. Do they recognize Castelar's name, or consider how his nineteenth-century republican advocacy did not impede the imperial ambitions and dreams of racial and commercial dominance in America and Africa? How do intellectuals feel about him when they are nominated for the recently minted Premio Emilio Castelar? What do the citizens of Melilla say about Calle General Buceta, named after a brutal and callous military figure from the colonial past? And what do Mexicans think about their own history as they stroll down Avenida Emilio Castelar in the capital or Calle Emilio Castelar in the country's second largest city, Guadalajara?

Other former dominions of the Spanish Monarchy also display a conflicted sense of history. Dominicans have yet to reconcile anti-Haitian rhetoric and a 2013 restrictive citizenship law with ideals of racial justice and equality, crucial components of their anticolonial war against Spain between 1863 and 1865. A controversial court ruling retroactively stripped citizenship from children born to foreign parents dating back to 1929. Supporters of the new law demonstrated in the streets, showing popular backing for the decision. Some held up signs with a widely circulated quote from the independence hero Juan Pablo Duarte that bluntly rejected Haitian and Dominican unity under the slogan "Defend your patria."[3] It reads, "A union [fusión] is not possible between the Dominicans and the Haitians." As one of the Dominican leaders who sought to establish a separate state and put forward a liberal nationalist agenda, Duarte did not express manifestly racist sentiment.[4] The quote, out of context, certainly makes it seem as if he did. But the fact that he had rebuffed the idea of bridging the two countries masks the next line in his oft-cited proclamation, revealing admiration for "the Haitian people" and their anticolonial struggles. He goes on to say that Haitians possessed two eminent virtues—courage and a love of liberty.[5] Today the slogan has been twisted to justify anti-Haitian policy. As Anne Eller has shown, nineteenth-century Dominican rebels actually joined forces with Haitian insurgents on the island's porous border throughout the course of the War of Restoration against Spanish forces and evinced a transnational commitment to freedom in the Caribbean.[6]

Yet white Hispanic discourse often upheld an emotional identification with race, culture, and religion that drove men and women to support the project of reclaiming an imperial mantle. A correspondent for the periodical *La Iberia*, Gaspar Núñez de Arce captured the longing and nostalgia many Spaniards felt for the distant past, an age of triumph epitomized by conquests from the Americas to the Pacific. In 1860 he wrote:

> I honestly confess that the question of Africa was not debated or discussed, it was felt; from the first announcement of war they removed the ashes from the tombs of their ancestors, and the spirit of race that passes from generation to generation like a river . . . lit a fire in our veins, and sped up all of our heartbeats. I joyfully followed this general impulse, not only because the captivating voice of our Christian traditions resonated in my soul, as it did in the souls of all the people, but because I knew that it was necessary to reconquer with a daring blow the regard of Europe, accustomed to see in us the Spain of civil wars, pronunciamientos, *ministerial crises*, misrule; a Spain, in sum, poor, drained, hungry, degraded, incapable of wielding the ancient sword of our heroes, and of disturbing the long sleep of our glory with an audacious stroke.[7]

A Dominican newspaper similarly presented the heroes of the Spanish-Moroccan War as "the dignified descendants of Pelayo and Hernán Cortés." Accordingly, the war against the imperium of Morocco, brought on by a sense of national honor and obligation, had resurrected the Spanish glory and strength that once had made the flags of all other nations tremble.[8] The historical precedent evoked images of the Reconquest, with Christians crusading against Saracen enemies on the Iberian Peninsula, incongruously drawing together disparate struggles separated by centuries of history. This "spirit of race," as Núñez de Arce called it, profoundly informed a teleological rendering of a racialized Spanish white identity. As Joshua Goode has demonstrated aptly, this kind of nonbiological rhetoric, along the lines of Miguel de Unamuno's mystical notion of intrahistory, had converged with scientific theories of race by the end of the nineteenth century.[9]

The same sentiment drove Manuel Iradier as he pursued Spanish colonial interests on the coasts of West Africa in the 1870s and 1880s. Contrasting European civilization, which he believed would be accepted and applauded universally, with the "moral defects" of an afflicted "black race," his accounts epitomize the civilizing logic of the age.[10] Unlike the ephemeral words that appeared in now obscure newspapers and diaries, however, Iradier's explorations brought artifacts back to Spain that ended up in the growing collection of the National Museum of Anthropology and are housed there today. There are Fang spears, axes, drums, necklaces, and a multiplicity of cultural objects transported directly by Iradier and his colleague Dr. Amado Ossorio. Questions of ownership and heritage will not fade, as museums grapple with the complex histories of their invaluable collections. Conversations on repatriation have been sparked in large part by African activists, political debates in France, and even provocative work done by scholars such as Adam Hochschild on Belgian colonialism.[11] What is the responsibility of those in power with regard to cultural objects that were carried to Europe during the age of imperialism?[12] Along similar lines, how do Spaniards conceive of their entanglements with Africa today in light of the past? For instance, a nongovernmental organization retains the name "Asociación Africanista Manuel Iradier."[13] An artisanal gin named "Iradier y Bulfy" likely does not find its consumers pondering the racial anxieties that drove Iradier to explore central Africa as they drink in his honor. But do they believe that he was "an admirable personality" who was intensely engaged in exploration, science, and invention, as the company's website proclaims?[14]

What popular culture crowned a heroic age of empire in the nineteenth century still continues to fascinate and spark imperial imaginations today. Empire building came with extreme violence, economic dislocation, and fantasies of racial domination, which too often have been elided in museums and commemorations. It provided a bridge from a largely inclusive liberal identity to the conservative underpinnings of the National-Catholicism that fueled Francisco Franco's brutal authoritarianism and nationalism. The imbricated histories of race, religion, and European culture must be at the center of both academic and public narratives of nineteenth-century imperialism as we continue to reexamine our collective past.

Almost all of the preceding pages of this book were written by the summer of 2020. The research and writing had begun well before a sea change reshaped our historical memories and people around the world started to tear down monuments built to honor those larger-than-life figures of the colonial past and to challenge public adulation of imperial "heroes" from a bygone age. Many of these memorials, as Richard Kagan explains, were erected in the late nineteenth century during what he calls a "Spanish craze," punctuated by the rehabilitation of conquistadors who spread civilization to the supposedly primitive peoples of the New World. Christopher Columbus, Juan Ponce de León, and Francisco Vázquez de Coronado became immortalized atop monuments and in festivals that celebrated Spanish colonial heritage from Washington DC to St. Augustine and Santa Fe.[15] When both Madrid and Chicago held Columbian Expositions in recognition of the quadricentennial of the European arrival in the New World, Spaniards and Americans unequivocally used the anniversary to illustrate the progressive ideals of Western civilization. In the early twentieth century Spain and the United States established the Día de la Raza and Columbus Day, respectively, as national holidays to be held on October 12.

Understandings of race have shifted in significant ways. Since the 1990s, with states like South Dakota and native peoples taking the lead, Columbus Day has fallen into disfavor. Many Indians have emphatically rejected the celebration and renewed a commitment to self-determination and autonomy, while additional states, cities, and universities now recognize Native American Day or Indigenous Peoples' Day in its place. Parallel to this, the public debate over reparations for slavery has intensified since the 1993 Abuja Proclamation, and Americans increasingly question the worth of monuments to the Confederacy. In June 2020 under the banner of Black Lives Matter, statues of Columbus, Ponce de León, and the sixteenth-century colonial governor Juan de Oñate, among so many others, were beheaded and toppled in the United States as symbols of continuing oppression and discrimination in our world today. In Palma de Mallorca, Spain, someone painted the word "racista" in bright red letters on a statue of the eighteenth-century Franciscan Junípero Serra, who opened missions and proselytized the Indigenous peoples of California.[16] Calling for reparations, protestors against racism burned and defaced statues of Belgian king Leopold II in Antwerp and Ghent, while British activists pushed a statue of a slave trader into Bristol's harbor. Politicians in Spain also have questioned the public veneration of imperialism. In Barcelona Jéssica Albiach has criticized the iconic Columbus statue, dating to the 1880s, that stands in the city center without any historical context whatsoever. Albiach, a parliamentary leader in Catalonia pushing for change from within the government, has highlighted the seemingly intractable issue of systemic racism, which she argues is not just a problem in the United States but in Spain as well.[17]

A complete retelling of these ongoing events can't be written comprehensively right now, as a cultural transition is beginning and reactions against the protest movements have grown. While scholars have been teaching and researching the interrelated issues of race and empire for a generation or more, the questions raised by this study and others like it certainly seem much more tangible than they did just ten years earlier when my research started. Uncovering the stories of liberal imperialism from the nineteenth century ultimately sheds light on both the past and the present and provides a unique opportunity to reflect on a history fraught with meaning and emotion for people around the world who have been affected profoundly by the violence and destruction of European colonization over the past five hundred years.

Notes

Acknowledgments

1. Boyd, *Praetorian Politics in Liberal Spain*.
2. Miller, *History of Modern Morocco*, xiii.

Introduction

1. *Aspecto diplomático de la cuestión de Marruecos, por un diplomático* (Madrid, 1859), 21–27, in BN. While these words constitute a paternalistic rhetoric, contemporaries such as Gonzalo de Reparaz clearly recognized that this discourse also "presupposes the ethnic superiority of the colonizers." See Martin-Márquez, *Disorientations*, 58.

2. *Confesión de Pedro Antonio de Alarcón al Obispo de Guadix*, cited in *Una imagen para la memoria*, 88. On the concept of "imperial nostalgia" and the loss of empire, see Lorcin, "Imperial Nostalgia," 97–111. While Alarcón recognized the historical contributions of Moriscos—those converted Muslims who stayed in Spain beyond 1492—his writing glossed over the "cultural violence" that came with their religious conversion. See Martin-Márquez, *Disorientations*, 103.

3. Martin-Márquez, *Disorientations*, 103.

4. One contemporary described Alarcón's chronicle as the "romantic account of that fight." Navarrete, *Desde Vad-Ras a Sevilla*, x.

5. For a list of the dozens of artists who had visited Morocco, see Martín Corrales, *La imagen del magrebí*, 55.

6. Berenson, *Heroes of Empire*, 12.

7. Jacobson, "Imperial Ambitions."

8. *La Correspondencia de España*, November 3, 1861.

9. *La Correspondencia de España*, November 9, 1861.

10. *Diario de las sesiones de las Cortes generales y extraordinarias* (DSCGE), September 2, 1811. Article 9 of the 1767 treaty between the Spanish Monarchy and the Moroccan Sultanate demarcated the "presidios of Ceuta, Melilla, Peñon and Alhucemas" as Spanish territory.

11. *El Corresponsal*, January 1, 1840.

12. Sundiata, "'Cuba Africana,'" 91; García Cantús, "Fernando Póo," 214.

13. *El Corresponsal*, November 25, 1843.

14. Hahs, "Scramble for Africa," 32–40.

15. Salom Costa, *España en la Europa de Bismarck*, 378–80.

16. Hobson, *Imperialism*, 22.

17. Upward of forty thousand attended his funeral services in 1899, according to Vilches García, *Emilio Castelar*, 302. Completed in 1908 with the help of thousands of city governments, banks, and individual donors, a plaza, with a statue as the centerpiece, commemorates his life and achievements in downtown Madrid. Streets are named after him all over Spain, from Seville to Vigo. But Castelar's influence extended far beyond peninsular Spain, with avenues named after him in Mexico City, Guadalajara, and Monterrey. A town bears his name in Argentina, and in Omaha, Nebraska, Castelar Elementary School and Castelar Street also honor his legacy.

18. Hobsbawm, *Nations and Nationalism*, 32.

19. Graham, *Donoso Cortés*, 105. Arthur de Gobineau advocated restoring "the word nation to its original signification, in which it expresses the same as the word race" in *Moral and Intellectual Diversity*, 65.

20. Cited in Álvarez Junco, "Nation-Building Process," 101.

21. Álvarez Junco, "Nation-Building Process," 100. On the convergence of liberal and conservative nationalist rhetoric in the early nineteenth century, see Eastman, *Preaching Spanish Nationalism*.

22. McClintock, *Imperial Leather*, 8.

23. Henry Hotze, in Gobineau, *Moral and Intellectual Diversity*, 149.

24. On the beliefs of neo-Lamarckian "environmentalists," see Haller's preface in *Outcasts from Evolution*, xi–xvi.

25. See the discussion of Geertzian concepts of culture in regard to European imperialism in Sessions, *By Sword and Plow*, 12–16.

26. Goode, *Impurity of Blood*.

27. Drescher, *Dilemmas of Democracy*, 172; Lorcin, *Imperial Identities*, 10–11.

28. *La Discusión*, June 6, 1861. Castelar narrated the rise of Western, Christian states that had eclipsed Asian despots characteristic of an earlier stage of historical development. Accordingly, such Oriental regimes resembled the intolerant empire that had crucified Christ to prevent the spread of his new ideas.

29. Castelar, *La fórmula del progreso*, 79. On Castelar's views of heterogeneity in Spanish history, see Goode, *Impurity of Blood*, 190.

30. Goode, *Impurity of Blood*, 15.

31. Carlos de España to Primer Secretario de Estado y del Despacho, July 6, 1858, Tangier, in MAEC, Correspondencia, Tangier, H 2075.

32. Garcia-Balañà, "Patriotismos trasatlánticos," 210.

33. Castelar, *La fórmula del progreso*, 16.

34. Castelar, *La civilización*, 50, 202. On the roots of the rhetoric of Christendom, see Mastnak, *Crusading Peace*, 93.

35. Iradier, *África*, 2:179.

36. Mariano Álvarez to Gobernador Capitán General de la Ysla de Cuba, April 8, 1862, Port-au-Prince, in AGI, Cuba, 984C.

37. Castelar et al., *Crónica del Ejército*, 188.

38. Anderson, *Imagined Communities*, 148.

39. To cement ideas of racial difference, the Spanish press commonly portrayed Moroccan troops as actual monkeys. See Martín Corrales, *La imagen del magrebí*, 62–63. On the stoking of racism and xenophobia, see Romero Morales, "Prensa y literatura," 619–44.

40. Drescher, *Dilemmas of Democracy*, 180.

41. Saturnino Calderón Collantes to Gobernador Capitán General de la Isla de Cuba, April 24, 1861, Aranjuez, in AGI, Cuba, 2266.

42. Sundiata, *From Slaving to Neoslavery*, 51.

43. Álvarez to Gobernador Capitán General de la Ysla de Cuba, December 8, 1860, no. 50, in AGI, Cuba, 2266.

44. Falcón, *Las rasgaduras de la descolonización*, 38.

45. *La Época*, December 22, 1868.

46. Kwame Anthony Appiah, "There Is No Such Thing as Western Civilisation," *Guardian*, November 9, 2016.

47. Said, *Orientalism*.

48. Bailyn, "Idea of Atlantic History," 19–44.

49. Nemesio Fernández Cuesta, "Revista de la quincena," *La América*, October 8, 1861.

50. Porter, *Absent-Minded Imperialists*. Brantlinger disputes the idea that the empire largely remained absent from British fiction of the mid-Victorian era in *Rule of Darkness*.

51. Álvarez Junco, "El nacionalismo español," 48.

52. Castelar et al., *Crónica de la Guerra*, 5.

53. The term dates to 1840 in France. See Sessions, *By Sword and Plow*, 6.

54. *El Español*, May 3, 1836.

55. *El Pensamiento de la Nación*, August 7, 1844.

56. Conklin, *Mission to Civilize*. On the "blind spots" of other European intellectuals regarding race and empire, see Pitts, *Turn to Empire*, 5.

57. *Aspecto diplomático de la cuestión*, 24. Sessions highlights the religious dimensions of Algerian war propaganda in *By Sword and Plow*, 40.

58. For Spaniards like Castelar, very little separated the ideals of the Spanish from other European colonial projects. See Schmidt-Nowara, *Conquest of History*, 37. On the other hand, Eric Calderwood builds on the concept of a Hispano-Moroccan brotherhood and the "ambivalence" of colonial relations. See *Colonial al-Andalus*, 22; Mateo Dieste, *La «hermandad» hispano-*

marroquí, 23. Sasha Pack argues in *Deepest Border* that in some respects, goodwill characterized Hispano-Moroccan relations.

59. Hobson, *Imperialism*, 19, 25.

60. Fradera, *Gobernar colonias*, 32.

61. One Spanish anthropologist suggests a discourse of "Hispanotropicalism" had advanced Christian ideals of equality between races rather than a colonialism bent on economic dominance. For a discussion of the debate, see Martin-Márquez, *Disorientations*, 73–80.

62. Muñoz Gaviria, *África*, 14–15.

63. Antonio Vivar, *Memoria*, November, 1871, Santa Isabel, in AGA, 81/8200; Álvarez to Gobernador Capitán General de la Ysla de Cuba, April 24, 1862, Port-au-Prince, in AGI, Cuba, 984C.

64. On the nineteenth-century Spanish economy, especially revenue and expenditures, see Tortella, *Development of Modern Spain*, 177. More on comparing and measuring monetary values can be found online at Measuring-Worth, https://www.measuringworth.com.

65. *La América*, April 8, 1860. The secondary cause of the war's popularity, accordingly, was the idea of extending civilization and Christianity to the other side of the strait.

66. Penny and Bunzl, introduction to *Worldly Provincialism*, 9.

67. "Condorcet on Human Progress," 157.

68. Castelar et al., *Crónica de la Guerra*, 7–8.

69. *La Discusión*, March 28, 1861; reprinted in *El Siglo Diez y Nueve*, October 9, 1861.

70. The idea of a tree of races similarly became an organizing principle of history, with its teleological notions premised upon progress and its antithesis in atavistic images of the primitive. See McClintock, *Imperial Leather*, 39, 44.

71. Castelar, *La fórmula del progreso*, 5. According to journalist Kate Field, who interviewed him in 1873, Castelar had a small statue of French revolutionary leader Mirabeau in his drawing room—one of his few decorations. See Field, *Ten Days in Spain*, 136.

72. *La Discusión*, founded by Rivero, was Spain's most important Democratic periodical. See Vilches García, *Emilio Castelar*, 33.

73. *El Eco del Comercio*, December 16, 1847. A later observer referred to them as "sad and desolate." See Jerez Perchét, *Impresiones de viaje*, 153.

74. Castelar et al., *Crónica de la Guerra*, 38.

75. *El Clamor Público*, January 18, 1848.

76. Cited in Lida, "Democratic and Social Republic," 53.

77. Cruz, "Moderate Ascendancy," 43.

78. Donoso Cortés, cited from an April 26, 1848, letter in Graham, *Donoso Cortés*, 144.

79. Lida, "Democratic and Social Republic," 57.

80. In addition to calling for an end to the monarchy, the Democratic Party espoused religious tolerance in place of Catholic uniformity. See Vilches García, *Emilio Castelar*, 19.

81. Garrido, *Historia del reinado*, 3:7. The full-page image at the beginning of volume 1 features Lady Liberty waving the republican flag and leading Spaniards away from tyranny and despotism, symbolized by victims of military repression and the slave trade.

82. Cited in Cowans, *Early Modern Spain*, 268–69.

83. Castelar et al., *Crónica de la Guerra*, 46.

84. Castelar, *La fórmula del progreso*, 36–38.

85. Riego's flag was green, yellow, and red, but blue replaced green to symbolize the idea of Iberian union in 1830. See Lida, "Democratic and Social Republic," 57.

86. Cited in Vilches García, *Emilio Castelar*, 38–39. *The Formula of Progress* received strong criticism from Mexican conservatives, who argued that his democratic vision would lead to chaos. See the book review in *La Sociedad: Periódico Político y Literario*, March 23, 1859.

87. See Sartorius, "Of Exceptions and Afterlives."

88. Burdiel, "Liberal Revolution," 27.

89. Castelar, *La fórmula del progreso*, 39.

90. Cited in Lida, "Democratic and Social Republic," 67.

91. Castelar et al., *Crónica de la Guerra*, 47.

92. *Dichos y opiniones de Espartero*, 15.

93. See Schmidt-Nowara, *Empire and Antislavery*, 15.

94. Castelar, *La fórmula del progreso*, 5.

95. Skocpol, *Social Revolutions*, 99.

1. The War of Africa

1. Juan Blanco del Valle to Primer Secretario de Estado y del Despacho, December 10, 1858, Tangier, in MAEC, Correspondencia, Tangier, H 2075. The importance of dress as a sign of European identity is emphasized in many of the letters sent from different consular posts in Morocco. See, for example, Isidoro Millas to Primer Secretario de Estado, December 4, 1862, in MAEC, Correspondencia, Tetuán, H 2077.

2. It should be noted that consular protection could include exemption from Moroccan taxation. See Bartlett, "Great Britain and the Spanish," 176. In addition, provisional protection also had been provided, to Jews in particular, with "the delivery of printed certificates . . . which declared them to be Spanish protected subjects." But Blanco del Valle did not want to worsen relations between the sultan and his subjects, claiming "the documents were not regular Passports; that [the sultan] should assume the right of jurisdiction over those persons, as Spanish protected subjects; that in consequence of the panic which existed amongst the Hebrew population that hostilities might ensue

between Spain & Morocco & in order to tranquillize [*sic*] the public mind, he had issued these temporary documents so as to enable those who possessed them—if they so desired—to leave the country, until peaceful relations were reestablished." Translation of a letter by Mr. Drummond Hay to Seed Muhammad Khateeb, March 14, 1859, in MAEC, Correspondencia, Tangier, H 2075.

3. There had been a coordinated persecution of Catholics in the early decades of the nineteenth century during the reign of Minh Mang (1820–41). The Vietnamese emperor banned the propagation of Christianity in 1825. Despite the official ban Christianity spread, with more than eighty thousand adherents by 1849. See Ramsay, "Extortion and Exploitation," 311–28.

4. The sovereign of the ruling Nguyen dynasty, Tu Duc, had 104 wives. Not a weak-willed ruler, he did in fact call for resistance to the combined Franco-Spanish force in 1859, although he subsequently signed the Treaty of Saigon of 1862. Truong Dinh, conversely, became a leading guerrilla fighter combating European advances even after the treaty had been formalized. McLeod, "Tru'o'Ng Dinh," 90–91.

5. Victor Esmenjaud, *Los mártires de Conchinchina: Zarzuela en 3 actos en verso* (Valladolid, ES, 1859), 5–43, in BN.

6. Lorcin maintains that nostalgia for empire is at its height following decolonization, which occurred in the context of Spain in the 1810s and 1820s. See Lorcin, "Imperial Nostalgia," 104.

7. Over eighty plays were written about the Spanish-Moroccan War in the second half of the nineteenth century. See Salgues, *Teatro patriótico*.

8. Handwritten correspondence with the Military Governor in Melilla from 1845 emphasizes the great "prestige enjoyed by Emir Abdel-Kader in this country." Letter to Coronel Gobernador de la Plaza de Melilla, April 30, 1845, Granada, in AGM, Fondo de África.

9. Cited in Martin-Márquez, *Disorientations*, 54.

10. Inarejos Muñoz, *Intervenciones coloniales*. Over six thousand men were injured, and almost seven hundred were killed in the Spanish-Moroccan War. The figures double if the sick are included. Castelar et al., *Crónica del Ejército*, 210.

11. The Spanish signed a treaty that stipulated Annam cede three provinces to the French and pay an indemnity to France and Spain. See R. S. Thomson, "Diplomacy of Imperialism," 345.

12. For the theories and practices related to the public sphere across the nineteenth-century Spanish Monarchy, see Eastman, *Preaching Spanish Nationalism*, chapter 3.

13. Álvarez Junco, "El nacionalismo español," 52.

14. Hennessy, *Federal Republic in Spain*, 13.

15. Garcia-Balañà, "Patria, plebe y política," 61.

16. Jover, "Caracteres del nacionalismo español," 15; Pennell, *Morocco since 1830*, 67.

17. Blanco del Valle to Primer Secretario de Estado y del Despacho, August 30, 1858, Tangier, no. 66, and September 9, 1858, Tangier, no. 72, both in MAEC, Correspondencia, Tangier, H 2075.

18. Carlos de España to Primer Secretario de Estado y del Despacho, July 4, 1858, Tangier, no. 53, in MAEC, Correspondencia, Tangier, H 2075.

19. Carlos de España to Primer Secretario de Estado y del Despacho July 6, 1858, Tangier, no. 54, in MAEC, Correspondencia, Tangier, H 2075.

20. Memorandum confidential, n.d., in MAEC, Correspondencia, Tangier, H 2075.

21. John Drummond Hay to Andrew Buchanan March 17, 1859, Tangier, in MAEC, Correspondencia, Tangier, H 2075.

22. The moniker "Guerra de África" was used early on in the conflict. See letter to Ministro de la Guerra en Real Orden, November 10, 1859, in AGM, Fondo de África.

23. Carlos de España to Primer Secretario de Estado y del Despacho, May 12, 1858, Tangier, no. 36, in MAEC, Correspondencia, Tangier, H 2075.

24. Letter to Primer Secretario de Estado y del Despacho, August 5, 1858, Tangier, no. 62, in MAEC, Correspondencia, Tangier, H 2075. Thirty-two cannons reportedly arrived by the end of May 1859, exacerbating tensions among all parties.

25. *La América*, July 24, 1858.

26. Diana, *Un prisionero en el Riff*, 18.

27. For a typical use of the term *kabila*, see, for example, "Un paseo por el Riff: a mi amigo Alarcón," *El Museo Universal*, November 1, 1859.

28. Diana, *Un prisionero en el Riff*, 18.

29. Carlos de España to Primer Secretario de Estado y del Despacho, April 15, 1858, Tangier, no. 28, in MAEC, Correspondencia, Tangier, H 2075.

30. Another Spaniard insisted that the salient issue was that elections were held at all rather than having a hereditary governing system. See Jerez Perchét, *Impresiones de viaje*, 157.

31. Buchanan to Calderón Collantes, March 6, 1859, Madrid, in MAEC, Correspondencia, Tangier, H 2075.

32. Diana, *Un prisionero en el Riff*, 114.

33. *Don Manuel Buceta del Villar*, 1882, Estado mayor general del ejército, in AGMS.

34. An 1856 image shows menacing "Moors of the Rif" victimizing innocent civilians with two white women front and center. See Martín Corrales, *La imagen del magrebí*, 59.

35. Blanco del Valle to Primer Secretario de Estado y del Despacho, October 20, 1858, Tangier, no. 91, in MAEC, Correspondencia, Tangier, H 2075.

36. On the "fly-swatter incident" as a pretext for war, see Sessions, *By Sword and Plow*, 25.

37. Drummond Hay, letter, October 11, 1858, Tangier, in MAEC, Correspondencia, Tangier, H 2075.

38. Cited in Martin-Márquez, *Disorientations*, 55. The peace treaty was derided in nationalist invective throughout Spain. See, for example, F. M. T. to "Paz," April 26, 1860, Tetuán, in BN.

39. Letter from Her Majesty's Government, October 22, 1858, Madrid, in MAEC, Correspondencia, Tangier, H 2075.

40. Drummond Hay, letter, October 27, 1858, Tangier, in MAEC, Correspondencia, Tangier, H 2075.

41. Blanco del Valle to Sidi Muhammad, December 31, 1858, in MAEC, Correspondencia, Tangier, H 2075.

42. Letter from the Embajada de España en Paris, no. 628, in MAEC, Correspondencia, Tangier, H 2075.

43. Blanco del Valle to Primer Secretario de Estado y del Despacho, January 22, 1859, Tangier, no. 16, and January 23, 1859, Tangier, no. 17, both in MAEC, Correspondencia, Tangier, H 2075. The borders of Alhucemas and el Peñón also would be extended.

44. Buchanan to Calderón Collantes, January 29, 1859, Madrid, in MAEC, Correspondencia, Tangier, H 2075.

45. Manuel Buceta to Vice Consul de España en Tetuán, February 20, 1859, Melilla, in MAEC, Correspondencia, Tangier, H 2075. Blanco del Valle disagreed with Buceta's strategy, and he convinced O'Donnell to support him. Blanco del Valle to Primer Secretario de Estado y del Despacho, February 24, 1859, Tangier, no. 47, in MAEC, Correspondencia, Tangier, H 2075.

46. Diana, *Un prisionero en el Riff*, 108.

47. Diana, *Un prisionero en el Riff*, 32, 162.

48. Letter to Blanco del Valle, February 20, 1859, in MAEC, Correspondencia, Tangier, H 2075.

49. Despacho telegráfico, February 26, 1859, Algeciras, in MAEC, Correspondencia, Tangier, H 2075.

50. Blanco del Valle to Primer Secretario de Estado y del Despacho, March 18, 1859, Tangier, no. 70, in MAEC, Correspondencia, Tangier, H 2075.

51. Ben-Srhir argues that the policy of expansion around Melilla dates to the early 1850s in *Britain and Morocco*, 64.

52. Blanco del Valle to Saturnino Calderón Collantes, February 1, 1859, Tangier, in MAEC, Correspondencia, Tangier, H 2075. On the debates between a military and diplomatic strategy, see Pennell, "Discovery of Morocco's Northern Coast," 230–31.

53. Blanco del Valle to Primer Secretario de Estado y del Despacho, December 31, 1858, Tangier, no. 131, in MAEC, Correspondencia, Tangier, H 2075.

54. Blanco del Valle to Primer Secretario de Estado y del Despacho, January 14, 1859, Tangier, in MAEC, Correspondencia, Tangier, H 2075.

55. Drummond Hay, letter, October 27, 1858, Tangier, in MAEC, Correspondencia, Tangier, H 2075.

56. Pennell, "Discovery of Morocco's Northern Coast," 229. Moroccans cited article 15 of the treaty between the two nations that gave Spain freedom to act militarily against hostile actors. See Muhammad el Jetib, letter, January 6, 1859, in MAEC, Correspondencia, Tangier, H 2075.

57. See, for example, Blanco del Valle to Siied Muhammad el-Jetib, January 13, 1859, in MAEC, Correspondencia, Tangier, H 2075.

58. Blanco del Valle to Primer Secretario de Estado y del Despacho, May 22, 1859, nos. 102 and 103, in MAEC, Correspondencia, Tangier, H 2075.

59. Buceta to Conde de Lucena, May 6, 1859, Melilla, in MAEC, Correspondencia, Tangier, H 2075.

60. Castelar et al., *Crónica del Ejército*, 158; Ventosa, *Españoles y marroquíes*, 2: 839–44.

61. *Times*, February 24, 1860.

62. *Buceta del Villar*, in AGMS.

63. El Vice Consul de S. M. interinamente Encargado de esta Misión de España to Primer Secretario de Estado y del Despacho, March 24, 1859, Tangier, no. 73, in MAEC, Correspondencia, Tangier, H 2075.

64. Letter to Primer Secretario de Estado y del Despacho, May 24, 1859, Tangier, in MAEC, Correspondencia, Tangier, H 2075. Spanish sources reported the arrival in Tangier, from England, of thirty-two cannons and a large number of munitions for the sultan.

65. *La Discusión*, April 8, 1859.

66. Castelar et al., *Crónica de la Guerra*, 48–49. The Anjera hailed from the Jebala Mountains.

67. Blanco del Valle to Sidi Muhammad El-Katib, September 5, 1859, in Castelar et al., *Crónica de la Guerra*, 50.

68. El Katib to Mr. Blanco, in Castelar, *Crónica de la Guerra*, 57.

69. Lord John Russell to Mr. Buchanam [sic], in Castelar et al., *Crónica de la Guerra*, 59.

70. Castelar et al., *Crónica de la Guerra*, 60.

71. Castelar et al., *Crónica de la Guerra*, 61. Álvarez Junco emphasizes that "the press unanimously presented the actions that were going to be undertaken in the north of Morocco as the occasion to demonstrate to Europeans the persistence of the Spanish Monarchy as a great power." Álvarez Junco, *Mater dolorosa*, 511. See also Serrallonga Urquidi, "La guerra de África," 140–43.

72. Letter to Cap. General, October 22, 1859, Málaga, in AGM, Fondo de África.

73. *El Mundo Pintoresco*, October 23, 1859, no. 43.

74. See, for example, "Isla de Cuba. Donativos que se ofrecen para contribuir a los gastos de la guerra con el Imperio de Marruecos," January 1860, in AHN, Ultramar, legajo 4668; *El Redactor*, December 9, 1859, no. 293.

75. Navarrete, *Desde Vad-Ras a Sevilla*, 25.

76. Castelar et al., *Crónica del Ejército*, 5–6, 26, 36, 58. The Tercios de Vizcaya petitioned for troops in 1859 in addition to Catalan volunteers: "Serán admitidos en ella los naturales de las tres Provincias Vascongadas comprendidos en la edad de 18 a 40 años, cuyas condiciones personales sean suficientes para el servicio." In AGM, Capitanía General de Vascongadas, sig. 5956.41.

77. Circular, November 19, 1859, Bilbao, in AGM, Capitanía General de Vascongadas, sig. 5956.41.

78. Castelar et al., *Crónica del Ejército*, 23. Departing from Málaga, soldiers reportedly sang parts of *El grumete* (The cabin boy).

79. Castelar et al., *Crónica del Ejército*, 68.

80. Schmidt-Nowara, *Conquest of History*, 37.

81. Castelar et al., *Crónica del Ejército*, 236–37.

82. On Castelar's "Hegelian" ideas of progress, see Vilches García, *Emilio Castelar*, 38–40.

83. Castelar et al., *Crónica de la Guerra*, 6–9.

84. Berenson, *Heroes of Empire*, 2, 199.

85. Castelar et al., *Crónica del Ejército*, 79.

86. Castelar et al., *Crónica del Ejército*, 80.

87. Castelar et al., *Crónica del Ejército*, 103.

88. Castelar et al., *Crónica del Ejército*, 106, 126.

89. Castelar et al., *Crónica del Ejército*, 100. Emphasis in the original. See also Marín, "Image of Morocco," 148. Similar stereotypes of a warlike Arab character and phenotype had emerged in France as well, according to Çelik in *Displaying the Orient*, 30.

90. Castelar et al., *Crónica del Ejército*, 120.

91. Castelar et al., *Crónica del Ejército*, 133.

92. Castelar et al., *Crónica del Ejército*, 120.

93. This was also the case with the Moroccan historian al-Nasiri, who explicitly compared Mulay al'Abbas to Muhammad XII (Boabdil), the Nasrid ruler who could not prevent the loss of Granada to the Christians in 1492. See Calderwood, "Beginning (or End) of Moroccan History," 407.

94. Pedro Niceto de Sobrado, *Escenas de campamento* (1860), in BN. The press drew on the same comparisons. See, for example, Havana's *Gaceta Oficial*, June 16, 1860. And the play was a success, according to Salgues in *Teatro patriótico*, 23.

95. Castelar et al., *Crónica del Ejército*, 129. This rhetoric dovetailed with that of the third Earl Grey, who said Britons had a duty to bring the arts of civilization and governance to Africa and uplift the inhabitants. See Hastings, "Christianity, Civilization, and Commerce," 75.

96. Castelar et al., *Crónica del Ejército*, 129.

97. On the congruence between liberalism and imperialism, see Mehta, "Liberal Strategies of Exclusion," 59–86.

2. The Taking of Tetuán

1. Cited in Martin-Márquez, *Disorientations*, 55. Scholars in Morocco generally favor the term "War of Tetuán" whether writing in Arabic or Tamazight. See Goikolea-Amiano, "Hispano-Moroccan Mimesis," 45.

2. *La España*, September 1, 1859.

3. Castelar et al., *Crónica del Ejército*, 35–36. He said, "No podía esperar otra cosa de soldados españoles que pelean por su Reina y por la honra de su país."

4. Berenson, *Heroes of Empire*, 11–12.

5. Núñez de Arce, *Recuerdos de la campaña*, 82.

6. Ben-Layashi and Maddy-Weitzman, "Myth, History and Realpolitik," 93–94.

7. In a caricature from *El Cañón Rayado*, a Jewish man, previously having had to bow and submit to Muslim authorities, now bows down deeply before a Spaniard. See Martín Corrales, *La imagen del magrebí*, 70.

8. Castelar et al., *Crónica del Ejército*, 150. Núñez de Arce called the "disgraced Jewish race" victims of Muslim oppression in *Recuerdos de la campaña*, 112.

9. Millas to Primer Secretario de Estado, July 17, 1861, in MAEC, Correspondencia, Tetuán, H 2077.

10. Castelar et al., *Crónica del Ejército*, 31–32, 72.

11. Castelar et al., *Crónica del Ejército*, 134.

12. Núñez de Arce, *Recuerdos de la campaña*, 110.

13. Al-Nasiri al-Salawi, *Versión árabe*, 45.

14. Castelar et al., *Crónica del Ejército*, 138.

15. Castelar et al., *Crónica del Ejército*, 138. Alarcón expressed similar sentiments. See Sánchez-Mejía, "Barbarie y civilización," 61. On Spanish views of race in Morocco, see Goode, *Impurity of Blood*, 89–91.

16. Castelar et al., *Crónica del Ejército*, 237.

17. Castelar et al., *Crónica del Ejército*, 138.

18. Castelar et al., *Crónica del Ejército*, 142. See also *El Cañón Rayado*, March 22, 1860, no. 22.

19. Castelar et al., *Crónica del Ejército*, 142.

20. Castelar et al., *Crónica del Ejército*, 163.

21. Castelar et al., *Crónica del Ejército*, 171.

22. Castelar et al., *Crónica del Ejército*, 164.

23. Castelar et al., *Crónica del Ejército*, 149.

24. Castelar et al., *Crónica del Ejército*, 163–64.

25. Al-Nasiri al-Salawi, *Versión árabe*, 47.

26. Castelar et al., *Crónica del Ejército*, 151.

27. Castelar et al., *Crónica del Ejército*, 118.

28. "Suplemento al Moro Muza," March 1, 1860.

29. Castelar et al., *Crónica del Ejército*, 146.

30. Castelar et al., *Crónica del Ejército*, 176.

31. *La Discusión*, February 7, 1860.

32. Castelar et al., *Crónica del Ejército*, 147–48.

33. Burdiel, *Isabel II*, 630.

34. Castelar et al., *Crónica del Ejército*, 124, 164.

35. *El asedio de Tetuán: Himno patriótico-popular*, 1860, Madrid, in BN.

36. Castelar et al., *Crónica del Ejército*, 118–19.

37. Castelar et al., *Crónica del Ejército*, 150.

38. Castelar et al., *Crónica del Ejército*, 157.

39. Letter from General en Gefe del Ejército, May 4, 1860, Tetuán, in MAEC, Obra Pía, Tetuán, OP 336.

40. Castelar et al., *Crónica del Ejército*, 174.

41. Castelar et al., *Crónica del Ejército*, 216.

42. Castelar et al., *Crónica del Ejército*, 174.

43. Castelar et al., *Crónica del Ejército*, 149. On the "colonized female body," see Martin-Márquez, *Disorientations*, 130–42.

44. Castelar et al., *Crónica del Ejército*, 150. Alarcón said it looked like Granada had four hundred years earlier. See Martin-Márquez, *Disorientations*, 106.

45. The proposed voyage never materialized, however. See Cerchiello and Vera-Rebollo, "Steamboats and Pleasure Travels," 32–34.

46. Castelar et al., *Crónica del Ejército*, 156. The first railroad line in Spain, built out from Barcelona, was inaugurated in 1848.

47. Castelar et al., *Crónica del Ejército*, 167.

48. Castelar et al., *Crónica del Ejército*, 164. Many Muslim residents did not return for the duration of occupation. See Goikolea-Amiano, "Hispano-Moroccan Mimesis," 47.

49. Castelar et al., *Crónica del Ejército*, 165.

50. Núñez de Arce, *Recuerdos de la campaña*, 130.

51. Castelar et al., *Crónica del Ejército*, 234–35.

52. Núñez de Arce, *Recuerdos de la campaña*, 112.

53. Castelar et al., *Crónica del Ejército*, 150.

54. Núñez de Arce, *Recuerdos de la campaña*, 132.

55. *La América*, April 8, 1860. Emphasis in the original.

56. Letter to Primer Secretario de Estado, September 20, 1861, Madrid, in MAEC, Obra Pía, Tetuán, OP 328.

57. Leopoldo O'Donnell to Ministro de Estado, August 12, 1860, in MAEC, Obra Pía, Tetuán, OP 336.

58. Miguel de la Puente, *Plaza de Tetuán*, November 8, 1861, in MAEC, Obra Pía, Tetuán, OP 336. Even though the estimate was revised downward on December 24 to 800,000 *reales de vellón*, a funding source from the Holy Land did not seem amenable to donating 120,000 *reales*. Letter to Primer Secretario de Estado, February 28, 1862, in MAEC, Obra Pía, Tetuán, OP 336.

59. *Cesión de aguas*, March 18, 1862, in MAEC, Obra Pía, Tetuán, OP 336.

60. *En la plaza de Tetuán*, n.d., in MAEC, Obra Pía, Tetuán, OP 336.

61. Millas to Primer Secretario de Estado, May 2, 1862, Tetuán, in MAEC, Obra Pía, Tetuán, OP 336. On the family of Ash'ash, see Miller, *Disorienting Encounters*, 13–15.

62. José Tenorio, *Obras del consulado*, April 30, 1862, Tetuán; letter from the Comisaría General de los Santos Lugares de Jerusalén, May 24, 1862, Madrid, both in MAEC, Obra Pía, Tetuán, OP 336.

63. *Palacio, 16 de Febrero 1863*, in MAEC, Obra Pía, Tetuán, OP 336.

64. Letter to Ministro de Estado, November 1, 1867, Tetuán, in MAEC, Obra Pía, Tetuán, OP 337. On the church, see Bravo Nieto, "Formas y modelos," 210.

65. Landa, *La campaña de Marruecos*, 152.

66. Millas to Primer Secretario de Estado, August 13, 1862, in MAEC, Correspondencia, Tetuán, H 2077.

67. Francisco Merry y Colom to Primer Secretario de Estado y del Despacho, September 21, 1861, Tangier, no. 164, in MAEC, Correspondencia, Embajadas y Legaciones, Marruecos, H 1638. The dangers of collaboration were demonstrated by the attempted assassination of Hamed Bencadar, the Arabic interpreter in Ceuta, although the motives for the act are not clear from the archival evidence. Letter to Comandante General de Ceuta, April 7, 1859, Ceuta, in MAEC, Correspondencia, Tangier, H 2075.

68. Millas to Primer Secretario de Estado, March 11, 1862, in MAEC, Correspondencia, Tetuán, H 2077.

69. Pennell argues that for "all intents and purposes, Moroccan sultans did not exercise any day-to-day control over the Rif in the eighteenth and nineteenth centuries." See Pennell, "Discovery of Morocco's Northern Coast," 229. The Spanish consul in Tangier makes the same point in correspondence from September 21, 1861.

70. *Reglamento de la compañía de moros tiradores del Rif,* October 15, 1859, Melilla, in AGM, Fondo de África.

71. *Campañas de África 1830–1909. Resumen,* in AGM, Fondo de África.

72. Letter to the Military Governor of Melilla, July 13, 1863; *Segun Rl. orn. de 20 Oct. de 1860,* both in AGM, Fondo de África.

73. Diplomatic correspondence expressed concern over desertion, with a list drawn up that included 240 names. See Merry y Colom to Primer Secretario de Estado, April 9, 1861, Tangier, no. 56, in MAEC, Correspondencia, Marruecos, H 1638. One letter describes Spanish soldiers "in a state of almost complete nudity," brought to the embassy by "Moors." See Merry y Colom to Primer Secretario de Estado y del Despacho, July 31, 1860, Tangier, in MAEC, Correspondencia, Marruecos, H 1638.

74. See, for example, *Traducción* (12 Shawwal 1280), in AGM, Fondo de África. Included with a number of items in Correspondencia árabe, this is from March 21, 1864.

75. Castelar et al., *Crónica del Ejército*, 75–76.

76. Merry y Colom to Primer Secretario de Estado y del Despacho, February 6, 1862, Tangier, in MAEC, Correspondencia, Marruecos, H 1638.

77. Diana, *Un prisionero en el Riff*, 77.

78. Merry y Colom to Primer Secretario de Estado, July 30, 1861, Tangier, in MAEC, Correspondencia, H 1638.

79. The British noted that Spain protected Muslims as well: "The Spanish Consular Agent has issued some 60 or 70 certificates to Moorish subjects that they are Spaniards." Extracts from a private letter from Drummond Hay to Buchanan, April 13, 1859, Tangier, in MAEC, Correspondencia, Tangier, H 2075.

80. Millas to Primer Secretario de Estado, August 23, 1862, in MAEC, Correspondencia, Tetuán, H 2077. Stories circulated of Spanish soldiers raping Jewish women, who were forced to deliver their children in a Franciscan missionary hospital. See Ben-Layashi and Maddy-Weitzman, "Myth, History and Realpolitik," 94.

81. Millas to Primer Secretario de Estado, August 5, 1862, in MAEC, Correspondencia, Tetuán, H 2077.

82. R. R. de M., *Crónica de la Guerra de África*, in BN, 203.

83. Castelar et al., *Crónica del Ejército*, 170–71.

84. Castelar et al., *Crónica del Ejército*, 240–43. One deputy insisted that Spain focus on internal turmoil such as the 1860 abortive Carlist rising of la Rápita, in which several thousand troops landed in Catalonia ostensibly to reestablish a traditional Catholic monarchy, rather than sending soldiers overseas. Liberal journalists decried the Carlist leader, Captain General of the Balearic Islands Jaime Ortega, as a traitor. See *La América*, April 8, 1860.

85. Castelar et al., *Crónica del Ejército*, 148.

86. Castelar et al., *Crónica del Ejército*, 248–54.

87. Castelar et al., *Crónica del Ejército*, 237–40.

88. Merry y Colom to Primer Secretario de Estado y del Despacho, August 9, 1860, Tangier, in MAEC, Correspondencia, Marruecos, H 1638.

89. *La España*, September 9, 1860.

90. Castelar reminded his readers that Moroccan ambassadors had visited Madrid during the reign of Charles III as well, in 1766 and 1780, bookended by two conflicts in North Africa. In 1774 the king sent General Alejandro O'Reilly to Ottoman Algeria with twenty thousand men, who disembarked near Algiers on July 8, 1775. Castelar declared it an unmitigated disaster, with hundreds of deaths, and Spain saw few gains or concessions. Castelar et al., *Crónica de la Guerra*, 27–28.

91. *Escenas Contemporáneas*, October 15, 1861; *La Correspondencia de España*, November 4, 1861.

92. *La América*, October 8, 1861.

93. *La España*, October 4, 1861.

94. Millas to Primer Secretario de Estado, May 9, 1862, in MAEC, Correspondencia, Tetuán, H 2077. Mulay al'Abbas visited a mountaintop shrine

that hosted Muslim pilgrims as a symbolic conclusion to hostilities. Millas to Primer Secretario de Estado, May 30, 1862, in MAEC, Correspondencia, Tetuán, H 2077.

95. Fradera, *La nación imperial*, 1:xvii.

96. *La Guerra de África y la toma de Tetuán: Episodio dramático-contemporáneo, en cinco actos y en prosa*, 1860, in BN.

97. Miller, *History of Modern Morocco*, 25.

98. Letter from El Ayuntamiento de la Habana, November 30, 1859, in AHN, Ultramar, legajo 4668.

99. Castelar et al., *Crónica del Ejército*, 169.

3. Visual Culture

1. Clayson, "Henri Regnault's Wartime Orientalism," 157.

2. González López and Martí Ayxelá, "La vida cotidiana," 18.

3. According to Tabbal, in "José Villegas y Cordero," 227, there are conflicting views on whether Villegas had traveled to Morocco. On the other hand, Ángel Castro Martín does mention a trip in his brief biographical essay, found online at Ángel Castro Martín, "Villegas y Cordero, José," Museo del Prado (website), https://www.museodelprado.es/aprende/enciclopedia/voz/villegas-y-cordero-jose/0169f7c9-53b5-4aff-aadc-36f101a6b5fa.

4. Schwartz and Przyblyski, "Visual Culture's History," 3.

5. Ginger, *Painting and the Turn*, 13.

6. Said, *Culture and Imperialism*.

7. Sinha, *Colonial Masculinity*, 15.

8. Álvarez Junco, "Formation of Spanish Identity," 18–19.

9. Clayson, "Henri Regnault's Wartime Orientalism," 135.

10. DeGuzmán, *Spain's Long Shadow*, 81.

11. R. Benjamin, *Orientalist Aesthetics*, 21–22.

12. Ruedy, *Modern Algeria*, 48.

13. On the idea that Hussein Dey was a quintessential Oriental despot, see Sessions, *By Sword and Plow*, 29–30.

14. *Aspecto diplomático de la cuestión*, 18.

15. Pitts, introduction to *Writings on Empire and Slavery*, xii–xx.

16. Tocqueville, in Pitts, *Writings on Empire and Slavery*, 20, 65.

17. Pitts, introduction to *Writings on Empire and Slavery*, xx.

18. R. Benjamin, *Orientalist Aesthetics*, 15–16.

19. Martín Corrales, *La imagen del magrebí*, 67.

20. R. Benjamin, *Orientalist Aesthetics*, 3.

21. *Una imagen para la memoria*, 152; López Mondéjar, *150 Years of Photography*, 80. According to accounts, the two did not get along well.

22. Palma Crespo, "Enrique Facio," 299.

23. Martin-Márquez, *Disorientations*, 104–5.

24. Palma Crespo, "Enrique Facio," 301.

25. Castelar et al., *Crónica del Ejército*, 172.

26. Cited in R. Benjamin, *Orientalist Aesthetics*, 24–25.

27. Castelar et al., *Crónica del Ejército*, 53.

28. Cited in Palma Crespo, "Enrique Facio," 302.

29. Castelar et al., *Crónica del Ejército*, 53.

30. Castelar et al., *Crónica del Ejército*, 44.

31. Castelar et al., *Crónica del Ejército*, 73.

32. Castelar et al., *Crónica del Ejército*, 78.

33. Castelar et al., *Crónica del Ejército*, 53–54.

34. Cited in R. Benjamin, *Orientalist Aesthetics*, 22.

35. *El Museo Universal*, June 12, 1864.

36. Alarcón acknowledged that his Africanist narrative allowed for "pure fantasy." See Martin-Márquez, *Disorientations*, 102.

37. Cited in R. Benjamin, *Orientalist Aesthetics*, 19.

38. On the history of the city's three cemeteries, see Calderwood, "Living and the Dead," 9. Facio photographed the Moorish cemetery, according to Palma Crespo, "Enrique Facio," 319.

39. Roberts, *Intimate Outsiders*, 8.

40. Martín Corrales, *La imagen del magrebí*, 69.

41. *El Mundo Pintoresco*, March 4, 1860, no. 10. Two pages later an artist's rendering of a bridge over the Júcar River with a train crossing from Valencia symbolizes the inauguration of an industrial age in Spain.

42. Martínez Gallego, "Entre el himno," 157.

43. Martín Corrales, *La imagen del magrebí*, 65.

44. *El Cañón Rayado*, December 11, 1859, no. 1.

45. *El Cañón Rayado*, March 15, 1860, no. 21.

46. Of course, during the uprising in India in 1857 rebels cut the telegraph wire and caused a communications blackout. Fears of similar sabotage certainly would have pervaded the Spanish camp. See Llewellyn-Jones, *Great Uprising in India*, 10.

47. Martín Corrales, *La imagen del magrebí*, 65.

48. Martín Corrales, *La imagen del magrebí*, 62–63.

49. Martín Corrales, *La imagen del magrebí*, 66.

50. Martín Corrales, *La imagen del magrebí*, 73.

51. Ginger, *Painting and the Turn*, 285.

52. Tabbal, "José Villegas y Cordero," 231.

53. "Condorcet on Human Progress," 157.

54. Blanco del Valle to Primer Secretario de Estado y del Despacho, May 22, 1859, no. 102, in maec, Correspondencia, Tangier, H 2075.

55. Letter from El Ayuntamiento de la Habana, November 30, 1859, in ahn, Ultramar, legajo 4668.

56. Santana's stationery features his name in bold characters, followed by "Libertador de la Patria, General en Gefe de los Ejércitos, Caballero

Gran Cruz de la Real Orden Americana de Isabel la Católica y Presidente de la República." A shield with a cross displayed prominently in the center adorns the top, and the words "Dios, Patria, Libertad" appear as the footer. Santana to Capitán General de la Ysla de Cuba, January 18, 1861, in AGI, Cuba, 2266.

4. Order, Progress, Civilization

1. Cortada, *Spain and the American Civil War*, 39.

2. Álvarez to Primer Secretario de Estado, August 8, 1862, Port-au-Prince, no. 71, in MAEC, Política, Dominicana, H 2375.

3. José de la Gándara y Navarro, *Dominicanos*, April 1, 1864, Santo Domingo, in AHS, Dominican Republic.

4. Anderson, "Creole Pioneers," in *Imagined Communities*, 47–65.

5. Sagás, *Race and Politics*, 33.

6. Martínez-Fernández, "Sword and the Crucifix," 70, 81.

7. Moya Pons, *Dominican Republic*, 152.

8. Martínez-Fernández, "Sword and the Crucifix," 73.

9. José Malo de Molina, *Memoria*, September 4, 1861, in AGI, Cuba, 2266.

10. Martínez-Fernández, "Sword and the Crucifix," 73.

11. Moya Pons, *Dominican Republic*, 168.

12. Cited in Sagás, *Race and Politics*, 32.

13. Javier de Istúriz to Presidente del Consejo de Ministros, September 11, 1863, Paris, in MAEC, Política, Dominicana, H 2375.

14. Earlier on Santana and the Dominican government had been open to Britain or France establishing a protectorate. See Bowen, *Spain and the American Civil War*, 85.

15. Juan del Castillo Jovellanos to Capitán General Gefe Superior Civil de la Ysla de Cuba, June 12, 1858, in AGI, Cuba, 984C.

16. Pedro Santana, Presidente de la República Dominicana, to S. M. la Regina de España, April 27, 1860, Santo Domingo, in AGI, Cuba, 2266.

17. Bowen, *Spain and the American Civil War*, 87.

18. Gabriel G. Tassara to Gobernador Capitán General de la Isla de Cuba, November 20, 1860, Washington DC, in AGI, Cuba, 2266.

19. Calderón Collantes to Gobernador Capitán General de la Isla de Cuba, June 27, 1860; Calderón Collantes to Consul General de España en Haiti, July 22, 1860, in AGI, Cuba, 2266.

20. *El Museo Universal*, June 23, 1861.

21. Letter to Ministro de la Guerra y de Ultramar, September 5, 1861, in AGI, Cuba, 2266.

22. Antonio Peláez Campomanes, *Memoria*, November 8, 1860, in AHN, Ultramar, legajo 3526.

23. Juan de Zavala to Ministro de la Guerra y de Ultramar, August 24, 1860, in AHN, Ultramar, legajo 3526.

24. Mariano Álvarez, *Memoria. Santo Domingo ó la República Dominicana*, April 20, 1860, in AHN, Ultramar, legajo 3526.

25. In 1844 the population had grown to 126,000. See Moya Pons, *Dominican Republic*, 185.

26. Álvarez, *Memoria*.

27. Álvarez to Primera Secretaria de Estado, September 18, 1860, in AGI, Cuba, 2266.

28. Bowen, *Spain and the American Civil War*, 88.

29. Malo de Molina, *Memoria*.

30. *El Museo Universal*, April 28, 1861.

31. Álvarez to Gobernador Capitán General de la Ysla de Cuba May 8, 1862, Port-au-Prince, in AGI, Cuba, 984C; Álvarez to Primer Secretario de Estado, August 8, 1862, Port-au-Prince, no. 71, in MAEC, Política, Dominicana, H 2375.

32. Álvarez to Gobernador Capitán General de la Ysla de Cuba, May 24, 1862, Port-au-Prince, in AGI, Cuba, 984C.

33. Malo de Molina, *Memoria*.

34. Francisco Fort to Capital General de la Ysla de Cuba December 4, 1860, Santo Domingo, in AGI, Cuba, 2266. On Fort, see Garcia-Balañà, "Patriotismos trasatlánticos," 214–16.

35. *La Discusión*, May 22, 1861.

36. Castelar et al., *Crónica de la Guerra*, 8. On the idea of the Latin race, see Goode, *Impurity of Blood*, 30.

37. An unsigned article published the following week, for example, again advocated the colonization of Tetuán and Tangier as a base for a larger imperial presence in North Africa. *La Discusión*, May 29, 1861.

38. *La Discusión*, May 23, 1861.

39. Inarejos Muñoz, *Intervenciones coloniales*, 68. Álvarez claimed the British had privately stated the same things in Álvarez to Primer Secretario de Estado, June 21, 1860, Santo Domingo, in MAEC, Política, Dominicana, H 2375.

40. Núñez de Arce, *Santo Domingo*, 43.

41. *La Discusión*, May 23, 1861.

42. A separate article suggested that Dominicans should be able to send representatives to the Cortes. See F. Díaz Quintero, "Cuestión de Santo Domingo," *La Discusión*, April 20, 1861.

43. *La Discusión*, March 21, 1861.

44. Félix de Bona, "Las leyes especiales," *La América*, September 24, 1861.

45. Santana to Capitán General de la Ysla de Cuba, January 18, 1861.

46. Álvarez to Primer Secretario de Estado, May 4, 1860, Santo Domingo, no. 46, in MAEC, Política, Dominicana, H 2375.

47. Álvarez to Gobernador Capitán General de la Isla de Cuba, August 4, 1860, Santo Domingo, in AGI, Cuba, 2266.

48. *Dominicanos!*, June 3, 1860, Santo Domingo, in MAEC, Política, Dominicana, H 2375. Santana had received the title "Liberator" in 1849. See Bowen, *Spain and the American Civil War*, 85.

49. Santana to Gobernador Capitán General de la Isla de Cuba, August 9, 1860, in AGI, Cuba, 2266.

50. Álvarez to Primer Secretario de Estado, July 3, 1860, Santo Domingo, in MAEC, Política, Dominicana, H 2375.

51. Istúriz to Primer Secretario de Estado, June 12, 1861, London, in MAEC, Política, Dominicana, H 2375.

52. F. Alfau to Primer Secretario de Estado August 2, 1860, Madrid, in MAEC, Política, Dominicana, H 2375.

53. Álvarez to Gobernador Capitán General de la Isla de Cuba, August 9, 1860, in AGI, Cuba, 2266.

54. Letter to the plenipotentiary in Washingthon [*sic*], October 16, 1860, in AGI, Cuba, 2266.

55. Álvarez to Gobernador Capitán General de la Ysla de Cuba, October 18, 1860, no. 31, in AGI, Cuba, 2266.

56. Tassara to Gobernador Capitán General, November 20, 1860, Washington DC, in AGI, Cuba, 2266.

57. Álvarez, letter, August 31, 1860, in AGI, Cuba, 2266.

58. While the official government proclamation of annexation definitively stated that "slavery . . . will not be reestablished," the document described Dominicans as "docile to the voice of authority," a people who gladly will accept the reorganization of the government under the auspices of Spain. See letter, May 19, 1861, Aranjuez, in Núñez de Arce, *Santo Domingo*, 73–74.

59. Calderón Collantes to Gobernador Capitán General de la Isla de Cuba, September 8, 1860, in AGI, Cuba, 2266.

60. Álvarez to Gobernador Capitán General de la Ysla de Cuba, September 20, 1860, in AGI, Cuba, 2266.

61. Álvarez to Gobernador Capitán General de la Ysla de Cuba, October 18, 1860, no. 30, in AGI, Cuba, 2266.

62. Pedro Ricart y Torres, Ministro de Relaciones Exteriores, de Hacienda y Comercio, to Gobernador y Capitán General de la Ysla de Cuba, November 1860, in AGI, Cuba, 2266.

63. Even Santana privately admitted to a demoralized clergy in correspondence with the Cuban captain general. See the classified letter from August 8, 1861, in AGI, Cuba, 2266. There were serious monetary issues as well, described by Moya Pons in *Dominican Republic*, 197–99.

64. Álvarez, "Observaciones que el infrascrito cree conveniente esponer al Exmo Señor Primer Secretario de Estado, para facilitar la resolución que debe darse á las delicadas cuestiones referentes á la República Dominicana," November 12, 1860, Havana, no. 38, in AGI, Cuba, 2266.

65. *La Discusión*, May 19, 1861.

66. Álvarez to Gobernador Capitán General de la Ysla de Cuba, November 12, 1860, Havana, no. 37, in AGI, Cuba, 2266.

67. *Proceso verbal levantado*, June 22, 1861; Santana to Gobernador y Capitán General de la Ysla de Cuba, July 5, 1861, both in AGI, Cuba, 2266.

68. Tassara to Gobernador Capitán General, November 20, 1860, Washington DC, in AGI, Cuba, 2266.

69. Álvarez to Gobernador Capitán General de la Ysla de Cuba, April 5, 1861, New York, no. 39, in AGI, Cuba, 2266.

70. Tassara, *Legación de España en Washington*, April 9, 1861, in AGI, Cuba, 2266.

71. Santana to Capitán General y Gobernador de la Isla de Cuba, February 4, 1861, in AGI, Cuba, 2266.

72. O'Donnell to Gobernador Capitán General de la Isla de Cuba, Muy reservado, December 8, 1860, in AGI, Cuba, 2266.

73. Eugenio Gómez Molinero to Gobernador Capitán General de la Ysla de Cuba, February 4, 1861, no. 19, in AGI, Cuba, 2266. In April, a month after reincorporation, the same diplomat repeated his claim, stating that with the arrival of four thousand troops from Cuba and Puerto Rico, the country was entirely tranquil. Eugenio Molinero to Primer Secretario de Estado, April 18, 1861, no. 18, in AGI, Cuba, 2266.

74. Santana, *Dominicanos!*, March 18, 1861, Santo Domingo, in AGI, Cuba, 2266.

75. Núñez de Arce, *Santo Domingo*, 76–106; Bowen, *Spain and the American Civil War*, 88. Haiti protested the annexation, while some in Spain promoted the French annexation of Haiti. See *La España*, May 9, 1861.

76. *La Correspondencia de España*, April 12, 1861. Even moderate periodicals issued veiled warnings concerning the "grave complications" that might arise from an attempt to unify the "Latin race" in America. See "Anexión de Santo Domingo," *La Época*, April 18, 1861.

77. *El Museo Universal*, May 12, 1861.

78. José María Cabral, *Dominicanos!*, April 6, 1861, Las Caobas, in AGI, Cuba, 984c.

79. J. M. Sánchez, B. González, *Como Dominicanos amantes de su patria*, January 15, 1861, in AGI, Cuba, 2266.

80. Molinero to Cap. General de la Ysla de Cuba, May 27, 1861; Antonio Alfau to Francisco Serrano, June 1, 1861, both in AGI, Cuba, 2266.

81. *Gaceta Oficial*, June 16, 1860.

82. Álvarez to Primer Secretario de Estado, June 18, 1860, Santo Domingo, no. 59, in MAEC, Política, Dominicana, H 2375. Evidence showed that Ramírez had sent "various Dominican families" to Haitian jails during the conflict.

83. Santana to Gobernador Capitán General de la Ysla de Cuba, July 5, 1861, in AGI, Cuba, 2266.

84. On Ramírez and Cabral, see Eller, "Let's Show the World," 116, 244.

85. Sang Ben, "Contradicciones en el liberalismo," 246.

86. William Seward, Department of State, letter, April 2, 1861, Washington DC, in AGI, Cuba, 2266.

87. Tassara, *Legación de España en Washington*, letter, April 4, 1861, in AGI, Cuba, 2266.

88. William Seward, Department of State, letter, April 5, 1861, Washington DC; William Seward, Department of State, letter, May 21, 1861, Washington DC, both in AGI, Cuba, 2266.

89. Tassara to Primer Secretaria de Estado, August 5, 1861, in AGI, Cuba, 2266.

90. Cited in *La América*, September 8, 1861.

91. R. Edwards to Calderón Collantes, May 23, 1861, Madrid, in MAEC, Política, Dominicana, H 2375.

92. Malo de Molina, *Memoria*.

93. Bienvenido Monzón y Martín, "Nos el Dr. D. Bienvenido Monzón y Martín por la gracia de Dios y de la Santa Sede Apostólica Arzobispo de Santo Domingo," March 7, 1863, in BN.

94. *Acta de Independencia*, September 14, 1863, Santiago de los Caballeros, in AGI, Cuba, 984C.

95. Letter to Ministro de la Guerra, October 28, 1863, in AGI, Cuba, 923B.

5. Anatomy of an Uprising

1. *Organización y planta de los gobiernos, comandancias militares y de armas de la isla de Santo Domingo*, June 26, 1862, Madrid, in AGI, Cuba, 923B.

2. Santana took the title of the Marquis de la Carreras with a monthly pension of two thousand "hard dollars" for life. *New York Herald*, November 7, 1863.

3. Álvarez to Gobernador Capitán General de la Ysla de Cuba, April 24, 1862, Port-au-Prince, in AGI, Cuba, 984C.

4. Álvarez to Gobernador Capitán General de Santo Domingo, March 2, 1862, Port-au-Prince, in AGI, Cuba, 984C.

5. Pedro Ezequiel Guerrero, *Capitanía General de Santo Domingo*, letter, August 8, 1863, in AHN, Ultramar, legajo 3525.

6. Álvarez to Primer Secretario de Estado, March 8, 1862, Port-au-Prince, in AGI, Cuba, 984C.

7. Álvarez, February 24, 1862, in AGI, Cuba, 984C. He singled out the ex-minister Salomon Soulouque, an émigré who had written against the government of Geffrard.

8. Álvarez to Gobernador Capitán General de la Ysla de Cuba, April 24, 1862, Port-au-Prince, in AGI, Cuba, 984C.

9. Moya Pons, *Dominican Republic*, 207; Eller, "Let's Show the World," 321.

10. Cited in Martínez-Fernández, "Sword and the Crucifix," 82.

11. *New York Herald*, March 17, 1863, in Tassara, March 20, 1863, Washington DC, no. 53, in MAEC, Política, Dominicana, H 2375.

12. Tassara, letter, March 23, 1863, Washington DC, in MAEC, Política, Dominicana, H 2375.

13. Álvarez to Gobernador Capitan General de la Ysla de Cuba, March 7, 1863, Port-au-Prince, in AGI, Cuba, 984C. The appeal was published by the Haitian authorities that month. Álvarez to Capitán General de la Ysla de Cuba, March 27, 1863, Port-au-Prince in AGI, Cuba, 984C.

14. Felipe Rivero y Lemoyne, Gobernador Capitán General de Santo Domingo, *Dominicanos*, May 29, 1863, in AGI, Cuba, 923B.

15. Rivero, *Bando*, May 29, 1863, in AGI, Cuba, 923B.

16. *Gaceta de Madrid*, May 30, 1863.

17. Rivero to Ministro de Estado y de Ultramar, June 10, 1863, in AHN, Ultramar, legajo 3525. López del Campillo was to root out rebels accused of robbing and pillaging towns.

18. Rafael Gómez Pérez, Julián Delgado, *Comisión militar permanente establecida en la ciudad de Puerto Plata*, in AGI, Ultramar, 881A.

19. *Don Juan Suero General de Brigada y Comandante Militar de esta plaza*, August 31, 1863, in AGI, Ultramar, 881A.

20. *Declaración del Capitán de las Reservas D. Julián de Lora*, September 20, 1863, in AGI, Ultramar, 881A.

21. *Declaración del Capitán de las Reservas Don Carlos Bastida*, September 20, 1863, in AGI, Ultramar, 881A.

22. *Declaración del Sargento 1.º de las reservas Manuel Rodríguez*, 1863, in AGI, Ultramar, 881A.

23. *Indagatoria del paisano Juan Francisco Merced* 1863, in AGI, Ultramar, 881A.

24. Gómez Pérez, Delgado, *Comisión militar permanente*; *Declaración del subteniente de las reservas D. Anastasio Fernández*, 1863, in AGI, Ultramar, 881A.

25. *Declaración de D. Rafael Leandro García*, 1863, in AGI, Ultramar, 881A.

26. Monzón y Martín, "Nos el Dr. D. Bienvenido Monzón y Martín," 5–6.

27. Buceta to General Philantrope Noël, *Legación Haitiana*, August 19, 1863, in AHN, Ultramar, legajo 3525.

28. Rivero to Ministro de Ultramar, September 3, 1863, in AHN, Ultramar, legajo 3525.

29. "Another Account. To the Editor of the Herald," *New York Herald*, November 2, 1863, in *Anexo al despacho no. 224*, Santo Domingo, in MAEC, Política, Dominicana, H 2375.

30. *World*, October 4, 1863, in *Anexo al despacho no. 206*, Santo Domingo, in MAEC, Política, Dominicana, H 2375.

31. Rivero, *Bando*, August 24, 1863, in AGI, Ultramar, 881A.

32. *Indagatoria del paisano preso Tomas Pacheco*, 1863, in AGI, Ultramar, 881A.

33. *Indagatoria del paisano José Agustín Bidó*, 1863, in AGI, Ultramar, 881A.

34. *Indagatoria del paisano preso D. Wenceslao de la Concha*, 1863, in AGI, Ultramar, 881A.

35. *Don Felipe Esguerra y Blasco*, 1863, in AGI, Ultramar, 881A.

36. *Declaración del preso Federico Scheffenberg*, 1863, in AGI, Ultramar, 881A.

37. *Don Felipe Esguerra y Blasco*, October 13, 1863, in AGI, Ultramar, 881A.

38. Benigno F. de Rojas, *To Her Majesty Queen Isabella II*, September 24, 1863, in AHN, Ultramar, legajo 3525.

39. *Acta de Independencia*, September 14, 1863, Santiago de los Caballeros, in AGI, Cuba, 984C.

40. *La Razón*, October 3, 1863, no. 74.

41. *Declaración indagatoria del paisano Juan Antonio del Rosario*, 1863, in AGI, Ultramar, 881A.

42. Eller, "Let's Show the World," 390–91. Some prisoners ultimately faced exile to Ceuta. See letter, August 9, 1864, Madrid, in AHN, Ultramar, legajo 3525.

43. *New York Herald*, October 5, 1863, in *Anexo al despacho no. 206*, Santo Domingo, in MAEC, Política, Dominicana, H 2375.

44. *New York Herald*, November 7, 1863.

45. *New York Herald*, October 30, 1863.

46. *New York Herald*, November 7, 1863.

47. Tassara to Capitán General de la Ysla de Cuba, *Legación de España en Washington*, November 18, 1863, Washington DC, in MAEC, Política, Dominicana, H 2375.

48. Tassara to Primer Secretario de Estado, November 9, 1863, Washington DC, in MAEC, Política, Dominicana, H 2375.

49. Gabriel Enríquez to Gobernador Capitán General de la Isla de Cuba, October 27, 1863, Madrid, in AGI, Cuba, 984C; Vizc. de la Vega to Ministro Plenipotenciario de S. M. en Washington, December 8, 1863, Boston, in MAEC, Política, Dominicana, H 2375.

50. Tassara to Gobernador Capitán General de la Isla de Cuba, November 3, 1863, Washington DC, in AGI, Cuba, 984C.

51. *The Royal Standard and Gazette of the Turks and Caicos Islands*, November 7, 1863, no. 45.

52. *Tribune*, October 3, 1863.

53. Carlos de Vargas to Ministro de Ultramar, Reservado, October 21, 1863, in AHN, Ultramar, legajo 3525.

54. Domingo Dulce to Ministro de Ultramar, September 14, 1863, Havana, in AHN, Ultramar, legajo 3525. Dulce had been captain general of the Catalan volunteers sent over to North Africa in 1860, and he later served in Cuba as war broke out in 1868. See Serrallonga Urquidi, "La Guerra de África," 152.

55. Joaquín Gutiérrez de Rubalcava to Ministro de Estado, January 23, 1864, Madrid, in MAEC, Política, Dominicana, H 2375.

56. Rivero, *Bando*, October 5, 1863, Santo Domingo, in MAEC, Política, Dominicana, H 2375; Vargas, *Bando*, November 7, 1863, Santo Domingo, in MAEC, Política, Dominicana, H 2375; *The Royal Standard and Gazette of the Turks and Caicos Islands*, November 7, 1863, no. 45.

57. John F. Crampton to His Excellency the Marquis of Miraflores, December 4, 1863, Madrid, in MAEC, Política, Dominicana, H 2375.

58. *London Gazette*, March 22, 1864.

59. Álvarez to Primer Secretario de Estado, March 24, 1864, Port-au-Prince, in MAEC, Política, Dominicana, H 2375.

60. *Anexo al despacho no. 198*, September 12, 1863, Havana, in MAEC, Política, Dominicana, H 2375.

61. Cited in a clip from an unnamed newspaper, in *Al no. 226*, in MAEC, Política, Dominicana, H 2375. Two years of war cost thirty-three million pesos, according to Moya Pons, *Dominican Republic*, 212.

62. Vargas to Ministro de Ultramar, December 23, 1863, in AHN, Ultramar, legajo 3525.

63. Santana to Ministro de Ultramar, October 10, 1863, in AHN, Ultramar, legajo 3525.

64. *Tribune*, January 1, 1865.

65. *El Constitucional*, November 17, 1864, no. 28, in MAEC, Política, Dominicana, H 2375.

66. *El Constitucional*, November 24, 1864, no. 31, in MAEC, Política, Dominicana, H 2375.

67. López de la Vega, *La cuestión de Santo Domingo*, 6–22.

68. López de la Vega, *La cuestión de Santo Domingo*, 6–26.

69. Tassara to Primer Secretaria de Estado, September 6, 1861, in AGI, Cuba, 2266.

70. On Tassara, see Sierra, "Política, romanticismo, y masculinidad," 203–26. The article does not discuss race or slavery in any detail.

71. *La Discusión*, August 5, 1863.

72. *La Discusión*, October 27, 1863.

73. *El Museo Universal*, February 28, 1864. He called for annexing the Samaná peninsula as compensation.

74. *El Museo Universal*, February 7, 1864.

75. Schmidt-Nowara, *Empire and Antislavery*, 115.

76. *Revista Hispano-Americana*, January 1, 1864.

77. Núñez de Arce, *Santo Domingo*, 6–7.

6. Death to Spain!

1. Fradera, "Juan Prim y Prats," 259; Inarejos Muñoz, *Intervenciones coloniales*, 98.

2. One report, in *La Correspondencia de España*, November 9, 1861, asserted that eighteen thousand Spaniards resided in Mexico.

3. Some periodicals lamented the news of Pacheco's departure. See *El Museo Universal*, February 17, 1861.

4. *El Siglo Diez y Nueve*, November 2, 1861.

5. Robertson, "Tripartite Treaty of London," 169. Falcón begins the story on July 17, 1861, with Juárez's suspension of debt payments in *Las rasgaduras de la descolonización*, 226.

6. Topik, "When Mexico Had the Blues," 714–38.

7. Falcón, *Las rasgaduras de la descolonización*, 225. Prim rebuffed the idea of intervention in Mexico in 1858, according to Oltra, "La visita del General Prim," 64.

8. Cortada writes that in July 1860 Calderón Collantes proposed the idea of an intervention to the British and the French in *Spain and the American Civil War*, 44.

9. J. F. Pacheco to Calderón Collantes, April 5, 1860, London, in RAH.

10. Pacheco to Calderón Collantes, March 28, 1860, Paris, in RAH.

11. *La Discusión*, April 6, 1861. See Schmidt-Nowara, *Empire and Antislavery*, 113–14.

12. *El Siglo Diez y Nueve*, October 9, 1861. The editorial first appeared in *La Discusión*, March 28, 1861. On Castelar's positive reception in Mexico, see Hale, *Transformation of Liberalism*, 41–47.

13. *El Siglo Diez y Nueve*, October 24, 1861.

14. *La América*, June 24, 1857. For more analysis, see Quijada, "Sobre el origen," 595–616.

15. On this subject, see Goode, *Impurity of Blood*, 60.

16. Castelar to Don Elías Montes, April 3, 1885, in BN.

17. Falcón, *Las rasgaduras de la descolonización*, 25–48. Garrido similarly decried the "degenerate" mestizo masses, whom he blamed for the violence and brutality of Mexico's midcentury wars. See García-Balañà, "Racializing the Nation," 272.

18. José María Gutiérrez de Alba, *Los Españoles en Mégico, drama original en tres actos y en verso* (1862), in BN, 14–48.

19. *El Siglo Diez y Nueve*, September 21, 1861. Mexican diplomats seconded the accusation. See J. A. de la Fuente, November 15, 1861, Paris, in AHGE, Francia 608.

20. *El Siglo Diez y Nueve*, September 21, 1861.

21. T. Benjamin, *La Revolución*, 40.

22. *El Siglo Diez y Nueve*, October 4, 1861. "Order and progress" was the mantra of the moderate government of Ignacio Comonfort in 1856, as well. See Krauze, *Mexico*, 168.

23. Fuente to Ministro de Relaciones Exteriores, June 3, 1861, New York, in AHGE, Francia 608.

24. Fuente to Ministro de Relaciones Exteriores, June 29, 1861, Paris, in AHGE, Francia 608.

25. Fuente, letter, September 11, 1861, Paris, in AHGE, Francia 608. The decision had been made and communicated to France on September 6, 1861. See Falcón, *Las rasgaduras de la descolonización*, 227.

26. Letter from the Legación de Méjico enviada á España, September 19, 1861, in AHGE, Francia 608.

27. Matías Romero to Fuente, October 27, 1861, Washington DC, in AHGE, Francia 608.

28. Cited in a clip from an unnamed newspaper, AHGE, Francia 608.

29. Fuente, Reservado, September 27, 1861, in AHGE, Francia 608.

30. Romero to Fuente, October 1, 1861, Washington DC, in AHGE, Francia 608. On Dunbar, see Curtin, *Atlantic Slave Trade*, 6–7.

31. Romero to Fuente, *Entrevista con Mr. Seward*, October 7, 1861, Washington DC, in AHGE, Francia 608.

32. See a discussion of the American press in *La América*, September 8, 1861.

33. Romero to Fuente, October 9, 1861, Washington DC, in AHGE, Francia 608.

34. Romero to Fuente, November 7, 1861, Washington DC, in AHGE, Francia 608. On the 1783 document incorrectly attributed to Aranda, see Escudero, *El supuesto memorial del Conde de Aranda*.

35. Romero to Fuente, October 12, 1861, Washington DC, in AHGE, Francia 608. See his subsequent statements in Romero to Fuente, November 3, 1861, Washington DC, in AHGE, Francia 608.

36. Fuente, Reservado, November 5, 1861, London, in AHGE, Francia 608. He wrote that he had thought of returning home to fight a thousand times.

37. Fuente, November 15, 1861, in AHGE, Francia 608.

38. *La Época*, September 12, 1861.

39. *La América*, September 24, 1861.

40. Falcón, *Las rasgaduras de la descolonización*, 230; Francisco Lozano Muñoz, "El principio de intervención," *La América*, September 24, 1861.

41. Fuente, Muy reservado, October 24, 1861, London, in AHGE, Francia 608.

42. Cited in *New York Times*, October 26, 1861.

43. Falcón, *Las rasgaduras de la descolonización*, 231.

44. Ramón Díaz, *Consulado Mexicano en la Habana*, letter, October 31, 1861, in SEDENA, expediente XI/481.4/8249.

45. José María de Mora, letter, November 19, 1861, Veracruz, in SEDENA, expediente XI/481.4/8249.

46. Circular, November 18, 1861, Toluca, in AGN, Mexico City, caja 7, 40222/3.

47. *Benito Juárez, Presidente Constitucional de los Estados Unidos Mexicanos, á sus habitantes*, December 17, 1861, in AGN, caja 7, 40222/3.

48. Romero to Fuente, November 3, 1861, Washington DC, in AHGE, Francia 608; Romero to Fuente, November 7, 1861, Washington DC, in AHGE, Francia 608.

49. *El Siglo Diez y Nueve*, November 2, 1861.

50. José María de Mora, letter, December 8, 1861, Veracruz, in SEDENA, expediente XI/481.4/8249.

51. *La América*, suplemento al número 4, April 26, 1862.

52. *Declaración tomada al desertor Silvestre Alonso*, December 30, 1861, in SEDENA, expediente XI/481.4/8249.

53. *Declaración tomada al desertor Juan López*, December 30, 1861, in SEDENA, expediente XI/481.4/8249.

54. Romero to Fuente, December 23, 1861, Washington DC, in AHGE, Francia 608.

55. G. P. C. Thomson, *Patriotism, Politics, and Popular Liberalism*, 75.

56. *El Siglo Diez y Nueve*, December 23, 1861.

57. Fuente, letter, Muy reservado, October 24, 1861, London, in AHGE, Francia 608; *La América*, October 8, 1861.

58. *La América*, October 8, 1861.

59. F. Hube to Fuente, January 22, 1862, Hamburg, in AHGE, Francia 608. Accordingly, "General Almonte, a Mexican, is now in Belgium conducting negotiations for placing the Archduke Maximilian on the throne." Cited in "France and Mexico," January 26, 1862, a clip from an unnamed newspaper, AHGE, Francia 608.

60. Romero, February 21, 1862, Washington DC, in AHGE, Francia 608.

61. Romero to Fuente, January 12, 1862, Washington DC, in AHGE, Francia 608.

62. *El Siglo Diez y Nueve*, November 14, 1862.

63. *¡El Moro Babú!* played at the Teatro de Oriente on the afternoon of January 27, 1861, in CEHM.

64. Fuente, February 4, 1862, Paris, in AHGE, Francia 608.

65. Romero to Fuente, February 21, 1862, Washington DC, in AHGE, Francia 608.

66. *El Siglo Diez y Nueve*, April 5, 1862.

67. *New York Times*, January 3, 1862.

68. Cited in a clip from an unnamed newspaper, AHGE, Francia 608.

69. *New York Times*, January 3, 1862.

70. *El Museo Universal*, December 29, 1861.

71. Cited in "The Mexican Intervention," January 15, 1862, a clip from an unnamed newspaper, AHGE, Francia 608.

72. Cited in "Spain," February 25, 1862, a clip from an unnamed newspaper, AHGE, Francia 608.

73. Letter to Napoleon III, March 17, 1862, Orizaba, in Piñol and Redondo, *Colección de cartas*, 152–54.

74. *La América*, March 24, 1862.

75. *Benito Juárez, Presidente Constitucional de los Estados-Unidos Mexicanos, á sus habitantes*, April 12, 1862, in AGN, caja 7, 40222/3; *El Siglo Diez y Nueve*, April 12, 1862.

76. Cited in Oltra, "La visita del General Prim," 68.

77. *La América*, June 24, 1862. Tassara espoused similar rhetoric according to Oltra, "La visita del General Prim," 66.

78. *El Constitucional*, November 19, 1864, no. 29, in MAEC, Política, Dominicana, H 2375. On the Spanish occupation of the Chincha Islands off the coast of Peru in 1864, see Inarejos Muñoz, *Intervenciones coloniales*, 99–134.

79. *La Discusión*, July 28, 1863.

80. Cited in Falcón, *Las rasgaduras de la descolonización*, 247.

7. The Traveling Society

1. See, for example, Antonio Caballero de Rodas, "La Guerra Civil," *Boletín Oficial del Principado de Cataluña*, March 10, 1875.

2. A 1778 treaty had delivered a base of operations to Spain in central West Africa, with potentially lucrative territories ceded by Portugal.

3. In the 1860s, according to Muñoz Gaviria, no Spanish government officials lived on Annobón or on Corisco. See *África*, 15. For developments in the last two decades of the nineteenth century on Fernando Po, see Sundiata, *From Slaving to Neoslavery*, 101–3.

4. Sierra, "Time of Liberalism," 41.

5. *La Iberia*, October 1, 1860.

6. Vilches García, *Emilio Castelar*, 86.

7. *La Iberia*, October 1, 1860.

8. *La Correspondencia de España*, September 30, 1868.

9. *La Época*, December 22, 1868. On the Grito de Yara, see Ferrer, *Insurgent Cuba*, 15.

10. For a discussion of the issue in the early nineteenth century, see Eastman, *Preaching Spanish Nationalism*, 99.

11. Ferry, "Speech before the French," 188.

12. *La Época*, December 22, 1868.

13. Cited in Field, *Ten Days in Spain*, 145.

14. Antonio Vivar, *Memoria*, November, 1871, Santa Isabel, in AGA, 81/8200.

15. Castillo Rodríguez, "Language and the Hispanization," 352.

16. Muñoz Gaviria, *África*, 14.

17. Vivar, *Memoria*, November, 1871, Santa Isabel, in AGA, 81/8200.

18. Vivar, *Memoria*, November, 1871, Santa Isabel, in AGA, 81/8200. An 1881 document lists 267 names of people taken on board the warship *Almansa*, who were then placed on the merchant vessel *Josefina*, and finally conducted to Fernando Po on December 27, 1880. This shows that the policy of bringing Cuban exiles to West Africa continued even though the *emancipado* scheme had ended in September 1866 and penal expeditions had been banned in 1867. See *Relación nominal de los deportados cubanos*, in AGA, 81/8201; Sundiata, "'Cuba Africana,'" 99. Joaquín Costa later elaborated a plan for a penal colony on Annobón in 1883. See Hahs, "Scramble for Africa," 147.

19. José Muñoz Gaviria estimated the entire island's population at thirty thousand inhabitants in his article in *El Museo Universal*, July 31, 1864. On the Moret Law, see Scott, *Slave Emancipation in Cuba*, 64.

20. Vivar, *Memoria*, November, 1871, Santa Isabel, in AGA, 81/8200.

21. Hahs, "Scramble for Africa," 6.

22. Vivar, *Memoria*, November, 1871, Santa Isabel, in AGA, 81/8200. Scholars estimate the population at 858 individuals at the time. See Castro and Calle, *La colonización española*, 16.

23. *El Museo Universal*, June 12, 1864.

24. "To the Governor General of the Colony," July 21, 1868, Santa Isabel, in AGA, 81/7958.

25. Vivar, *Memoria*, November, 1871, Santa Isabel, in AGA, 81/8200.

26. *El Museo Universal*, August 7, 1864.

27. *El Museo Universal*, July 24, 1864.

28. Vivar, *Memoria*, November, 1871, Santa Isabel, in AGA, 81/8200.

29. Sundiata, "'Cuba Africana,'" 100.

30. Vivar, *Memoria*, November, 1871, Santa Isabel, in AGA, 81/8200. Muñoz Gaviria estimated the annual cost at close to one million *reales*, whereas customs dues brought in a scant fourteen thousand *reales*. Muñoz Gaviria, *África*, 14.

31. *El Museo Universal*, August 7, 1864.

32. *El Museo Universal*, July 31, 1864.

33. Muñoz Gaviria, *África*, 12.

34. *El Museo Universal*, July 31, 1864.

35. Alejo Angel Medina, letter, December 28, 1859, Fernando Po, in AGA, 81/7209; Anselmo Garulla, *Infermería de la Viva Santa María*, January 31, 1860, Santa Isabel, in AGA, 81/7209.

36. *El Museo Universal*, June 19, 1864.

37. For an overview of the snake-god Dangbe, sacred trees, and Dahomian religious practices in general, see Law, *Ouidah*, 88–98.

38. *El Museo Universal*, July 24, 1864.

39. *El Museo Universal*, July 31, 1864.

40. *El Museo Universal*, July 31, 1864.

41. García Cantús, "Fernando Póo," 320; Iradier, *África*, 1:216.

42. Based on scholarship and primary source material, Bonkoro II sat for the portrait taken by Muñoz Gaviria. Alonso Fernández identifies him as Bonkoro I in "La presencia de España," 54.

43. *El Museo Universal*, July 31, 1864.

44. Muñoz Gaviria, *África*, 14; Salom Costa, *España en la Europa de Bismarck*, 323–24.

45. Berenson, *Heroes of Empire*, 2.

46. Iradier, *África*, 1:iv.

47. Iradier, *África*, 1:v, 377.

48. Berenson, *Heroes of Empire*, 57–58.

49. Iradier, *África*, 1:163–65; Majó Framis, *Las generosas y primitivas empresas*, 47.

50. Iradier, *África*, 2:201; Martin-Márquez, *Disorientations*, 80.

51. Iradier, *África*, 1:154.

52. Iradier, *África*, 1:145; Sundiata, *Equatorial Guinea*, 21.

53. Iradier, *África*, 1:247.

54. Iradier, *África*, 2:261. Rumors of cannibalism proved false. See Young, "Fang," 460.

55. Iradier, *África*, 2:438.

56. Jefferson wrote, "I advance it therefore as a suspicion only, that the blacks, whether originally a distinct race, or made distinct by time and circumstances, are inferior to the whites in the endowments both of body and mind," in *Notes on the State of Virginia*, 150.

57. Departing in late 1874, Iradier traveled with his wife Isabel and her sister Manuela, who both remained on Elobey Chico for eight months. On their scientific achievements, see Benita Sampedro Vizcaya, "The Colonial Politics of Meteorology."

58. Martin-Márquez, *Disorientations*, 68.

59. Cited in Goode, *Impurity of Blood*, 185.

60. Iradier, *África*, 1:376–77.

61. Mosse, *Toward the Final Solution*, 27. Scholars presented a great deal of research on subjects such as craniometry at the Congreso Geográfico-Hispano-Portugués-Americano held in October 1892. See Blanco, "Theorizing Racial Hybridity," 86–90.

62. Goode, *Impurity of Blood*, 52–62.

63. Iradier, *África*, 2:175–87.

64. Iradier, *África*, 2:188–89.

65. Iradier, *África*, 2:190.

66. Iradier, *África*, 2:193–96.

67. Iradier, *África*, 2:198–99.

68. *El Globo*, December 8, 1877.

69. Berenson, *Heroes of Empire*, 50.

70. *El Globo*, May 1, 1881.

71. *El Globo*, May 1, 1881.

72. Berenson, *Heroes of Empire*, 63.

73. *El Globo*, May 1, 1881.

74. Iradier, *África*, 1:376.

75. Iradier, *África*, 1:193.

76. Salom Costa has argued that Britain had prevented Spain from exerting its influence in Morocco by the early 1880s, whereas Bartlett views France as the major obstacle to Spanish expansion in the Maghreb and highlights instances of collaboration with the British. See Salom Costa, *España en la Europa de Bismarck*, 378–80; Bartlett, "Great Britain and the Spanish," 179.

77. Iradier, *África*, 2:249.

78. Varela Ortega, *Los amigos políticos*, 172.

79. Castelar, "Discurso pronunciado el 7 de Agosto de 1881 en Huesca sobre la politica democrática ante una reunión electoral," in *Discursos parlamentarios*, 4:38.

80. Castelar, "Discurso pronunciado," 14–35.

81. Hahs, "Scramble for Africa," 157–61.

82. For contextualization, see Dalmau, "Clientelism, Politics and the Press," 144–45.

Epilogue

1. Berenson, *Heroes of Empire*, 17.

2. On the bias of Dominican nationalist historiography, see Venator Santiago, "Haitian Revolutionary Ideology," 103.

3. "Miles de dominicanos de origen haitiano pierden sus derechos políticos," *El País*, November 10, 2013.

4. Eller, *We Dream Together*.

5. Moya Pons, *La dominación haitiana*, 119.

6. Eller, *We Dream Together*.

7. Núñez de Arce, *Recuerdos de la campaña*, 9.

8. *Gaceta Oficial*, June 16, 1860.

9. Goode, "Genius of Columbus," 63–83.

10. Iradier, *África*, 1:81, 383.

11. Hochschild, *King Leopold's Ghost*. On representations of the horrors and violence of colonialism in Congo, see "Revamped Museum Takes New Look at Belgium's Colonial Past," *Philadelphia Tribune*, December 5, 2018.

12. "El incierto retorno de los tesoros africanos," *El País*, December 14, 2018. The article does not mention Spanish museums at all. On controversies in Britain, see "The Ethiopian Treasures in the v&a May Have to Return Home," *Guardian*, April 9, 2018.

13. Found online at Asociación Africanista Manuel Iradier, "Quiénes Somos," Asociación Africanista Manuel Iradier (website), https://www.iradier.org /quienes-somos/.

14. Found online at Iradier y Bulfy, "Dry Gin," Iradier y Bulfy (website), https://www.iradierybulfy.es/en/dry-gin/.

15. Kagan, *Spanish Craze*.

16. Found online at "La estatua de fray Junípero Serra de Palma amanece con la palabra 'racista' pintada," *La Vanguardia*, July 22, 2020, https:// www.lavanguardia.com/local/baleares/20200622/481909011696/estatua -fray-junipero-serra-pintada-palma-racista.html.

17. "Jéssica Albiach: 'Desmontar la estatua de Colón en Barcelona sería una buena medida,'" *ABC*, June 13, 2020.

Bibliography

Archives

AGA. Archivo General de la Administración, Alcalá de Henares

AGI. Archivo General de Indias, Seville

AGM. Archivo General Militar de Madrid

AGMS. Archivo General Militar de Segovia

AGN. Archivo General de la Nación, Mexico City

AGP. Archivo General de Palacio, Madrid

AHGE. Archivo Histórico Genaro Estrada de la Secretaría de Relaciones Exteriores, Mexico City

AHN. Archivo Histórico Nacional, Madrid

AHS. Archivo Histórico de Santiago, Dominican Republic

BN. Biblioteca Nacional, Madrid

CEHM. Archivo del Centro de Estudios de Historia de México

MAEC. Archivo General del Ministerio de Asuntos Exteriores y de Cooperación, Madrid

RAH. Real Academia de la Historia, Biblioteca, Madrid

SEDENA. Archivo Histórico de la Secretaría de la Defensa Nacional, Mexico City

Published Works

Alonso Fernández, Guillermo. "La presencia de España en África." *Reales sitios* 36, no. 139 (1999): 52–63.

Álvarez Junco, José. "The Formation of Spanish Identity and Its Adaptation to the Age of Nations." *History and Memory* 14, nos. 1–2 (Spring–Winter 2002): 13–36.

——— . *Mater dolorosa: La idea de España en el siglo XIX.* Madrid: Taurus, 2001.

——— . "El nacionalismo español como mito movilizador. Cuatro guerras." In *Cultura y movilización en la España contemporánea,* edited by Rafael Cruz and Manuel Pérez Ledesma, 35–67. Madrid: Alizanza Universidad, 1997.

———. "The Nation-Building Process in Nineteenth-Century Spain." In *Nationalism and the Nation in the Iberian Peninsula: Competing and Conflicting Identities*, edited by Clare Mar-Molinero and Angel Smith, 89–106. Oxford, UK: Berg, 1996.

Anderson, Benedict. *Imagined Communities: Reflections on the Origin and Spread of Nationalism*. Rev. ed. London: Verso, 1991.

Bailyn, Bernard. "The Idea of Atlantic History." *Itinerario* (1996): 19–44.

Bartlett, Christopher John. "Great Britain and the Spanish Change of Policy towards Morocco in June 1878." *Historical Research* 31, no. 84 (1958): 168–85.

Benjamin, Roger. *Orientalist Aesthetics: Art, Colonialism, and French North Africa, 1880–1930*. Berkeley: University of California Press, 2003.

Benjamin, Thomas. *La Revolución: Mexico's Great Revolution as Memory, Myth, and History*. Austin: University of Texas Press, 2000.

Ben-Layashi, Samir, and Bruce Maddy-Weitzman. "Myth, History and Realpolitik: Morocco and Its Jewish Community." *Journal of Modern Jewish Studies* 9, no. 1 (2010): 89–106.

Ben-Srhir, Khalid. *Britain and Morocco during the Embassy of John Drummond Hay, 1845–1886*. Translated by Malcolm Williams and Gavin Waterson. London: RoutledgeCurzon, 2005.

Berenson, Edward. *Heroes of Empire: Five Charismatic Men and the Conquest of Africa*. Berkeley: University of California Press, 2011.

Blanco, Alda. "Theorizing Racial Hybridity in Nineteenth-Century Spain and Spanish America." In *Empire's End: Transnational Connections in the Hispanic World*, edited by Akiko Tsuchiya and William G. Acree Jr., 84–106. Nashville TN: Vanderbilt University Press, 2016.

Bowen, Wayne H. *Spain and the American Civil War*. Columbia: University of Missouri Press, 2011.

Boyd, Carolyn P. *Praetorian Politics in Liberal Spain*. Chapel Hill: University of North Carolina Press, 1979.

Brantlinger, Patrick. *Rule of Darkness: British Literature and Imperialism, 1830–1914*. Ithaca NY: Cornell University Press, 1988.

Bravo Nieto, Antonio. "Formas y modelos de la arquitectura religiosa española en Marruecos." *Boletín de arte*, no. 19 (1998): 205–29.

Burdiel, Isabel. *Isabel II: Una biografía (1830–1904)*. Madrid: Taurus, 2010.

———. "The Liberal Revolution, 1808–1843." In *Spanish History since 1808*, edited by José Álvarez Junco and Adrian Shubert, 17–32. London: Arnold, 2000.

Calderwood, Eric. "The Beginning (or End) of Moroccan History: Historiography, Translation, and Modernity in Ahmad B. Khalid Al-Nasiri and Clemente Cerdeira." *International Journal of Middle East Studies* 44, no. 3 (2012): 399–420.

———. *Colonial al-Andalus: Spain and the Making of Modern Moroccan Culture*. Cambridge MA: Harvard University Press, 2018.

———. "The Living and the Dead." *American Scholar* 78, no. 4 (2009): 7–11.

Castelar, Emilio. *La civilización en los cinco primeros siglos del Cristianismo. Lecciones pronunciadas en el Ateneo de Madrid*. Madrid: Manuel Gómez Marín, 1858.

———. *Discursos parlamentarios y políticos de Emilio Castelar en la Restauración*. Vol. 4. Madrid: Librerías de A. de San Martín, 1885.

———. *La fórmula del progreso*. Madrid: Establecimiento tipográfico de J. Casas y Díaz, 1858.

Castelar, Emilio, Francisco de Paula Canalejas, Gregorio Cruzada Villaamil, and Miguel Morayta, ed. *Crónica de la Guerra de África*. Madrid: Imprenta de V. Matute y B. Compagni, 1859.

———, ed. *Crónica del Ejército y Armada de África*. Madrid: Imprenta de V. Matute y B. Compagni, 1859.

Castillo Rodríguez, Susana. "Language and the Hispanization of Equatorial Guinea." In *A Political History of Spanish: A Making of a Language*, edited by José del Valle, 350–63. Cambridge, UK: Cambridge University Press, 2013.

Castro, Mariano L. de, and María Luisa de la Calle. *La colonización española en Guinea Ecuatorial (1858–1900)*. Barcelona: Ceiba Ediciones, 2007.

Çelik, Zeynep. *Displaying the Orient: Architecture of Islam at Nineteenth-Century World's Fairs*. Berkeley: University of California Press, 1992.

Cerchiello, Gaetano, and José Fernando Vera-Rebollo. "Steamboats and Pleasure Travels: Success and Failure of the First Spanish Initiatives in the Mid-Nineteenth Century." *Journal of Tourism History* 7, no. 1–2 (2015): 18–35.

Clayson, Hollis. "Henri Regnault's Wartime Orientalism." In *Orientalism's Interlocutors: Painting, Architecture, Photography*, edited by Jill Beaulieu and Mary Roberts, 131–78. Durham NC: Duke University Press, 2002.

"Condorcet on Human Progress." *Population and Development Review* 21, no. 1 (1995): 153–61.

Conklin, Alice L. *A Mission to Civilize: The Republican Idea of Empire in France and West Africa, 1895–1930*. Stanford: Stanford University Press, 1997.

Cortada, James W. *Spain and the American Civil War: Relations at Mid-Century, 1855–1868*. Philadelphia PA: American Philosophical Society, 1980.

Cowans, Jon, ed. *Early Modern Spain: A Documentary History*. Philadelphia: University of Pennsylvania Press, 2003.

Cruz, Jesus. "The Moderate Ascendancy, 1843–1868." In *Spanish History Since 1808*, edited by José Álvarez Junco and Adrian Shubert, 33–47. London: Arnold, 2000.

Curtin, Philip D. *The Atlantic Slave Trade: A Census*. Madison: University of Wisconsin Press, 1969.

Dalmau, Pol. "Clientelism, Politics and the Press in Modern Spain. The Case of the Godó Family and the Founding of 'La Vanguardia.'" PhD diss., European University Institute, 2015.

DeGuzmán, María. *Spain's Long Shadow: The Black Legend, Off-Whiteness, and Anglo-American Empire*. Minneapolis: University of Minnesota Press, 2005.

Diana, Manuel Juan. *Un prisionero en el Riff. Memorias del ayudante Álvarez*. Madrid: Imprenta Nacional, 1860.

Dichos y opiniones de Espartero en conversación con sus amigos. N.p., 1868.

Drescher, Seymour. *Dilemmas of Democracy: Tocqueville and Modernization*. Pittsburgh PA: University of Pittsburgh Press, 1968.

Eastman, Scott. *Preaching Spanish Nationalism across the Hispanic Atlantic*. Baton Rouge: Louisiana State University Press, 2012.

Eller, Anne. "Let's Show the World We Are Brothers: The Dominican Guerra de Restauración and the Nineteenth-Century Caribbean." PhD diss., New York University, 2011.

———. *We Dream Together: Dominican Independence, Haiti, and the Fight for Caribbean Freedom*. Durham NC: Duke University Press, 2016.

Escudero, José Antonio. *El supuesto memorial del Conde de Aranda sobre la independencia de América*. 2nd ed. Madrid: Agencia Estatal Boletín Oficial del Estado, 2020.

Falcón, Romana. *Las rasgaduras de la descolonización: Españoles y mexicanos a mediados del siglo XIX*. Mexico: El Colegio de México, 1996.

Ferrer, Ada. *Insurgent Cuba: Race, Nation, and Revolution, 1868–1898*. Chapel Hill: University of North Carolina Press, 1999.

Ferry, Jules. "Speech before the French National Assembly (1883)." In *Sources of the Making of the West: Peoples and Cultures Volume II: Since 1500*, edited by Katharine J. Lualdi, 186–90. 4th ed. Boston: Bedford, 2012.

Field, Kate. *Ten Days in Spain*. Boston: James R. Osgood, 1875.

Fradera, Josep M. *Gobernar colonias*. Barcelona: Ediciones Península, 1999.

———. "Juan Prim y Prats (1814–1870)." In *Liberales, agitadores y conspiradores: Biografías heterodoxas del siglo XIX*, edited by Isabel Burdiel and Manuel Pérez Ledesma, 239–66. Madrid: Espasa, 2000.

———. *La nación imperial: Derechos, representación y ciudadanía en los imperios de Gran Bretaña, Francia, España y Estados Unidos (1750–1918)*. Vol. 1. Barcelona: Edhasa, 2015.

Garcia-Balañà, Albert. "Patria, plebe y política en la España Isabelina: La Guerra de África en Cataluña (1859–1860)." In *Marruecos y el colonialismo español (1859–1912). De la Guerra de África a la "penetración pacífica,"* edited by Eloy Martín Corrales, 13–78. Barcelona: Edicions Bellaterra, 2002.

———. "Patriotismos trasatlánticos. Raza y nación en el impacto de la Guerra de África en el Caribe español de 1860." *Ayer* 106, no. 2 (2017): 207–37.

———. "Racializing the Nation in Nineteenth-Century Spain (1820–65): A Transatlantic Approach." *Journal of Iberian and Latin American Studies* 24, no. 2 (2018): 265–77.

García Cantús, Dolores. "Fernando Póo: Una aventura colonial española en el África occidental (1778–1900)." PhD diss., Universitat de Valencia, 2004.

Garrido, Fernando. *Historia del reinado del ultimo Borbón de España.* Vol. 3. Madrid: Librería de Antonio de San Martín, 1869.

Ginger, Andrew. *Painting and the Turn to Cultural Modernity in Spain: The Time of Eugenio Lucas Velázquez (1850–1870).* Selinsgrove PA: Susquehanna University Press, 2007.

Gobineau, Arthur de. *The Moral and Intellectual Diversity of Races, with Particular Reference to Their Respective Influence in the Civil and Political History of Mankind.* Philadelphia PA: J. B. Lippincott, 1856.

Goikolea-Amiano, Itzea. "Hispano-Moroccan Mimesis in the Spanish War on Tetuán and its Occupation (1859–1862)." *Journal of North African Studies* 24, no. 1 (2019): 44–61.

González López, Carlos, and Montserrat Martí Ayxelá. "La vida cotidiana de los pintores españoles en Roma durante la estancia de José Villegas." In *José Villegas Cordero (1844–1921)*, edited by Ignacio Cano Rivero, Virginia Marqués Ferrer, 17–36. Córdoba: Publicaciones de la Obra Social y Cultural Cajasur, 2001.

Goode, Joshua. "The Genius of Columbus and the Mixture of Races: How the Rhetoric of Fusion Defined the End and Beginning of Empire in Nineteenth- and Early Twentieth-Century Spain." In *Empire's End: Transnational Connections in the Hispanic World*, edited by Akiko Tsuchiya and William G. Acree Jr, 63–83. Nashville TN: Vanderbilt University Press, 2016.

———. *Impurity of Blood: Defining Race in Spain, 1870–1930.* Baton Rouge: Louisiana State University Press, 2009.

Graham, John T. *Donoso Cortés: Utopian Romanticist and Political Realist.* Columbia: University of Missouri Press, 1974.

Hahs, Billy Gene. "Spain and the Scramble for Africa: The Africanistas and the Gulf of Guinea." PhD diss., University of New Mexico, 1980.

Hale, Charles. *The Transformation of Liberalism in Late Nineteenth-Century Mexico.* Princeton NJ: Princeton University Press, 1989.

Haller, John S., Jr. *Outcasts from Evolution: Scientific Attitudes of Racial Inferiority, 1859–1900.* Carbondale: Southern Illinois University Press, 1995.

Hastings, Adrian. "Christianity, Civilization, and Commerce." In *European Imperialism, 1830–1930*, edited by Alice L. Conklin and Ian Christopher Fletcher, 74–81. Boston: Houghton Mifflin, 1999.

Hennessy, C. A. M. *The Federal Republic in Spain: Pi y Margall and the Federal Republican Movement 1868–74.* Oxford, UK: Clarendon Press, 1962.

Hobsbawm, Eric. *Nations and Nationalism since 1780: Programme, Myth, Reality.* New York: Cambridge University Press, 1990.

Hobson, J. A. *Imperialism: A Study.* New York: James Pott, 1902.

Hochschild, Adam. *King Leopold's Ghost: A Story of Greed, Terror, and Heroism in Colonial Africa.* Boston: Houghton Mifflin, 1999.

Una imagen para la memoria: La carte de visite. Colección de Pedro Antonio de Alarcón. Madrid: Fundación Lázaro Galdiano, 2011.

Inarejos Muñoz, Juan Antonio. *Intervenciones coloniales y nacionalismo español: La política exterior de la Unión Liberal y sus vínculos con la Francia de Napoleón III (1856–1868).* Madrid: Sílex, 2010.

Iradier, Manuel. *África: Viajes y trabajos de la Asociación Euskara La Exploradora.* 2 vols. Vitoria: Imprenta de la viuda é hijos de Iturbe, 1887.

Jacobson, Stephen. "Imperial Ambitions in an Era of Decline: Micromilitarism and the Eclipse of the Spanish Empire, 1858–1923." In *Endless Empire: Spain's Retreat, Europe's Eclipse, America's Decline,* edited by Alfred W. McCoy, Josep M. Fradera, and Stephen Jacobson, 74–91. Madison: University of Wisconsin Press, 2012.

Jefferson, Thomas. *Notes on the State of Virginia.* Boston: Wells and Lilly, 1829.

Jerez Perchét, Augusto. *Impresiones de viaje: Andalucía, el Riff, Valencia, Mallorca.* Málaga: Correo de Andalucía, 1870.

Jover, José María. "Caracteres del nacionalismo español, 1854–1874." *Zona abierta* 31 (April–June 1984): 1–22.

Kagan, Richard L. *The Spanish Craze: America's Fascination with the Hispanic World, 1779–1939.* Lincoln: University of Nebraska Press, 2019.

Krauze, Enrique. *Mexico: Biography of Power. A History of Modern Mexico, 1810–1996.* Translated by Hank Heifetz. New York: Harper Collins, 1997.

Landa, Nicasio. *La campaña de Marruecos.* Madrid: Imprenta de Manuel Álvarez, 1860.

Law, Robin. *Ouidah: The Social History of a West African Slaving "Port" 1727–1892.* Oxford, UK: James Currey, 2004.

Lida, Clara. "The Democratic and Social Republic of 1848 and Its Repercussions in the Hispanic World." In *The European Revolutions of 1848 and the Americas,* edited by Guy Thomson, 46–75. London: Institute of Latin American Studies, 2002.

Llewellyn-Jones, Rosie. *The Great Uprising in India, 1857–58: Untold Stories, Indian and British.* Woodbridge, UK: Boydell Press, 2007.

López de la Vega, José. *La cuestión de Santo Domingo.* Madrid: D. Zacarias Soler, 1865.

López Mondéjar, Publio. *150 Years of Photography in Spain.* Barcelona: Lunwerg, 2000.

Lorcin, Patricia M. E. *Imperial Identities: Stereotyping, Prejudice and Race in Colonial Algeria.* London: IB Tauris, 1995.

———. "Imperial Nostalgia; Colonial Nostalgia: Differences of Theory, Similarities of Practice?" *Historical Reflections (Reflexions Historiques)* 39, no. 3 (Winter 2013): 97–111.

Majó Framis, Ricardo. *Las generosas y primitivas empresas de Manuel Iradier Bulfy en la Guinea española: El hombre y sus hechos.* Madrid: CSIC, 1954.

Marín, Manuela. "The Image of Morocco in Three 19th Century Spanish Travellers." *Quaderni di Studi Arabi* 10 (1992): 143–58.

Martín Corrales, Eloy. *La imagen del magrebí en España: Una perspectiva histórica siglos XVI–XX.* Barcelona: Edicions Bellaterra, 2002.

Martínez-Fernández, Luis. "The Sword and the Crucifix: Church-State Relations and Nationality in the Nineteenth-Century Dominican Republic." *Latin American Research Review* 30, no. 1 (1995): 69–93.

Martínez Gallego, Francesc Andreu. "Entre el himno de Riego y la marcha real: La nación en el proceso revolucionario español." In *Revoluciones y revolucionarios en el mundo hispano,* edited by Manuel Chust, 115–72. Castelló de la Plana, ES: Universitat Jaume I, 2000.

Martin-Márquez, Susan. *Disorientations: Spanish Colonialism in Africa and the Performance of Identity.* New Haven: Yale University Press, 2008.

Mastnak, Tomaž. *Crusading Peace: Christendom, the Muslim World, and Western Political Order.* Berkeley: University of California Press, 2002.

Mateo Dieste, Josep Lluís. *La «hermandad» hispano-marroquí: Política y religión bajo el Protectorado español en Marruecos (1912–1956).* Barcelona: Bellaterra, 2003.

McClintock, Anne. *Imperial Leather: Race, Gender and Sexuality in the Colonial Contest.* New York: Routledge, 1995.

McLeod, Mark W. "Tru'o'Ng Dinh and Vietnamese Anti-Colonialism, 1859–1864: A Reappraisal." *Journal of Southeast Asian Studies* 24, no. 1 (March 1993): 88–105.

Mehta, Uday S. "Liberal Strategies of Exclusion." In *Tensions of Empire: Colonial Cultures in a Bourgeois World,* edited by Frederick Cooper and Ann Laura Stoler, 59–86. Berkeley: University of California Press, 1997.

Miller, Susan Gilson, ed. *Disorienting Encounters: Travels of a Moroccan Scholar in France in 1845–1846: The Voyage of Muhammad As-Saffār.* Berkeley: University of California Press, 1992.

———. *A History of Modern Morocco.* Cambridge, UK: Cambridge University Press, 2013.

Mosse, George L. *Toward the Final Solution: A History of European Racism.* New York: Howard Fertig, 1985.

Moya Pons, Frank. *La dominación haitiana 1822–1844.* 3rd ed. Santiago: Universidad Católica Madre y Maestra, 1978.

———. *The Dominican Republic: A National History.* Princeton NJ: Markus Wiener, 1998.

Muñoz Gaviria, José. *África: Islas de Fernando Póo, Corisco, y Annobón*. Madrid: Rubio, Grilo y Viturri, 1871.

al-Nasiri al-Salawi, Ahmad ibn Khalid. *Versión árabe de la Guerra de África (años 1859–60)*. Translated by Clemente Cerdeira. Madrid: Tip. Moderna, 1917.

Navarrete, José. *Desde Vad-Ras a Sevilla: Acuarelas de la campaña de África*. Madrid: Imprenta a cargo de Víctor Saiz, 1880.

Núñez de Arce, Gaspar. *Recuerdos de la campaña de África*. Madrid: Imprenta a cargo de José M. Rosés, 1860.

———. *Santo Domingo*. Madrid: Imprenta de Manuel Minuesa, 1865.

Oltra, Joaquín. "La visita del General Prim a los Estados Unidos." *Atlántida* 9, no. 49 (1971): 61–70.

Pack, Sasha. *The Deepest Border: The Strait of Gibraltar and the Making of the Modern Hispano-African Borderland*. Stanford: Stanford University Press, 2019.

Palma Crespo, Antonio David. "Enrique Facio y el nacimiento de la fotografía de guerra en España." *Fotocinema: Revista científica de cine y fotografía*, no. 9 (2014): 298–324.

Pennell, C. R. "The Discovery of Morocco's Northern Coast." *British Journal of Middle Eastern Studies* 20, no. 2 (1993): 226–36.

———. *Morocco since 1830: A History*. New York: New York University Press, 2000.

Penny, H. Glenn, and Matti Bunzl. "Introduction: Rethinking German Anthropology, Colonialism, and Race." In *Worldly Provincialism: German Anthropology in the Age of Empire*, edited by Penny and Bunzl, 1–30. Ann Arbor: University of Michigan Press, 2003.

Piñol, Daniel, and Alfredo Redondo, eds. *Colección de cartas del General Juan Prim (1834–1870)*. Madrid: De Librum Tremens Editores, 2014.

Pitts, Jennifer. *A Turn to Empire: The Rise of Imperial Liberalism in Britain and France*. Princeton NJ: Princeton University Press, 2005.

———, ed. *Writings on Empire and Slavery: Alexis de Tocqueville*. Baltimore: Johns Hopkins University Press, 2001.

Porter, Bernard. *The Absent-Minded Imperialists: Empire, Society, and Culture in Britain*. Oxford, UK: Oxford University Press, 2004.

Quijada, Mónica. "Sobre el origen y difusión del nombre 'América Latina' (o una variación heterodoxa en torno al tema de la construcción social de la verdad)." *Revista de Indias* 58, no. 214 (1998): 595–616.

Ramsay, Jacob. "Extortion and Exploitation in the Nguyen Campaign against Catholicism in 1830s–1840s Vietnam." *Journal of Southeast Asian Studies* 35, no. 2 (June 2004): 311–28.

Roberts, Mary. *Intimate Outsiders: The Harem in Ottoman and Orientalist Art and Travel Literature*. Durham NC: Duke University Press, 2007.

Robertson, William Spence. "The Tripartite Treaty of London." *Hispanic American Historical Review* 20, no. 2 (May 1940): 167–89.

Romero Morales, Yasmina. "Prensa y literatura en la Guerra de África (1859–1860). Opinión publicada, patriotismo y xenophobia." *Historia contemporánea* 49 (2014): 619–44.

Ruedy, John. *Modern Algeria: The Origins and Development of a Nation.* Bloomington: Indiana University Press, 1992.

Sagás, Ernesto. *Race and Politics in the Dominican Republic.* Gainesville: University Press of Florida, 2000.

Said, Edward W. *Culture and Imperialism.* New York: Knopf, 1993.

———. *Orientalism.* New York: Vintage Books, 1978.

Salgues, Marie. *Teatro patriótico y nacionalismo en España: 1859–1900.* Zaragoza, ES: Prensas Universitarias de Zaragoza, 2010.

Salom Costa, Julio. *España en la Europa de Bismarck: La política exterior de Cánovas (1871–1881).* Madrid: CSIC, 1967.

Sampedro Vizcaya, Benita. "The Colonial Politics of Meteorology: The West African Expedition of the Urquiola Sisters." In *Unsettling Colonialism: Gender and Race in the Nineteenth-Century Global Hispanic World*, edited by N. Michelle Murray and Akiko Tsuchiya, 19–53. Albany: State University of New York Press, 2019.

Sánchez-Mejía, María Luisa. "Barbarie y civilización en el discurso nacionalista de la Guerra de África." *Revista de estudios políticos* 162 (October–December 2013): 39–67.

Sang Ben, Mu-Kien Adriana. "Contradicciones en el liberalismo Dominicano del siglo XIX: Un contraste entre el discurso y la práctica." *Ciencia y sociedad* 16, no. 3 (July–September 1991): 240–51.

Sartorius, David. "Of Exceptions and Afterlives: The Long History of the 1812 Constitution in Cuba." In *The Rise of Constitutional Government in the Iberian Atlantic World: The Impact of the Cádiz Constitution of 1812*, edited by Scott Eastman and Natalia Sobrevilla Perea, 150–76. Tuscaloosa: University of Alabama Press, 2015.

Schmidt-Nowara, Christopher. *The Conquest of History: Spanish Colonialism and National Histories in the Nineteenth Century.* Pittsburgh PA: University of Pittsburgh Press, 2006.

———. *Empire and Antislavery: Spain, Cuba, and Puerto Rico, 1833–1874.* Pittsburgh PA: University of Pittsburgh Press, 1999.

Schwartz, Vanessa R., and Jeannene M. Przyblyski. "Visual Culture's History: Twenty-First Century Interdisciplinarity and Its Nineteenth-Century Objects." In *The Nineteenth-Century Visual Culture Reader*, edited by Vanessa R. Schwartz and Jeannene M. Przyblyski, 3–14. New York: Routledge, 2004.

Scott, Rebecca J. *Slave Emancipation in Cuba: The Transition to Free Labor, 1860–1899.* Pittsburgh PA: University of Pittsburgh Press, 2000.

Serrallonga Urquidi, Joan. "La Guerra de África. Una revision." *Ayer* 29 (1998): 139–59.

Sessions, Jennifer E. *By Sword and Plow: France and the Conquest of Algeria.* Ithaca NY: Cornell University Press, 2011.

Sierra, María. "Política, romanticismo, y masculinidad: Tassara (1817–1875)." *Historia y política* (January–June 2012): 203–26.

———. "The Time of Liberalism: 1833–74." In *The History of Modern Spain: Chronologies, Themes, Individuals,* edited by José Álvarez Junco and Adrian Shubert, 31–45. London: Bloomsbury, 2018.

Sinha, Mrinalini. *Colonial Masculinity: The 'Manly Englishman' and the 'Effeminate Bengali' in the Late Nineteenth Century.* Manchester, UK: Manchester University Press, 1995.

Skocpol, Theda. *Social Revolutions in the Modern World.* Cambridge, UK: Cambridge University Press, 1994.

Sundiata, Ibrahim K. "'Cuba Africana': Cuba and Spain in the Bight of Biafra, 1839–1869," *Americas* 34, no. 1 (July 1977): 90–101.

———. *Equatorial Guinea: Colonialism, State Terror, and the Search for Stability.* Boulder CO: Westview Press, 1990.

———. *From Slaving to Neoslavery: The Bight of Biafra and Fernando Po in the Era of Abolition, 1827–1930.* Madison: University of Wisconsin Press, 1996.

Tabbal, Sarah. "José Villegas y Cordero (1844–1921) in Rome: Orientalist Fantasies, Lifestyle, and Networks." *Art in Translation* 11, no. 2 (2019): 223–40.

Thomson, Guy P. C. *Patriotism, Politics, and Popular Liberalism in Nineteenth-Century Mexico.* Wilmington DE: Scholarly Resources, 1999.

Thomson, R. Stanley. "The Diplomacy of Imperialism: France and Spain in Cochin China, 1858–1863." *Journal of Modern History* 12, no. 3 (September 1940): 334–56.

Topik, Steven C. "When Mexico Had the Blues: A Transatlantic Tale of Bonds, Bankers, and Nationalists, 1862–1910." *American Historical Review* 105, no. 3 (June 2000): 714–38.

Tortella, Gabriel. *The Development of Modern Spain: An Economic History of the Nineteenth and Twentieth Centuries.* Translated by Valerie J. Herr. Cambridge MA: Harvard University Press, 2000.

Varela Ortega, José. *Los amigos políticos: Partidos, elecciones y caciquismo en la Restauración (1875–1900).* Madrid: Marcial Pons, 2001.

Venator Santiago, Charles R. "Race, the East, and the Haitian Revolutionary Ideology: Rethinking the Role of Race in the 1844 Separation of the Eastern Part of Haiti." *Journal of Haitian Studies* 10, no. 1 (Spring 2004): 103–19.

Ventosa, Evaristo. *Españoles y marroquíes: Historia de la Guerra de África.* Vol. 2. Barcelona: Librería de Salvador Manero, 1860.

Vilches García, Jorge. *Emilio Castelar, la patria y la república.* Madrid: Biblioteca Nueva, 2001.

Young, Eric. "Fang." In *Encyclopedia of Africa,* Vol. 1, edited by Kwame Anthony Appiah and Henry Louis Gates Jr., 460. Oxford, UK: Oxford University Press, 2010.

Index

Page numbers in italics indicate illustrations.

Ab'ayir, Ahmad, 52, 53, 54
'Abd al-Qadir, 25, 74, 75
'Abd al-Rahman, 27, 36, 87
abolition, 9, 125, 160; Emilio Castelar and, 175; in Santo Domingo, 95, 96, 103, 106; of slave trade, 18, 131, 160. *See also* antislavery movement; slavery
Africa: land ownership in, 174; northern, 24, 28–34, 97, 101, 148, 196n90; slave trade in, 160; stereotypes of, 38, 166; western, 12–13, 156, 163, 167–68, 180, 210n2. *See also* Africans and people of African descent; Algeria; Fernando Po (Bioko); Morocco; race; Río Muni
Africanistas, 4, 156, 176, 180
Africans and people of African descent, 46, 130; agency of, 180; as childlike, 171–72; evangelization of, 159; exclusion from citizenship, 18; of Fernando Po, 160–61; race and, 101, 114; religion and, 164; sexualized, 171, 174; stereotypes of, 1, 7, 8, 87, 89, 92. *See also* race war; racism; slavery
Afro-Hispanics. *See* Africans and people of African descent
Agüero, Francisca, 152
al'Abbas, Mulay, 59, 62, 87, 192n93, 196n94; denigration of, 49; diplomacy of, 52, 55, 62, 64, 65; military service of, 35, 45
Alarcón, Pedro Antonio de, 1, 183n4,

193n15, 194n44, 198n36; *Diary of a Witness to the War of Africa*, 2, 77, 89; religious ideology of, 2, 183n2; travel to Morocco, 57, 76, 77
Albiach, Jéssica, 182
Alcántara, Valentín, 110
Alfau, Antonio Abad, 104
Algeria, 27, 60, 62, 101; French army in, 30; French commerce with, 173; French conquest of, 1, 4, 9, 15, 25, 73; Oran, 29; stereotypes of, 75, 77
Álvarez, Francisco, 29, 32–33, 61
Álvarez, Mariano, 5, 96, 98–99, 100, 200n39; diplomacy of, 102, 104–7, 110, 113, 115, 127; racism of, 9, 103, 114
Álvarez Junco, José, 191n71
La América, 28, 137, 138, 144, 146, 152; on Spanish-Moroccan War, 53
Anderson, Benedict, 94
Anjera, 36, 39, 66, 191n66
Annam, 3, 24–25, 157, 188n11; resistance to European imperialism, 188n4. *See also* Vietnam
Annobón, 156, 210n3, 210n18
Anthropological Society, Spanish, 169, 173
anticolonial resistance, 5, 118–29, 177, 178; in Algeria, 73; in Vietnam, 188n4
antiracism, 182
antislavery movement, 103, 137, 142
Appiah, Kwame Anthony, 10

Arab culture: French denigration of, 60, 74, 81, 192n89; stereotypes of, 39–40, 51, 66, 68

Aranda, Count of (Pedro Pablo Abarca de Bolea), 165, 208n34

art and artists, 2, 46, 57, 76–91. *See also* Fortuny, Marià; photography; Villegas y Cordero, José

Ash'ash, 'Abd al-Qadir, 55

Asian contract labor: trade in, 160

Asociación Africanista Manuel Iradier, 180

Azemmour, 27, 35

Azua, 99, 103, 128; military district of, 113

Báez, Buenaventura, 95–96, 98, 115, 128; followers of, 99

Bailyn, Bernard, 10

Balaguer, Victor, 75

Barcelona, 16, 26, 68, 175, 182; railroad in, 194n46

Basque Country: autonomy and, 176; troops from, 192n76

The Battle of Tetuán (Fortuny), 68–69

Belgium: imperialism of, 174–75, 176, 180, 182, 213n11

Bengas, 8, 171; of Elobey, 165

Benisidel, 29, 32, 34

Berbers, 9, 10, 28–29, 33; stereotypes of, 66

Berenson, Edward, 2, 42, 166, 174

Berlin Conference, 173, 175, 176

Bernal, Calixto, 132

Bible, 77, 81, 91, 95

Blanco del Valle, Juan, 5, 23–24, 39, 90; diplomacy of, 32–34, 36–37, 105, 187n2, 190n45

Bonkoro II, 165, 211n42

Bouchard, Paul, 85

Bourbon dynasty, 148; expulsion from Spain, 157; Spanish, 16, 21

Brazza, Pierre Savorgnan de, 39, 167, 172, 174

Britain, 4, 26, 73; Dominican diplomacy of, 102, 104, 106–7, 111, 126, 199n14; East India Company, 71; imperialism of, 1, 10, 174, 185n50, 192n95; loan to Morocco, 66; Mexican affairs of,

12, 135, 141–43, 144–45, 153, 207n8; Moroccan diplomacy of, 25, 27–28, 29, 31–35, 37, 62–63, 212n76; press in, 127, 145, 150; in West Africa, 159–61

Bubis, 160, 163; king of, *164*; stereotypes of, 164–66

Buceta del Villar, Manuel, 5, 190n45; commemoration of, 178; Dominican Republic campaigns of, 112–13, 116, 118–21, 123, 126, 128; post in Melilla, 30–32, 34–35, 59

Butler, Eduardo, 60

Cabral, José María, 109–10

Cadalso, José, 10

Calderón Collantes, Saturnino, 5, 106; Dominican diplomacy of, 97, 105; Mexican diplomacy of, 135–36, 148, 207n8; Moroccan diplomacy of, 26, 37, 59, 63

Canary Islands, 53, 162, 171; Guanches, 171; people of, 9

El Cañón Rayado, 84, 86–89, 193n7

Carlism, 19, 146; Carlist Wars, 19, 167, 196n84

Castelar y Ripoll, Emilio, 5, 7, 11–12, 74, 177–78, 186n71; abolitionism of, 137, 175; *Chronicle of the War of Africa*, 38–39, 48–49, 53, 76–78, 80, 196n90; *The Formula of Progress*, 18, 184n29, 187n86; funeral of, 184n17; Hegelianism of, 14; involvement in the "Glorious Revolution," 157–58; liberal imperialism of, 8, 12, 41, 67, 101, 176; Plaza de Castelar, 177, 184n17; Premio Emilio Castelar, 178; progressive ideals of, 14–21, 140, 169, 184n28; racism of, 21; recolonization and, 136–38

Castillejos, 77

Catholicism, 11–12, 13, 24; conversion to, 23, 159; Dominican nationalism and, 95, 109; in Fernando Po, 165; imperialism and, 8, 41, 65, 157; liberal Mexican views of, 140; in popular culture, 66; and religious tolerance, 187n80; Spanish-Moroccan War and, 50, 52–57; Spanish nationalism and, 5–6, 181; traditionalism and, 19, 114,

170; in Vietnam, 24–25, 188n3. *See also*
National-Catholicism

Céspedes, Carlos Manuel de, 157

Ceuta, 24, 33–34, 59, 64, 183n10, 195n67;
exile to, 205n42; history of, 28; hospital in, 78, 89; Spanish-Moroccan War
and, 38, 44, 62, 81; Treaty of Wad-Ras
and, 53; unrest in, 16, 27, 36

Chacón, Carlos, 159

Chafarinas Islands, 4, 15, 32, 61

Charles III, 1, 196n90

Chincha Islands, 154, 210n78

Chivo, Manuel, 121, 127

Chronicle of the War of Africa, 38–39,
48–49, 53, 76–78, 80. *See also* Castelar
y Ripoll, Emilio

Cibao, 5, 109, 113, 114; *campesino
cibaeño*, 94, 99; constitutional movement in, 99; economy of, 98–99;
insurgency in, 118–29

Cisneros, Wenceslao, 90

civilizing mission, 4, 8, 11, 24, 25,
192n95; French, 11, 63; history of, 11;
in Morocco, 35, 45, 51, 64, 90; religion and, 6, 12, 41, 65, 66–67; in West
Africa, 157, 173, 180

colonialism. *See* imperialism

colonization: European history of,
182; Spanish history of, 14. *See also*
imperialism

Columbus, Christopher, 109, 132, 139,
181, 182; Columbus Day, 181

Combenyamango, 167

Condorcet, Marquis de, 14, 90; *Sketch
for a Historical Picture of the Progress
of the Human Mind*, 14

Conference of Madrid, 4

Conservatives: Mexican, 134, 139, 144,
152, 187n86; Spanish, 11, 16, 18, 19

constitutionalism, 19, 99, 104, 152, 158

Constitution of 1812, Cádiz, 16–19, 20,
139

Constitution of 1845, 16, 102, 157

Constitution of 1869, 175

Corisco, 4, 156, 167, 168, 170, 173; Spanish officials living on, 210n3

Cortes, 4, 16, 19, 20, 26, 57; of Cádiz, 4,

18; conscription and, 35; Dominican
annexation and, 100; Dominican representation in, 200n42; Emilio Castelar as a deputy of, 175; occupation
of Veracruz and, 145, 155; Spanish-
Moroccan War and, 38, 62–63

Cortés, Donoso, 6

Cortés, Hernán, 40, 81, 148, 179

Corwin, Thomas, 141, 142, 143

Costa, Joaquín, 176, 210n18

Courtet de L'Isle, Victor, 7

craniometry, 169–70, 212n61. *See also*
phrenology

Cuba, 102, 106, 108, 139; Cádiz Constitution and, 19; deportees from, 160,
161, 210n18; Dominican annexation
and, 110, 122, 202n73; occupation
of Veracruz and, 141, 145, 153; slavery in, 9–10, 21, 103, 175; support for
Spanish-Moroccan War, 37, 90; Ten
Years' War in, 157–58, 176, 205n54

Dahomey, 163, 168

Darmon, Víctor, 15

Dayton, William, 142

DeGuzmán, María, 72

Delacroix, Eugène, 74

Democratic Party, Spanish, 17, 63, 175,
186n72, 187n80

deserters: in Mexico, 147; in Morocco,
58, 60, 61, 195n73

La Discusión, 15, 20, 35, 101, 136, 157,
186n72; the Dominican question and,
131–32

Dominican Republic, 3, 25, 91, 178,
201n58; annexation of, 3–4, 9, 96–100,
138, 139, 140; anticolonial resistance
in, 5, 118–29; anti-Haitian sentiment
in, 94, 178; constitutionalism in, 20,
145; economy of, 13, 103, 106; independence of, 95, 109; law in, 95, 100, 103,
111; national identity of, 94, 99, 103,
116, 178; population of, 95, 98; race in,
7, 9, 102, 123; slavery and, 9, 105, 106,
118; white emigration to, 132

Drescher, Seymour, 9

Drummond Hay, John, 27, 30–31, 33, 34

Duarte, Juan Pablo, 95, 178
Dulce, Domingo, 126, 157, 205n54
Dunbar, Edward, 142

Echagüe, Rafael, 42
El Eco del Comercio, 15
elections, Spanish, 16, 18
Eller, Anne, 178
Elliot, Jonathan, 105
Elombuangani, 167
El Seibo, 115, 127; military district of, 113
empire: nostalgia for, 2, 97, 133, 179, 183n2, 188n6. *See also* imperialism
Enlightenment: and ideas of progress, 14–15, 90; imperialism and, 14–15
La Época, 10, 158
Espaillat, Ulises, 110
Espartero, Baldomero, 19–20, 53
La Exploradora, 169, 173–74

Fabrés Costa, Antonio María, 85–86
Facio Fialo, Enrique, 2, 50, 76–77, 82, 85, 198n38
Falcón, Romana, 138, 144, 207n5
Fangs (Pamues), 160, 180; reputed cannibalism of, 168
Felipó, 87
Ferdinand VII, 18
Fernando Po (Bioko), 4, 9, 13, 92, 156; population of, 211n19; Spanish colonization of, 158–66, 168, 210n18
Ferry, Jules, 158
First Republic: in Spain, 5, 27
Floridablanca, Count of (José Moñino y Redondo), 1
The Formula of Progress (Castelar), 18, 187n86
Fortuny, Marià, 2, 68, 69, 75; *The Battle of Tetuán*, 68, 69
Fradera, Josep Maria, 12
France: Algeria and, 4, 60, 62, 73–74; Charles X of, 73; civilizing mission of, 11–12, 63, 138, 185n53; colonial legacy of, 180; Constitution of 1793, 140; diplomacy of, 15, 32, 33, 106, 107, 142; Haiti and, 95, 202n75; imperialism of, 1, 2, 3, 25, 173–74; invasion of Mexico, 20, 128, 133, 135, 144–45, 148–53;

invasion of Vietnam, 24–25, 188n11; July Monarchy of, 12; Maghreb and, 15, 27, 47, 192n89, 212n76; Napoleon III of, 140–41; Orientalist art, 75–76, 81. *See also* Brazza, Pierre Savorgnan de; Ferry, Jules
Francis II (Naples), 141, 148
Franco-Prussian War, 12
French Revolution, 14, 17, 138, 186n71
Fromentin, Eugène, 75, 81
Fuente, Juan Antonio de la, 5, 140–42, 144, 208n36

Gándara y Navarro, José de la, 5, 92, 93, 130, 159, 162
Garcia-Balañà, Albert, 26
Garrido, Fernando, 17, 19, 21, 187n81, 207n17
Gasset, Manuel, 147, 149, 150–51
Geffrard, Fabre Nicolas, 109–10, 114, 203n7
gender, 6; masculinity and, 42–43, 66, 69, 77, 154; paternalism and, 23–24; race and, 6
Germany: imperialism of, 2, 13, 175; race and, 101, 137, 170; unification of, 12
Gérôme, Jean-Léon, 74, 83
Gibraltar, 33, 37
Ginger, Andrew, 71, 89
"Glorious Revolution" of 1868, 10, 27, 157, 175
Gobineau, Arthur de, 7, 169, 184n19
González, Bruno, 129
González Bravo, Luis, 63
González de Velasco, Pedro, 169
Goode, Joshua, 7, 179
Guernica, 38
Gulf of Guinea, 3, 167, 169–70. *See also* Fernando Po (Bioko); Río Muni

Haiti, 94–97, 99, 178, 202n75, 202n82, 204n13; border strife, 92, 104, 108, 109–10, 113, 118–19; Dominican insurgency and, 121, 125, 126; European diplomacy with, 8, 13, 100, 105, 114, 115; race and, 9, 95–96, 103, 106; war with France, 112
Hartzenbusch, Juan Eugenio, 66

Havana, 106, 115; *ayuntamiento* of, 67, 90; occupation of Veracruz and, 134, 145, 147, 150; periodical press of, 48, 192n94. *See also* Cuba

Hegel, Georg Wilhelm Friedrich, 14, 18, 103, 130

Hennessy, C. A. M., 26

Hispaniola, 3, 9, 107, 113–14, 130, 132; racism and, 100, 103

Hispanism, 136–37, 154, 176

Hobsbawm, Eric, 6

Hobson, J. A., 4, 12

Hochschild, Adam, 180

Holy Alliance, 18

Hugo, Victor, 72

humanitarianism, 2, 23, 137, 175; Spanish imperialism and, 35, 39, 46, 89, 98, 130

hybridity, 61, 106

La Iberia, 146, 179

Ifni, 53

imperialism, 2–4, 10–12, 145, 173, 177; art and, 68–91; Catholicism and, 8, 41, 65, 157; cost of, 12–13; culture of, 2–5, 69, 138, 180–81; in Fernando Po, 158–66; Joaquín Costa and, 176; liberal, 4, 13, 41–42, 45, 137, 157–58, 182; in Morocco, 23–67; narratives of, 24; "new," 12, 75, 154; paternalism and, 24–25; racial supremacy and, 158; rivalries and, 174–75; Spanish, 14, 15, 20–21, 90, 154–55, 159–62; Spanish nationalism and, 42; United States, 131. *See also* race; racism; recolonization

Inquisition, 17, 19, 149

Iradier y Bulfy, Manuel, 8, 156, 166–76, 180, 212n57

Isabel I (La Católica), 26, 37, 46, 67, 90, 109; Spanish identity and, 127

Isabel II, 26, 40, 54, 64, 90; and Dominican annexation, 91, 97, 100, 102, 109, 121; intervention in Mexico and, 145; "War of Africa" and, 49, 67

Istúriz, Javier, 96, 135

Italy, 144

Jacobson, Stephen, 3

Jefferson, Thomas, 168–69, 212n56

Jesuits, 19, 26, 159

Jewish community: consular protection of, 61, 187n2; *convivencia* and, 47, 51; images of, 44, 82, 85, 86; Sephardic, 7, 58; Spanish troops and, 45, 46; stereotypes of, 43, 193n7; in Tetuán, 43, 46, 50, 53, 193n8, 196n80

Jones, William, 71

Jovellanos, Gaspar Melchor de, 17

Juárez, Benito, 129, 134, 140, 144, 152; government of, 139, 144, 145

kabilas, 29, 33

Kagan, Richard, 181

Kalaya, 29

Kant, Immanuel, 14

Kossuth, Lajos, 140

Kru, 159, 161

Landa, Nicasio, 50

Larache, 28, 35, 80

Latin race, 202n76; contrasted with Anglo-Saxon race, 137; idea of, 101, 176

Leopold II, King, 174–75, 182

Lepanto, Battle of, 28, 52

Lerena, Juan José de, 4, 159, 165

liberalism: Hispanic, 15, 16, 18, 21, 131; imperialism and, 4, 13, 41–42, 45, 137, 157–58; legacy of, 182

Liberal Union, 10, 12, 26, 65, 155, 157; fall of, 4, 27, 133, 134–35

Lincoln, Abraham, 106, 107, 110, 142

López de la Vega, José, 130

López del Campillo, Juan, 112, 116, 204n17

Lora, Gregorio de, 5, 114, 116, 121

Louis XVI, 17

Lucas Velázquez, Eugenio, 89–90

Macaulay, Thomas Babington, 51, 72

Madrid, 53, 92, 138, 169, 181, 196n90; Cortes in, 26; diplomacy in, 65, 96; Plaza de Castelar, 177, 184n17; Prado, 69; protest in, 16, 63, 92; railroad in, 52; Retiro Park, 71; welcoming of troops in, 48, 49. *See also* Spain

Maghrebis, 8, 75; consular protection of, 196n79; and stereotypes of "Moors," 40, 66, 68, 89–90, 189n34

Malo de Molina, José, 91, 95, 100, 111, 158–59

Martínez, Benito, 121

Martínez, Ignacia, 44–45

Martínez Campos, Arsenio, 69, 71

Martínez-Fernández, Luis, 94

Martínez Muller, Victoriano, 102–3

Martin-Márquez, Susan, 2

The Martyrs of Cochin China (play), 24–25, 66

masculinity, 6, 42–43, 69, 77, 154. *See also* gender

Maximilian, Archduke Ferdinand, 148, 149, 152, 209n59

Mazuza, 29

Mazzini, Giuseppe, 101

McClintock, Anne, 6

Melilla, 15, 24, 27, 60–61, 178; Buceta and, 5, 30, 34, 112, 118; conflict in, 29–33; diplomacy and, 53, 59, 62; history of, 28

Menéndez y Pelayo, Marcelino, 6, 170

Mexico, 3, 5, 7, 178; 1829 Spanish invasion of, 3, 108; 1860–61 occupation of Veracruz, 25, 113, 134–55; Catholicism in, 94, 140; constitutionalism in, 20; diplomacy of, 19, 140–44; European intervention in, 12, 20, 128, 135, 144; military of, 147, 150, 153; nationalism in, 139, 148; population of, 137, 206n2; race and, 138; stereotypes of, 150; views of Emilio Castelar in, 207n12; white emigration to, 9, 138. *See also* Juárez, Benito

Mill, James, 71

Millas, Isidoro, 55

Miramón, Miguel, 134, 135, 147

missionaries: in North Africa, 61; in Vietnam, 24; in West Africa, 159, 165, 169. *See also* Catholicism

Moca, 109, 119, 121, 129

Moderates, 11, 15, 19, 20, 27

Moliné, 87

Monzón y Martín, Bienvenido, 114–15, 118

Mora, Juan de Dios, 101

Morayta, Miguel, 157

Moret Law, 160

Morocco, 2–3, 13, 15, 25–26, 101, 185n58; 1844 French invasion of, 12, 28, 74; caricatures of, 86–87, 185n39; Catholicism in, 52–57; diplomacy with Spain, 23, 27–37, 52, 60–62, 183n10, 191n56; diplomatic delegations of, 64, 196n90; economic development in, 173; European travel to, 69, 72, 197n3; indemnity of, 53, 66; military of, 45, 78; Orientalism and, 71, 77; spies in, 57–59; stereotypes of, 1, 8, 38, 40, 45, 51. *See also* Maghrebis; Rif; Spanish-Moroccan War; Tetuán

Muhammad IV (Sidi Muhammad), 36, 53, 62

El Mundo Pintoresco, 85

Muñoz Gaviria, José, 159, 162–66, 167, 210n3, 211n30

El Museo Universal, 76, 132, *151*, 163, *164*, 191; José Muñoz Gaviria and, 165–66

Nador, 29

Napoleon Bonaparte, 73; wars of, 4

Napoleon III, 135, 152, 153; designs on Mexico, 141

Narváez, Ramón María, 15, 27, 129

National-Catholicism, 6, 156, 176, 181

nationalism, 4, 6, 12, 155; Dominican, 94–95, 178; honor and, 1, 15, 23, 131–32, 154, 179; Latin American, 129, 154; Mexican, 139–41, 148; race and, 138, 155; religion and, 24, 181; Spanish, 5–6, 15, 92, 157–58, 176; Spanish imperialism and, 42, 49, 63. *See also* National-Catholicism

National Museum of Anthropology (Madrid), 169, 180

New York Herald, 119, 123–24

Núñez de Arce, Gaspar, 43, 45, 53, 133, 179, 193n8

O'Donnell, Leopoldo, 26–27, 37, 38, 54, 77, 173; administration of, 13, 20, 26, 37; diplomacy of, 62; Dominican affairs and, 107–8, 113; Mexico and, 135, 145, 151; military service of, 44, 46–48, 63, 81. *See also* Liberal Union

Olóriz, Federico, 170

Oñate, Juan de, 182

Orientalism, 8, 10, 43, 51, 103, 168; art and, 57, 71–73, 75–90; Emilio Castelar and, 40, 184n28

Ortiz de Pinedo, Manuel, 28

Ossorio, Amado, 180

Ottoman Empire, 1, 73, 83; sixteenth-century history of, 28, 52; eighteenth-century history of, 196n90

Pacheco, Joaquín, 134–36, 142, 150, 154

Pamues. *See* Fangs (Pamues)

Paris, 95, 134, 135, 141–42, 144, 149; revolution in, 17, 19; Spanish refugees in, 16

Peláez Campomanes, Antonio, 91, 97–98, 158–59

Penny, H. Glenn, 13

Peñón de Vélez de la Gomera, 28–29, 32, 183n10, 190n43

periodical press, 28, 159, 167; British, 3, 145, 150–52; Cuba in, 157–58; Cuban, 192n94; Dominican, 110, 179; Dominican annexation and, 97, 115, 122, 127–28, 139, 156; freedom and, 16, 19, 157; Hispanism in, 154; imperialism and, 24, 25, 42, 155, 165; Iradier in, 172–74; Latin American, 129, 154; Mexican, 134, 136, 138, 145, 149–50; Mexico in, 141, 144, 146, 148, 150; prisoners and, 80; public opinion and, 4, 106, 109; racism in, 8, 53, 84, 123–24, 132, 185n39; Spanish, 11, 20, 37, 138, 141, 191n71; Spanish Moderate, 10, 15, 138, 202n76; Spanish-Moroccan War and, 8, 37–39, 43–45, 46–52, 64, 75; United States, 110, 119, 123–24, 143

Peru, 3, 129, 148, 154

Philippines, 26

photography, 64, 71, 163–65, 191; Enrique Facio and, 2, 50, 76–77, 82, 85, 198n38. *See also* art and artists

phrenology, 8, 163, 169–71; Franz Joseph Gall and, 170. *See also* craniometry; racism

piracy, 29, 62, 63; Riffian, 30, 34; smuggling and, 27

Pitts, Jennifer, 74

Pizarro, Francisco, 148

Polanco, Gaspar, 129

Ponce de León, Juan, 181, 182

Pope Eugene IV, 28

Port-au-Prince, 100, 114, 115. *See also* Haiti

Porter, Bernard, 10–11

Portugal: history of expansion in Africa, 28, 210n2

Prim y Prats, Juan, 5, 68, 157, 207n7; diplomacy of, 52; military service in Mexico, 150–53; military service in Morocco, 44–45, 46

prisoners, 104, 117, 160, 205n42; images of, 78–80, 79; in North Africa, 31, 32–34, 39, 59, 60, 61

Progressives, 11–12, 15, 17, 19–20, 26

Puebla, 147; Battle of, 153

Puerto Plata, 99, 101, 116, 117, 126; rebellion in, 120–23, 125

Puerto Rico, 122, 126, 202n73; slavery in, 9, 21, 103

Pulido, Ángel, 169

race, 20, 46, 58, 63, 133; caste and, 138; empire and, 6–11, 13–14, 177, 182, 185n56; history of, 74, 186n70; Iberia and, 170; miscegenation, 94, 114; nationalism and, 138, 155, 184n19; religion and, 1, 65, 155, 179, 181, 186n61; sexualized bodies and, 171; stereotypes, 100–106, 166, 168; Tocqueville and, 74. *See also* Latin race; phrenology; race war; racism

race war: anxieties about, 46, 125–26, 130, 133

racism, 6, 8, 73, 100, 123–24, 158; imperialism and, 21; in press, 53, 84; scientific, 7–8, 156, 163, 168–72; 180; Spanish, 114, 132, 142, 168, 185n39; Thomas Jefferson and, 168–69, 212n56; tropes and caricatures, 86–89, 95–96

realpolitik, 107

recolonization, 100, 132, 136

Regalado, Baldomero, 121
Regnault, Henri, 72
republicanism: Dominican, 5; Emilio
 Castelar and, 11, 19, 158, 177, 187n81;
 French, 12; Mexican, 5, 152; Spanish,
 15, 17, 90, 157
Republican Party: in United States, 143
Retzius, Anders, 170
Revolutions of 1848, 15, 16–17, 18, 19,
 140
Riego, Rafael, 16, 18, 187n85
Rif, 28–35, 43, 195n69; mountains of, 54;
 people of, 40, 45, 59–61, 64
Río Muni, 8, 156, 174–75; people of, 167,
 171–72. See also Gulf of Guinea
Ríos, Santiago de los, 52
Rivero, Felipe, 115–16, 120, 125–26
Rivero, Nicolás María, 16–17, 21, 38,
 46, 63–64, 157; La Discusión and, 15,
 186n72
Rochegrosse, Georges, 81
Rojas, Benigno Filomeno de, 99, 121, 129
Romanticism, 71, 74, 76
Romero, Matías, 142–43, 148, 149
Ros de Olano, Antonio, 44
Russell, John, 64, 104, 111, 144, 145

Sagás, Ernesto, 94
Said, Edward, 10, 71
Saint James: Reconquest and, 37
Salcedo, José, 121, 128–29
Samaná, 98, 121, 125, 206n73; military
 district of, 113
Samí, Mamado, 117
Sánchez, Francisco, 109–10
Santa Isabel (Malabo), 158–59, 162, 165;
 population of, 160
Santana, Pedro, 96–98, 102–6, 107–10,
 128, 198n56, 201n48; Báez and, 99;
 clergy and, 201n63; European diplo-
 macy of, 97, 100, 121, 199n14; resigna-
 tion of, 113, 203n2
Santiago de los Caballeros, 99, 119–20,
 123, 124, 127, 128; military district of,
 113; rebel capital of, 117, 121–22
Santo Domingo, 98, 125; military district of, 113. See also Dominican
 Republic

Scheffenberg, Federico, 121
Schmidt-Nowara, Christopher, 38
Schreyer, Adolph, 75–76
Scramble for Africa, 12, 156, 166, 174
Serra, Junípero, 182
Serrano, Francisco, 91, 95, 101, 107–8,
 126, 151–52; diplomacy of, 97, 106
Seville, 16, 37, 69, 184n17
Seward, William, 110, 142–43, 145, 149
El Siglo Diez y Nueve, 136, 145, 153
Sketch for a Historical Picture of the
 Progress of the Human Mind (Condorcet), 14
slavery, 9–10, 18, 21, 100, 117, 124; abolition of, 95, 96, 103, 106, 157; Britain and, 111; history of, 107; images of,
 78–80, 79, 84–85; narratives of, 139;
 patronato system, 175; persistence of,
 131–32; racism and, 133, 142; reparations for, 182; rumors of, 105, 112, 117–
 18; United States and, 106, 131, 141; in
 West Africa, 160, 161
slave trade, 182, 187n81; abolition of, 18,
 131, 160
Spain: Catholicism and, 11; diplomacy of, 61–65, 102, 104–6, 107–
 8, 134, 143; Dominican annexation
 and, 4, 96–100; Foreign Ministry of,
 33, 107, 130; imperialism of, 1–4, 11–
 13; national identity of, 6, 27, 49, 71;
 nineteenth-century history of, 5, 15–
 21; nineteenth-century political parties in, 11; occupation of Veracruz
 and, 134–55; presidios of, 4, 5, 15, 28,
 183n10; race and, 7–8, 137–38; revolution in, 15–16, 19; slavery and, 9;
 stereotypes of, 72; as threat to Latin
 American sovereignty, 148, 154; "War
 of Africa" and, 23–67, 76–81, 86–90;
 West African imperialism, 156–76. See
 also Constitution of 1812; liberalism;
 periodical press; racism
Spanish Congress of Colonial and Mercantile Geography, 176
The Spanish in Mexico (play), 138–39
Spanish-Moroccan War, 1, 5, 20, 23–67,
 86–90, 158; beginnings of, 27–37, 86–

87, *88*; casualties of, 188n10; Catalan volunteers in, 8, 101, 192n76, 205n54; Dominican press and, 179; images of, 68, 75, *78*, 89; nationalism and, 11, 92; plays about, 65–66, 188n7; praise of, 67, 138, 156; press coverage of, 8, 37–39, 43–45, 46–52, 64, 75; racism and, 163; veterans of, 114, 119; writers and journalists in, 2, 57, 76–77. See also *Chronicle of the War of Africa*
Stanley, Henry Morton, 166–67, 173, 175
Suero, Juan, 116, 120–21, 122–23

Tabbal, Sarah, 90, 197n3
Tangier, 29, 35, 64, 78, 191n64; French bombardment of, 28, 74; Spanish consulate in, 23–24, 30, 33, 36, 59; Spanish imperialism and, 37, 63, 89, 101, 200n37
Tassara, Gabriel, 5, 96–97, 115, 143, 145, 147; North America and, 105, 107, 110, 131, 140; race war and, 125
Ten Years' War, 157–58, 176, 205n54. *See also* Cuba
Tetuán, 40, 42–67, 81, 89, 157, 200n37; *Battle of Tetuán*, 68–69; church and consulate in, 52–57, 67; economy of, 46; images of, *47–48*, *55*, *58*, 75, *82–83*, 85; parish of, 26; protectorate, 156; rumors in, 30; Spanish seizure of, 3–5, 20, 97, 101, 136, 200n37; "War of Tetuán," 193n1
Thouvenel, Antoine-Edouard, 142
Times, 35
Tocqueville, Alexis de, 7, 9, 74, 160; *Essay on Algeria*, 74
Treaty of Aranjuez, 113

Treaty of Mon-Almonte, 134, 150
Treaty of Wad-Ras, 31, 53, 62, 66
Tribune, 143
Trienio Liberal, 16, 18
tripartite alliance, 135, 142, 149, 153, 155
turno pacífico, 175

Unamuno, Miguel de, 180
United States: Civil War, 107, 130, 131, 136; Columbus Day and, 181; diplomacy with Mexico, 142–43, 152; imperialism and, 1, 10; Monroe Doctrine of, 108, 129, 140–41; racism in, 182; relationship with Dominican Republic, 96, 99, 104–5, 110, 114, 125; scientific racism and, 170; slavery and, 18, 106

Vallejo, José, 46, 57, 76–78, 80–83, 85
Vargas, Carlos de, 126
Vázquez de Coronado, Francisco, 181
Venezuela: anti-imperialism in, 129
Veracruz, 5, 111, 134–35, 142; occupation of, 145, 147, 149–50, 152
Vietnam, 3; Catholic proselytization in, 24, 188n3. *See also* Annam
Villegas y Cordero, José, 2, 69, 73, 85–86, 90, 197n3
Vivar, Antonio, 13, 158–61, 176

The War of Africa and the Taking of Tetuán (play), 65–66
War of Restoration, 94, 116, 178; racism and, 163
War of the Reform, 134, 152
Weeks, Edwin Lord, 81

Zarco, Francisco, 145
zarzuela, 24, 38
Zavala, Juan de, 44

Lightning Source UK Ltd.
Milton Keynes UK
UKHW020411090322
399769UK00002BA/78